# Ten Thousand Working Days

# Ten Thousand Working Days

Robert Schrank

The MIT Press
Cambridge, Massachusetts, and London, England

Second printing, 1978
Copyright © 1978 by
The Massachusetts Institute of Technology

This book was set in Palatino by dnh typesetting, printed on R & E Book by Halliday Lithograph, and bound in G.S.B. Bookcloth Style 535 by Halliday Lithograph in the United States of America.

Library of Congress Cataloging in Publication Data

Schrank, Robert.
    Ten thousand working days.

    Includes bibliographical references.
    1.   Schrank, Robert.   2.   Labor and laboring classes—United States—Biography.   I.   Title.
HD8073.S34A37       301.44'42'0973       77—14521
ISBN 0—262—19169—5

# Contents

Preface    ix

Acknowledgments    xv

Furniture Factory    1

Plumber    10

Coal Miner and Farmhand    23

Packard Motor Car    51

Machinist    69

Union Organizing    85

Union Official  93

Politics  113

Management  133

Human Services  145

City Commissioner  174

Sociologist  211

References  245

# Preface

This is a book about what goes on in different kinds of jobs. I have worked for forty-two years now and have not been much of a success when it comes to "hanging in there." I have held dozens of different jobs and pursued half as many varied careers. By most conventional standards I should be considered a failure because at sixty I am still not sure what I want to do.

At fourteen I was sent off to work because I was unable to cut the mustard as a student in P.S. 34, an old neighborhood school with an auditorium created by sliding back the classroom walls. I lived in an Italian community in the northeast corner of the Bronx next to the zoo. My father was a German immigrant who jumped ship in 1905 to escape service in the Kaiser's army. He loved zoos. He considered living next door to a zoo the closest one could get to Valhalla. Father was an anarcho-syndicalist and he would explain much of what that meant in our almost churchlike Sunday visits to the zoo. He was a big man with large hands that he said came from doing real work, and when he would hold my hand and explain to me how all wealth was created by workers, I would get a most wonderful feeling of being. Father worshiped nature and work. For him, they were the twin source of all our benefits. He would depict the zoo as representing nature's good works, and every house, bridge, trolley car, automobile, the subway, a radio, a skyscraper, and its plumbing as representing man's good works. People who built these things were good; "the idle rich were evil, contributing and doing nothing but exploiting workers." Father hated bureaucrats, the people who "sat on their behinds and got fat on the backs of the workers." He was an anarchist to the extent that he believed that most bureaucracies were self-serving, and he would say "workers could run the world quite well if government, private ownership, and managers just got off their backs."

Father's great sense of the world's injustices would be stated as "You see, Bobby, the trouble with our most beautiful world is that too many workers strain their backs getting very little in return to support a very few who sit on their fat behinds and do nothing." As I recall those walks holding Papa's huge warm reassuring hand I was learning not only about who is exploited but the difference between manual and nonmanual work.

The house I grew up in as a child was a place of endless discussion, conversation, and argument. Mother died when I was six, and my two older sisters, my father, and I moved in with an aunt. Not a real one, but one of those who out of association became an aunt. They were Austrian, but like my father, were also somehow socialists—or anarchists or some mixture. There were eight for dinner every night and Sundays seemed to me as a little boy to bring an endless stream of interesting and excited people who argued about freedom, fascism, Stalinism, Goethe, Bukharin, August Bebel, Isadora Duncan, Marx, and Engels. It was a time of colony building. There were anarchist colonies like Stelton, New Jersey and progressive schools and camps like Manumit and around these and many others there seemed to be endless arguments. Father would say you cannot build islands of socialism and anarchism in a capitalist sea, because if it shows any promise of success the "ruling class" will see to it that it sinks. The arguments went on and on and most often ended with some beer drinking and singing. They were people full of ideas about what society should look like, and they had songs of protest about the old and praise for the new. They would intersperse them with tales of working class heroism until the early hours of the morning when each excused himself, explaining that he had to be in the factory at eight. Most of these men who sang of the future were skilled craftsmen—toolmakers, machinists, and mechanics—and they had a great pride in their work. Many were members of the International Workers of the World, the IWW, called Wobblies.

Dinner discussions usually started with a current-event or religious subject. Father was an atheist, and as was so true of many of them, he was a biblical scholar. His whole object seemed to be to prove from the Bible itself that religion was a false hope and the real hope for man lay in "knowing the truth." The arguments within the various radical approaches to revolutionary change were forever renewed by the publication of another article by Trotsky or Radek or Bukharin. In retrospect I see that I learned how to think critically about problems, and that socialists, anarchists, and communists were full of endless disagreements among themselves as well as with others about what the future world of brotherhood should look like.

The social gatherings at our house were often turned into political meetings, as there always seemed to me to be someone in jail who needed cigarettes and defending. I remember the desperate drives to raise money to defend Sacco and Vanzetti at the same time that they were most critical of the attorney's defense tactics. Mooney and Billings were rotting in jail, as were the McNamara brothers. All were put there, as father and his friends explained, by the ruling class "to terrorize and scare the hell out of the workers." It was listening to these endless arguments on defense strategies or about whether socialists should run for office that would give me my first glimmerings about the enormous complexities of social change, and these complexities would continue to grow in a lifetime involved with changing the world.

Of all the anarchists I remember, the Italians were my favorites and Arturo Giovanetti the most. I recall him as a tall man with a flaming bow tie who would sweep me up in the air and bounce me over his head, proclaiming, "Is one of our new kind of man—a revolutionist, a free man, loving, and always a worker." Then he would put me down and, holding my shoulders, in a whispered voice as in a sort of great confidence between two men, he would ask, "You like da girls yet?" I would be embarrassed and say, "No," and he would smile with his big face lit up close to mine, look me straight in the eyes, and say, "Little boy, you gotta da best ting coming. After da revolution, da women is da best of all."

Part of the freedom many of these people sang about was the

freedom to love, and for many the radical movements they participated in gave them the opportunity to live this love among themselves. Whenever I was at the socialist-anarchist freethinker picnics in their camps and schools, I always felt I was part of a huge extended family of working people so very proud of who they were. I never experienced the phenomenon of working class self-hate as a child, but would come to learn about it much later. Giovanetti was the epitome of the radical men I knew as a child. They were tough, and so hard in their beliefs it seemed that they could easily commit murder for them. Yet they were also poets who loved women, ate with gusto, sang endlessly, believed in hard work and strong bodies, and were eternally optimistic about the world—until three things happened. The terror of Stalinism, the Great Depression, and nazism created a pall of great personal disillusionment that finally led to the disintegration of the Left.

In the meantime I was in endless trouble in P.S. 34, and out of desperation my teachers had dubbed me a disruptive child. That resulted in talk of sending me to a "protectory," which just scared the daylights out of me. But it so happened that in P.S. 34 I had an unseen friend in Mr. Finerty, the school shop teacher. He wore a bow tie, had a very kind face, and once I overheard him talking with another teacher about me. He said, "I don't know, he is not so bad. Why don't we let him work with me in the woodshop and see if I can handle him?" I just loved Mr. Finerty for that. I was assigned to the woodworking shop where I was to experience my first great teacher, who not only handled this "disruptive child" but taught me some of the most useful things I have learned. Father, speaking in German, began to tell other people in my presence that, "Bobby here is very good with his hands. In fact, they are golden. He can fix anything, but in his head there is not much." I, of course, accepted that and began to wonder and fantasize about what kind of work I could do with my hands.

Father's sadness over the failure of the Russian Revolution to produce a truly free society engulfed him like a vine that finally overtakes the tree. Some years later when I was fifteen and had joined a local chapter of the Young Communist League, he would throw me out of the house because "No Stalinist will live in this house—there is no apology for murder. So out!" And he meant it. But before that came the slow but steady division of this radical German community into Nazis and anti-Nazis. Father was in the vanguard of the antifascists. I would come to see nothing but hate and violence between father and his old friends as he slowly but surely withdrew from his world of lofty ideals.

Our family survived the depression by simply pooling resources with others in similar straits, and in a way the depression wasn't so bad, as father said. Karl Marx had been right, capitalism was collapsing, but father was terribly troubled by the alternatives that seemed to loom so powerful: Stalin and Hitler.

I left home and, as predicted for me, worked with my hands for the next ten years. During this time father and I hardly spoke to each other. Father watched his dream of socialism, the beloved brotherhood of man, turn into a nightmare of trials as his "old Bolshevik" heroes whimpered their confessions in the courtroom. He became more and more withdrawn and began to paint pictures of landscapes, scenes from his youth in Germany. He and I became friends again when I apologized to him for being wrong about the dictatorship of the proletariat. As I talked, he listened so quietly that I could feel all his pain; we never spoke of the revolution again.

While I was working with my hands over the years, it was slowly dawning on me that I could use my head. Eventually I had jobs that did not require the skill of my hands at all, and in some I just sat on my behind. This is a book about the jobs I have held and how life was lived at the different kinds of workplaces where I was employed. I will try to tell what is the same and what is different about being a commissioner, a plumber, a sociologist, a machinist, an auto mechanic, a union official, a plant manager and engineer, an antipoverty program bureaucrat, a foundation professional, or a truck driver. In forty-two years of working, these are the jobs I have held.

I was moved to write this book as a result of listening to and reading about what behavioral scientists, academics, and other literati had perceived at places of work. I felt that in the pursuit of psychology or sociology they had missed the humanity, the poetry, and the community of people that is created by the workers at their workplaces. I hope in this book to catch some of that sense of community, camaraderie, conflict, and humor. Much of my lifetime has been involved with workplace problems, starting as a trade unionist with a concern over wages, hours, working conditions, and the right to organize. Later, as a sociologist, I have concentrated on the problem of the distribution of amenities at the workplace—such as who gets which parking space. Or put another way, I have been deeply concerned with the unequal distribution of the benefits of work in our society, benefits that may start with wages and end with who has the use of a telephone.

Economists have dubbed the eighty-seven million people in the United States who are employed "the work force." Most of the people in this work force go to what is called a "job." The name work force may be all that some of these people have in common because under the work force rubric come coal miners, toe dancers, clerks, truck drivers, doctors, foundrymen, and professionals. I will be tempted from time to time to write in my present profession as a sociologist. But I will do my best to resist that in favor of trying to catch the language and the feel of the workplaces I am writing about. I will try to differentiate between the job and the actual work on tasks. The job I define as the container, the institution, or the structure in which a person performs something for which he or she gets paid. If we think about the job as a container, what interests me in this book is what goes on inside that container. This includes the work tasks, physical surroundings, the benefits, the amenities, and most important, the social milieu of the community.

As I moved from job to job, the concept of job amenities began to dawn on me. I began to feel the differences in what was permitted and granted in different jobs. I relate the narrative of working in different places in the hope that the reader might share the experience of the amenities as well as the work.

# Acknowledgments

My thanks to all of you who read the manuscript, made suggestions and comments, and mostly urged me to keep on with this project: Roy Fairfield, S. M. Miller, Mike Sviridoff, Eli Ginsberg, Susan Berresford, Bobbi McKellar, Pat Sexton, and Basil Whiting, more than anyone else my nagging mentor. Many of you may be surprised how this ended up, considering how it started, but I thank you for your suggestions and encouragement. Special thanks to my dear friend Shoshonna Zuboff, who did the final reading and made so many valuable suggestions, and to Jeanine Bryan, who so patiently dealt with the manuscript.

Robert Schrank

# Ten Thousand Working Days

# Furniture Factory

It was 1932 and we were in the depths of the depression. If you were lucky enough to find a job, it was usually through a friend, and that was how I got my first full-time job in a Brooklyn factory that made frames for upholstered furniture. I was fifteen years old and lived in the Bronx, traveling on the subway for an hour and fifteen minutes each way, every day, six days a week for twelve dollars. I considered myself to be the luckiest boy in the world to get that job. When Mr. Miller, the owner of the Miller Parlor Frame Company, interviewed me and agreed to hire me, he made it quite clear that he was doing a favor for a mutual friend and did not really care much about giving me a job.

Like most small factory offices, Mr. Miller's was cluttered with catalogs, samples of materials, some small tools, a rolltop desk with a large blotter pad worn through the corners. The whole place was in a sawdust fog with a persistent cover of dust over everything. Mr. Miller was a short fat man who chewed cigars and sort of drooled as he talked to me. He sat on the edge of his big oak swivel chair. I had a feeling he might slip off anytime. He never looked at me as we spoke. He made it clear that he was annoyed at people asking favors, saying that he did not like people who were "always trying to get something out of me."

The sour smell of the oak sawdust comes back to fill my nose as I recall the furniture factory. It is a smell I always welcomed until I had to live in it eight hours a day. There were days, especially when it was damp or raining, when the wood smell was so strong you could not eat your lunch. Next to the smell I remember getting to the factory and back as being an awful drag. But the New York subway that I rode to and from work for many years had two marked positive effects on me. First, I felt part of a general condition that nobody seemed to like. I was part of a group and we were all in the same fix, busting our asses to get to work in the morning and home at night. While I felt unhappy, it was made easier through the traditional "misery loves company," and there was plenty of that. And second, if I had a lucky day, there was the chance of seeing or being pressed up against some sweet-smelling, young, pretty thing who would get me all excited. Sometimes I tried a pickup, but it usually did not work because the situation was too public. With each person rigidly contained, it was surprising if anyone tried to move out of his shell. Everyone in the train would be staring to see what would develop. Almost nothing did.

To be at the furniture factory in Brooklyn by 8 A.M., I would leave my house in the Bronx by 6:30 A.M. While it was always a bad trip it became less so in the long spring days of the year as contrasted with December, when I most hated getting up in the dark. It was very important to be very quiet as I would feel my way around our old frame house, so as not to wake people who had another thirty or forty minutes to sleep. I would sleepily make a sandwich for lunch, preferably from a leftover or just bologna, grab a cup of coffee— always with one eye on the clock—and run for the station. Luckily, we lived at the end of a subway line, and in the morning I was usually able to get a corner seat in the train. The corner seat was good for sleeping because I could rest against the train wall and not have the embarrassment of falling asleep on the person sitting next to me. It meant being able to sleep the hour-long trip to Brooklyn, and it was critical to set my "inner clock" so it would wake me up at the Morgan Avenue station in Brooklyn. If it failed or was a little late, which sometimes happened, panic would ensue, as I usually would wake up just as the train was pulling out of Morgan Avenue. I would make a quick, unsuccessful dash for the door, and people would try to help by grabbing at the door. Then I would burn with anger for being late and maybe losing the job. When I would end up past my stop, I would have to make a fast decision to either spend another nickel and go back or go on to a double station where I could race down the steps to the other side of the tracks and catch a train going the other way without paying an additional fare.

The trip home from work on the New York subway in the evening rush hour is an experience most difficult to describe. The train, packed full of people, hurtles into a station. The doors slide open. There is always an illusion that someone may be getting out. That never seems to happen while a mass of people begin to push their way in. All strangers, we are not packed like sardines in a can, as is often suggested; the packing of sardines is an orderly process. The rush hour subway is more like a garbage compacter that just squeezes trash and rubbish into a dense mass and then hurtles it at very high speeds through a small underground tube. Unlike the morning, at night when I was exhausted from the day's work I never was able to get a seat, and that meant standing on my dog-tired feet for more than an hour and trying not to lean on the person next to me, an almost impossible thing to do. Sometimes I would get ridiculously excited pressed against the behind of a complete stranger, and get an erection that I could not control and be sure I would be arrested for molesting or something. What if the woman just let off and whacked me? What could I do? It was a beautifully terrible thing, but it sometimes made the subway ride seem less violent.

As I walked from the subway in the morning I could smell the furniture factory a block away. It was a powerful smell; as I said, I loved that oak at first. It was a perfume from the woods: a combination of skunk, mushrooms, and honeysuckle blended to a musk, a sweet contrast to the steel-and-oil stink of the subway. Yet, by the end of a day's work, the factory, its smells, its noise, its tedium all became so terribly tiresome and exhausting that leaving every day was an act of liberation.

The factory was a five-story loft building about half a city block long. The making of the furniture frames began on the bottom floor where the rough cuts were made from huge pieces of lumber. As the cut wood moved along from floor to floor, it was formed, shaped, carved, dowled, sanded, and finally assembled on the top floor into completed frames. The machines in the plant included table saws, band saws, planers, carving machines, routers, drills, hydraulic presses, all run by 125 machine operators who were almost all European immigrants. My job was to keep the operators supplied with material, moving the finished stuff to the assembly floor, a sort of human conveyor. When I wasn't moving pieces around, I was supposed to clean up, which meant bagging sawdust into burlap bags. Sometimes the foreman would come and say, "Hey, kid, how would you like to run the dowling machine?" At first I thought that was a real break, a chance to get on a machine and become an operator. I told him enthusiastically, "Yeah, that would be great." I would sit in front of this little machine, pick up a predrilled piece, hold it to the machine, which would push two glued dowels into the holes. I soon found that I preferred moving parts around the plant and cleaning up to sitting at that machine all day, picking up a piece of wood from one pile, locating the holes at the dowel feeder that pushed in two preglued dowels, then dropping it on the other side. The machine had a sort of gallump, gallump rhythm that made me sleepy and started me watching the clock, the worst thing you can do in a factory. It would begin to get to me, and I would just sit and stare at the machine, the clock, the machine, the clock.

Those first few weeks in that factory were an agony of neverending time. The damn clock just never moved, and over and over again I became convinced that it had stopped. Gradually, life in the furniture factory boiled down to waiting for the four work breaks: coffee, lunch hour, coffee, and quitting time. When the machines stopped, it was only in their sudden silence that I became aware of their deafening whine. It was almost impossible to hear each other talk while they were running, and all we were able to do was to scream essential information at one another.

The breaks were the best times of the day, for I could become intoxicated listening to the older men talk of rough, tough things in the big world out there. Being accepted was a slow process, and I was just happy to be allowed to listen. When I had been there for a couple of weeks, Mike the Polack said, "Hey, kid, meet in the shit house for talk." I was making it all right.

The coffee- and lunch-break talks centered around the family, sports, politics, and sex, in about that order. The immigrants from Middle Europe, and especially the Jews, were the most political. Most of them seemed to believe that politicians were crooks and that's how it is. The Jews talked the least about sex and the Italians the most. Luigi would endlessly bait Max (who would soon be my friend), saying that what he needed most was "a good woman who make you forget all dat political shit." There were a whole variety of newspapers published in New York at that time and one way workers had of figuring out each other's politics, interests, and habits was by the papers they read.

Max Teitelbaum would say to me, "See Louie over there. You can tell he's just a dummy, he reads that *Daily Mirror*. It fills his head with garbage so he can't tink about vot is *really* happening in the vorld." Arguing strongly in the defense of Franklin Roosevelt, probably too strongly, Mike the Polack told me with his finger waving close to my nose, "Listen, kid, vot I tink and vot I do is my business, and nobody, no politician or union or smart-ass kid like you is gonna butt into dat. You got it? Don't forget it!"

As people began to trust me, I was slowly making friends. Their trust was expressed in small ways, like when Luigi called me over to his workbench, held up a picture of Jean Harlow for me to look at as he shook his big head of black hair, all the time contemplating the picture together with me, and said, "Now, whaddya tink, boy? You getta your face between those legs, boy, you got someting. Dis is too pretty to fuck, boy. You remember dat, kid." Then he said, "OK, kid, you gotta work hard and learn something. See all those poor bastards out there outa work. Watch out or you could be one of dem." Luigi was a wood-carver who made the models for the multiple-spindle carving machine and was probably the only real craftsman in the place.

I wasn't sure what Luigi was talking about, especially his advice about Jean Harlow, but trying to hide my embarrassment, I said, "Of course, I understand." I ate all this conversation up, especially the talk about who was "banging" whom and in what manner. They talked about ways of doing it that in my wildest fantasies I had never dreamed of.

One day as I distributed work in process to the operators and picked up their finished stuff, I received one of my first lessons in the fundamentals of working that I would relearn again and again in almost every job I have had: How to work less hard in order to make the task easier.

Max Teitelbaum, a band saw operator just a few years out of Krakow, Poland, a slightly built man with sort of Mickey Mouse ears, twinkling eyes, and a wry smile, would upbraid me repeatedly with such passing comments as, "You are a dummy," or "You're not stupid, so what's da matter vit you?" Finally one day he stopped his machine, turned to me, and said, "Look, come over here. I vant to talk vit you. Vy you are using your back instead your head? Max Teitelbaum's first rule is: Don't carry nuttin' you could put a veel under. It's a good ting you wasn't helpin' mit der pyramids—you vould get crushed under the stones."

I said, "But Max, if the hand truck is on the third floor and I'm on the fifth, I can't go all the way down there just for that."

"You see," he said, "you are a dummy. Vy you can't go down dere? Huh, vy not? You tell me!"

"Well," I said, "it would take a lot of time—"

He cut me off. "You see, you are vorrying about da wrong tings, like da boss. Is he vorrying about you? Like da Tzar vorried about Max Teitelbaum. Listen, kid, you vorry about you because no von else vill. Understand? You vill get nuttin' for vorking harder den more vork. Now ven you even don't understand someting, you come and ask Max. OK?" Max became my friend, adviser, and critic.

By the end of my first weeks in the factory I began to feel as if I was crushed under stones. My body helped me to understand what Max was saying. I would come home from work on Saturday afternoon and go to bed expecting to go out later that night with a girl friend. For some weeks when I lay down on Saturday I did not try, nor was I able, to move my body from the bed until some time on Sunday. The whole thing just throbbed with fatigue: arms, shoulders, legs, and back were in fierce competition for which hurt the most. I began to learn what Max meant by "Always put a veel under it and don't do more than you have to."

My third or fourth week at the factory found me earnestly launched in my quest for holding the job but doing less work—or working less hard. This was immediately recognized and hailed by the men with "Now you're gettin' smart, kid. Stop bustin' your ass and only do what you have to do. You don't get any more money for bustin' your hump and you might put some other poor bastard outa a job." Remember this was the depression. Most workers, while aware of the preciousness of their jobs, felt that doing more work than necessary could be putting someone else, even yourself, out of a job. "Only do what you have to" became a rule not only to save your own neck but to make sure you were not depriving some other soul like youself from getting a job.

In the next few weeks, I was to be taught a second important lesson about working. One day while picking up sawdust, I began to "find" pieces in the sawdust or behind a woodpile or under a machine. The first few times, with great delight, I would announce to the operator, "Hey, look what I found!" I should have figured something was wrong by the lack of any similar enthusiasm from the operator. Sam was a generally quiet Midwesterner who never seemed to raise his voice much, but now when I showed him my finished-work discovery behind his milling machine he shouted, "Who the fuck asked you to be a detective? Keep your silly ass out from behind my machine; I'll tell you what to pick up. So don't go being a big brown-nosing hero around here."

Wow, I sure never expected that. Confused, troubled, almost in tears, not knowing what to do or where to go, I went to the toilet to hide my hurt and just sat down on an open bowl and thought what the hell am I doing in this goddamned place anyway? I lit a cigarette and began pacing up and down in front of the three stalls, puffing away at my Camel. I thought, What the hell should I do? This job is terrible, the men are pissed off at me. I hate the place, why don't I just quit? Well, it's a job and you get paid, I said to myself, so take it easy.

While I'm pacing and puffing, Sam comes in, saying, "Lissen, kid, don't get sore. I was just trying to set you straight. Let me tell you what it's all about. The guys around, that is the machine operators, agree on how much we are gonna turn out, and that's what the boss gets, no more, no less. Now sometimes any one of us might just fall behind a little, so we always keep some finished stuff hidden away just in case." The more he talked, the more I really began to feel like the enemy. I tried to apologize, but he just went on. "Look, kid, the boss always wants more and he doesn't give a shit if we die giving it to him, so we [it was that "we" that seemed to retrieve my soul back into the community; my tears just went away] agree on how much we're going to give him—no more, no less. You see, kid, if you keep running around, moving the stuff too fast, the boss will get wise about what's going on." Sam put his arm on my shoulder. (My God! I was one of them! I love Sam and the place. I am in!) "So look," he says, "your job is to figure out how to move and work no faster than we turn the stuff out. Get it? OK? You'll get it." I said, "Yes, of course, I understand everything." I was being initiated into the secrets of a work tribe, and I loved it.

I was beginning to learn the second work lesson that would be taught me many times over in a variety of different jobs: Don't do more work than is absolutely necessary. Years later I would read about how people in the Hawthorne works of Western Electric would "bank work" and use it when they fell behind or just wanted to take it easy. I have seen a lot of work banking, especially in machine shops. In some way I have felt that banking work was the workers' response to the stopwatches of industrial engineers. It is an interesting sort of game of hide the work now, take it out later. In another plant, would you believe we banked propellor shafts for Liberty ships!

I learned most of the rules, written and unwritten, about the furniture factory, but I never got to like the job. After I had been there six or seven months, the Furniture Workers Union began an organizing drive. I hated the furniture factory, the noise, the dust, and the travel, so I, too, quickly signed a union card. I was just as quickly out on my ass. It was a good way to go, since my radical friends considered me a hero of sorts, having been victimized for the cause. The first time I ever considered suicide in my life was in that furniture factory as I would stare at the clock and think to myself, "If I have to spend my life in this hellhole, I would rather end it." Well, of course, I didn't; and as I look back, it was not the worst place I worked, but I was young and unwilling to relinquish childhood.

# Plumber

In 1934, I was seventeen and worked as a plumber's helper for the Hoffelmeyer Plumbing and Heating Company. That winter was one of the coldest on record. As a result I learned to keep warm by drinking some cheap booze called Green River and even tried chewing tobacco. The liquor did seem to warm me outside by burning my insides, and the tobacco made me greener and sicker than I have ever been before or since, because none of those bastards who coaxed me into chewing the damn stuff told me to keep spitting and not to swallow it.

Hoffelmeyer, as the company was known, did contract work on new construction and rehabilitation of old buildings. The number of men employed depended on the number of contracts the company held at any one time, yet there was a small group of steady men for whom I became a helper. The depression was still on in 1934 and the rehabilitation work on the West Side of Manhattan consisted mostly of breaking up large twelve- to fifteen-room apartments that people could no longer afford into small three- and four-room apartments.

I was referred to Mr. Hoffelmeyer by an IWW friend of my father's who was a building superintendent on the West Side of Manhattan. Hoffey, as he was called, was over six feet tall, weighed over 300 pounds, had absolutely no neck and a perfectly round bowling-ball head. The job interview with Hoffey was held in a basement that was a combination of office and shop. There was a rolltop desk up front toward the street that was loaded with slips of papers, many of them so soiled that you knew they had been there for a long time. On the top of the rolltop there were piles of heavily used plumbing catalogs. This was "the boss's place" and the rest of the basement was the "shop." Hoffey had a heavy German accent. He looked me over sort of approvingly and said, "Oscar [my father's friend] says you're a good German kid, so you know how to vuerk. Is dat right?"

"Well," I said, "yes, I think so."

"Tink so," said Hoffey. "You better fuckin' vell know if you're gonna come here to vuerk. Ve don't vant you to tink, ve vant you to vuerk."

Hoffey was not as scary as he sounded, because he had sort of a way of giggling at the end of each opinion as though, in afterthought, he considered what he had heard himself say as funny. During the depression job interviews were a very serious business. It was as though your life were at stake. Hoffey's giggles eased some of the pain in my stomach and for that I liked him.

The shop smelled from pipe compound, a sort of heavy paint odor. There were various pipe fittings strewn on the floor. Without any preparation Hoffey just let his huge hand swing away from his chair and pointed to one of the fittings. "OK, if you're so schmart, vot is dat?"

"An elbow."

"And dat?"

"A Y." And then he just kept pointing to different pipe fittings and I ticked off, "A forty-five, a trap, an S trap, an expansion joint, a male plug, a female cap, a nipple." These were pretty common, but then he pointed at a less-known fitting that I happened to know the name of because it had stuck in my head, and as I found myself repeating it I felt good. Wow, here was my big moment. Gleefully, I jumped in with "a tucker fitting!"

He looked at me, more surprised by my enthusiasm than my knowledge. A little annoyed, he said, "OK, don't be too schmart now. Ve don't need vize guys around here. Ve got dem already."

I had learned the names of fittings from plumbers who worked in the neighborhood where I grew up. My community was one where I knew the local plumber, and when school was out I could say, "Hey, Smitty, can I ride your truck? I'll help out." And Smitty would say, "Sure come on," and I would jump in and help out some times just a little, for which I got a quarter or sometimes even a half a buck. And I learned the names of pipe fittings.

Hoffey said, "OK, you're hired at thirty cents an hour and don't let me catch you fuckin' doze Vest Side vidows. You gotta vuerk here, uttervize out, you hear?"

"Yes sir," I said. I could have hugged and kissed him not only for the job but for seeing me as a Vest Side vidow fucker. Wow, that was real he-man talk. Wait until I tell my buddies on Tremont Avenue about this. I was absolutely euphoric, hoping he would not want me to start right away so I could go back and tell my friends. They just won't believe it and at thirteen dollars a week! I was not sure what to do at that point, so I just stood there waiting while Hoffey answered the phone.

In the opposite corner of the basement, facing the street, there was an old man sitting in front of a small rickety typewriter desk. He seemed nervous about Hoffey and extremely anxious to respond to anything he might ask for. He listened and watched the interview almost as though he was being questioned. I later learned from the plumbers that John, the old man in the corner, was "an old steam-fitter who can't work anymore because his back is gone. So we call him the office manager. Be nice to John," they said, "he can do you a lot of good or harm if he wants to." Hoffey called over to John, saying, "Give dis kid da can and let him get some beer at the corner." And to me, "And tell dat cheap bartender not all foam. Und get some pretzels, too. Hey, kid, do you know vot foam is?"

"Well, it's the white stuff on the top of the beer," I said.

"You see, already you are shtupid. Dat's air und ve don't pay for air, unless you vant to pay for farts. OK, get beer not air, and tell him plenty pretzels, too." I took the can, went over to the corner, told the Irish bartender what Hoffey said about foam and pretzels. He laughed, filled the can, gave me a handful of pretzels, and said, "If you're working for Hoffey, kid, what's your name, we're going to see you aplenty." He wished me good luck and said, "Hoffey's a fine feller, but don't cross him up."

I returned with the beer. We all drank, and almost right off I loved Hoffey for his tough talk and his rare sense of humor, such an unusual quality in the boss-worker relationship. For a seventeen-year-old kid, this was a dream of men's stuff. After some more beer drinking and filling out of papers I was told to "beat it now, and show up 7:30 tomorrow ready for vuerk vit no fooling around."

I showed up on time the next morning at the plumbing shop, where every morning there were about fifteen men drinking coffee, picking up fittings and tools, and loading trucks. I had hoped to get on new construction, but was told to work with Reggie's crew on a rehabilitation job in a twenty-story building requiring forty new bathrooms and kitchens. Reggie was a young man in his early thirties, about six feet, clean shaven, carefully dressed in clean dungarees and a woolen shirt, and he seemed very reserved. While most of the other men were picking up tools and supplies they were expounding their views on sports, sex, and politics, but Reggie seemed pretty aloof from all the talk. He just told me what fittings to pick up, then said, "Get the bag and let's go."

The bag was a huge leather tool case that looked like a mailman's bag that you slung on your back. It was full of heavy plumbing tools. It must have weighed fifty pounds, but seemed to gain a pound every ten minutes. The helper carried the bag, and it never mattered that you had such other items as the gasoline torch, a bag of fittings, and sometimes some pipe to carry—you still carried the bag. An amenity of being a journeyman plumber was to have a helper who was a combination mule, personal attendant, and general support system.

Reggie said that I was to cut floors and walls and run the roughing (the pipe that goes inside the walls). He was soft-spoken, and I liked him. He never swore nor was he abusive, which was not true of any of the other plumbers. He showed me how to cut floors and walls, using a drill, saw, hammer, and chisel. It seemed easy, until in a few hours my arm began to feel like a piece of wood. By noon I was sure it would fall off. Fortunately I was rescued by being sent out on my first plumbing supply-house pickup. This would become a regular routine that I loved because I was out on my own. I would walk along the street or would sometimes drive the truck. I could daydream, kind of just setting my own pace without any supervision. What a feeling of freedom that was to be out of the job site on my own like a truck driver.

Because Hoffelmeyer did emergency work, sometimes I was given odd supply-house pickups. Once I had to carry a toilet bowl in a bus around rush hour. First, the driver looked at me in disbelief, and I said, "What can I do? My boss sent me for it." In those days that statement called forth a certain kind of instant solidarity. If you were trying to make a living, no matter what you did, people seemed to be sympathetic to any endeavor. He said, "OK, get in the back door." The passengers on the bus looked at me in utter disbelief, then someone made a crack about this being the best-equipped bus he had ever been on. Everybody had a good laugh, including the driver who yelled, "Kid, make sure you bring the bathtub tomorrow."

At lunch, the plumbing crew usually gathered in the basement. I would sit with the men. At first I was self-conscious and unsure, but in time I became accepted and could join in the conversation. In contrast to the furniture factory workers, plumbers seemed much more argumentative and less intellectual, probably because there were no Jews among them. It occurs to me now that one of the reasons the furniture factory had been so oppressive was the high noise level that prevented conversation during working hours. Not so with the plumbers. Since they tended to work in groups, they argued about everything almost all the time. Sports, physical prowess, cars, boats, politics, sex, and plumbing. The conversation filled a void caused by boredom and this made the time pass much faster.

The political discussions were less intellectual than those in the furniture factory. One day I made a comment about what an evil bastard Hitler was. Well, my quiet friend Reggie came to life and to the fuehrer's defense on the grounds that he had eliminated unemployment and was getting rid of Jewish bankers.

This argument proved to be one of the most difficult ones that I would become involved in with workers over and over again in the thirties. Many decent workers like Reggie were looking for some way out of the mire of the depression, and Hitler and Mussolini seemed to offer simple solutions. By combining Jews and bankers, Hitler appealed to a legitimate, antibanker feeling and then married this idea to the Jews. My problem as a helper was not to be a smart-ass kid. If I was, I'd be dead. On the other hand my radicalism demanded that I challenge any sympathy with fascism, which I did.

Many workers have a real desire for some kind of order in the social-economic world. Ambiguity tends to create fear of economic insecurity. Most of the work they do is orderly and predictable, and I think it influences their life outlook. Ibn Khaldun describes this phenomenon in the *Muqaddimah* as a "coloring of the soul."

If arguments got out of hand or a little too hot, someone could always switch the topic to sex. They would then argue about how many times can you do it in one night or are fat women better than skinny women. Can you get the syph from a blow job? A rhinoceros horn is an aphrodisiac that'll make you fuck till you bleed. It was fantastic talk, full of challenge and certainty. By God, this gang made me feel like I could lick the world.

Reggie ever so patiently showed me how to cut open floors and walls to receive pipe. "Never more than you have to," he would say, "because remember, we have to close them up again." I learned how to cut and thread pipes to dimensions given by the plumber. Since the pipe vise, dies, and fittings were usually kept in the basement, there was a ceaseless muling of stuff up and down stairs, unless I was lucky and worked in a building where I could use the elevator. As the helper I was the go-fer, running for fittings, pipe, fixtures, coffee, beer, Coke, and so forth, for eight hours every day. Reggie was good to work with. He would try to give me a bunch of assorted pipe orders so I could work out my own system of cutting and threading. The trick was to mix up sizes—do some half inch, then one or two inch. The one- and two-inchers were back busters. Threading and cutting two-inch pipes all day left me a limp rag by quitting time.

I would have wanted more than anything to use the pipe-threading machine around there, but the union did not permit them on the job site. It could be used only in the shop. When I was on a job near the machine, I would sneak into the shop and thread a bunch of pipes. I would think what a relief this machine is, how stupid to break my back when I can just sit and let the machine do it. I thought how proud Max would be of me if he saw me just sitting there watching the machine do the work. I understood the reasons for the union protecting my job from the machine; in 1934 a job was more important than a sore (or even a broken) back. But my back hurt so much I felt the union was nuts.

One day five men started drinking Green River on the roof of a thirty-story Fifth Avenue building, with the temperature somewhere around zero. We were trying to chop out a fire line from a roof tank that had frozen. It was so cold up there we were not able to move around to do the work, so after considerable discussion, I was sent for a pint of Green River. I was happy to get off that roof. When I returned, it was passed around. I tried ducking my turn, for I had not cultivated a whiskey taste as yet, but no way was I to be let out of this.

"Come on, kid, we'll make a man outa ya. Have a good shot of this." So I took a sip, which warmed so well that I took another. So we drank, chopped some ice off the fire line to the tank, and drank some more. By evening we got the covering cleared off the broken fire line. I was amazed to see the power of ice that had split a four-inch pipe open as if it were paper and someone had run a razor down it.

We had done our job. All seemed well until I got in the warm cellar to change my clothes. Vaguely I remember hearing the men say, "Just leave him there. He'll be all right. Let him sleep it off." Socko, like a huge carousel the whole place began to turn. I woke up some time that night with my head in the mop sink, convinced I had been poisoned. Somehow I dragged myself out of there. Finding my way home was one of those great tributes to the human spirit. Next day, to my surprise, nothing happened when I showed up for work. Nobody mentioned or said a thing; it was considered to be a part of the making-a-man-of-me routine, a sort of worker's rite of passage.

This kind of ritual of passage happened many times, including one experience on a Saturday afternoon that ended with me running

out of a whorehouse on 116th Street while it was being raided. I had
gone with two guys from the plant, Tony and Karl. Not being
terribly enthusiastic about the whole thing, I finished quickly to get
it over with and prove I was a man. I was sitting in my car across the
street when suddenly I saw my friend Tony come out the window
onto the fire escape in his shorts, wearing a tie and a jacket. I was
sitting in my 1932 Chrysler roadster pissing in my pants, laughing,
as my bewildered friend jumped in, Tony yelling, "It's a raid. Let's
go. If my mother finds out, Christ, she'll kill me."

"But your pants," I said. "You can't go home like that, and
besides Karl is still in there."

We waited but Karl never showed, so we left. We went to my
house, where we decided that Tony would borrow a pair of my
pants even though they were many sizes too big for his five-foot-
five frame (I was five foot eleven). He looked like a scarecrow, but
no matter; he told his mother some ridiculous story about how his
pants caught on fire. The next day we were the plant heroes. "Did
you hear about the two kids running and beating the cops out of the
whorehouse?" I was one of them—wow—talk about being men. That
was some rite of passage. As manual work continues to decrease, I
am not sure what will happen to this kind of ritual.

One day I was pulled off a job I was working on to help a crew
with a main sewer stoppage in a 75- or 100-family, 20-story
building. I should have suspected that something was up as the guys
greeted me with, "We'll see what this kid's made of." And, "This is
a big job for a big man," and to each other, "Don't know if we got
one. Well, this will tell." I was being challenged, and I knew if I
shriveled and ran away, I would be shunned like a skunk. Though
scared to death, I kept whistling in the dark, saying to myself, Don't
worry. This challenge has to be answered. That is that. Besides it
will be good for me. I hoped.

We unloaded the tools and snakes from the truck and carried
them into the cellar, which because of the stoppage was already
under a foot of water with all kinds of junk floating around. One of
the men said, "OK, kid, here are the boots; put them on. See that
plug over there in the corner? Take it off and start working the

snake into the sewer line as we feed it to you." All the men kind of hung back toward the door. That should have been a clue that there was something fishy going on. But I just forged ahead.

Off I went by myself in my hip boots across the cellar to the sewer line. The line must have been a foot in diameter. I needed a three-foot wrench just to screw out the plug. Then I took the end of the steel snake that the men were feeding to me and began to push it into the pipe. Well, it hadn't gone but six feet when the whole thing let go with a huge geyser that hit the ceiling. A deluge of toilet paper and shit rained all over that basement, and it seemed like it would never stop. I ran, but there was no escaping.

Covered from head to foot with pieces of toilet paper and shit, I finally found a way out of that flooded room, and there were the guys holding their noses and rolling with laughter. I was filled with rage, tears, and fury. I could have killed one of those men, and if I had had a wrench in my hands, I might have, but I had dropped it in the panic of running.

I picked up a hose and was beginning to wash myself off when Hoffey arrived. Looking around, he quickly surmised what had happened and began to roll with laughter, but he looked at me, saw I was in trouble, then shifted quickly to, "One of you guys go get dat kid some dry clothes so he can vosh da shit off himself, or he'll get pneumonia. Hurry up." He further announced to me, "You can go tank some fat-ass lady in da building for sticking her Kotex in da shit house and blocking up da whole place." According to Hoffey, all the world's troubles originated with women's toilet practices.

I recovered from the "Old Faithful Shit Shower," as it became known; and in some way I became a legend around the shop, with Old John going over and over the details so many times with anyone who would listen that after a while I wasn't exactly sure what did happen.

The longer I worked as a plumber's helper, the physically more powerful I became until I felt like I could lick the world and behaved that way. The work made me extremely aware of my body. I had a sense of having discovered every inch of my being, and I strutted that body around for all the girls to see. It was a period of intensive sensuality with anything a good excuse to undress with a chick and do show and tell.

Hoffey once sent me on a mission to placate an opera singer on 96th Street who was complaining about a job that his brother Joe had done. She reported that he had not cleaned up properly. This was another assignment I should have been suspicious of, since Joe was a drunk whom all the plumbers were ashamed of, saying that he was an insult to their professional pride. Not that most of them did not drink. They did. But they had a fierce pride, as do most workers, in their ability to hold their liquor. Joe could not.

I went to 96th Street and was welcomed by a screaming 250-pound Brunhild in her nightgown with her huge teats rolling back and forth across her barrel chest. She was screaming something about her bathtub upstairs. When she took a bath, all the water ran into her closet downstairs and ruined her clothes.

She kept moaning, "I'm ruined. All my clothes are destroyed." As she tore at herself, her nightgown kept opening up more and more. What was there was being exposed, and there was lots of it. I was not sure whether to jump on her or out the window. It was hard for me to believe that even in her hysterics she was not aware of how she was presenting herself. I asked her if I could use the phone, and without waiting for an answer I ran downstairs and in a panic called Hoffey to tell him what was going on. His response was, "See maybe if you could fuck her a little. Dis maybe vill calm her down and ve could talk vit her about da leak. Look, kid, just go dig up da tub und see vot is vit it."

I dug up the tub. There was no trap pipe or anything in the drain, so when Brunhild took her afternoon bath and pulled the plug the water just ran down into her closet. It was beyond belief. I couldn't understand it.

Hoffey came, took one look, closed the door, sat down on the edge of the tub with his head in his hands, mumbling, "Vot am I gonna do vit dat son of a bitch of a brudder. He vill ruin me. Bankrupt me."

I asked him, "What happened?"

"Vot happened?" he yelled. "Dat drunken bum sold da trap for a bottle of cheap vine. Dat's vot he done."

I felt sorry for Hoffey because his brother had made a fool of him, and his German dignity really hurt. This was my first experience with a drunk, but there were many more to come and all seem now as unexplainable as the bathtub with no drainpipe.

Hoffey was sad, all his jolly humor was gone. He told me how to repair the tub and left me there. As I did it, I marveled at Joe's ingenuity in getting booze. By now Brunhild had calmed down and was becoming friendly and very seductive. I thought to myself, I prefer her screaming. As much as I really wanted to fuck a Vest Side vidow, I just couldn't get serious with all that flesh flying around. I was never to have much luck with fat ladies, because I feel very silly being way up there. I have to spend too much time balancing to have any real fun, and besides that makes me giggle. How can you giggle and fuck?

Hoffey was sued by Brunhild. Not for ruining her clothes, but because I made too much dust. I complained to the lawyer that I was in the dust, while she was four rooms away. The lawyer said, "You're just a plumber, and she is an opera singer. Nobody will care about how much dust you swallowed."

He was right. The opera singer won; we lost. Hoffey blamed me. "You're von of dem dumb Americans who like skinny vimmin. Vot you know about a good zaftig ding dere? Dat opera zinger could teach you a few dings." Plumbing, like most construction work, has a high socializing, or schmooze, element.

The kind of plumbing work I have described at Hoffelmeyer is much more reflective of the service end of plumbing than of new construction. However, the work is never completely routine, though on new buildings a lot of pipe is now precut and prethreaded, which means that many plumbers are becoming installers.

One morning on a new construction job I was told to run lead into cast iron pipe joints, and I just kept going from one joint to the next. Around noon I had finished a couple of dozen or so when a plumber came up to me and said, "Who the hell do you think you are, Gunga Din or somebody?" I had no idea what was up, so I just waited, and sure enough he came back with, "What the hell you goin' to do the rest of the day now that you finished the day's work? Now listen. You watch for when the snapper leaves for lunch, get a torch, and get that lead outa half those goddamned joints or we'll put it up your ass."

I was somewhat scared. Horrified, I did them all over again, wondering about all the games that are played out at work. This was another tough lesson in "limiting, soldering, banking, feather-bedding, or holding." All of this means doing less work or maintaining unnecessary tasks in order to stretch it out. Father used to say that if I just worked hard, I would be OK, I would make it. Now I thought he was a liar. It began to seem to me that being successful on a job had more to do with knowing the written and unwritten rules than with how hard you worked. Occasionally it appears to me that many jobs have a sort of a Japanese kabuki character in which each person assumes a role that has little or nothing to do with work.

Some of my best days on the job were ones with humorous moments like the toilet bowl incident on the bus. Most blue-collar workers have a phenomenal ability to create a world of humor at work with in-jokes and lots of teasing, and some good-natured trick playing. I find I miss this kind of humor. It is still very much a part of me and is often not understood by the people I work with now.

Physical prowess was more important in plumbing than in most of the other jobs I have had. Plumbers handle huge wrenches that are three or four feet long, heavy lengths of two- or three-inch pipes, sixteen feet long, which weigh 60 to 100 pounds, and they have to jackass bathtubs, sinks, and toilet bowls. Handling this stuff for eight hours at a time requires a degree of skill, but brawn is also an essential ingredient and plumbers know this.

Plumbers used to argue in a most aggressive way. I wonder now if that is a result of their work. The arguments, like the work, were never vague. It was always: Babe Ruth is the best player who ever lived. Roosevelt is a goddamned socialist. Father Coughlin is the only one who knows what the hell he is talking about. Packard is the best car ever made in the U.S. You can get the syph from kissing a broad.

I believe that workers who do plumbing, construction, or any heavy physical type of work tend to be more aggressive than, say, office machine repairmen. Ibn Khaldun talks about how a craft influences people's thinking and behavior. My experience tends to confirm that. For instance, it is essential that a construction worker make decisions and act. When I had to cut pipe and thread it, I was scared as hell at first to cut a three-inch pipe. Suppose it is too long or too short, and it may well be. However, you learn to act aggressively, you cut it. Occasionally I was wrong (but not too often), that was OK. Unlike intellectual jobs, this work does not permit much time for reflection; it requires action or nothing gets done. I learned to act. That made me aggressive.

Construction workers also tend to be conservative, and that may be related to the unambiguous nature of their work. They have a sense that if one works, one gets results. In spite of their limits on productivity, they still build skyscrapers. Workers do not suffer from the malaise of "who am I," because their work affirms who they are. They are also anxious to protect their jobs for fear of being unemployed, and so run tight membership controls on their unions.

Construction work pays well, offers variety, has plenty of schmooze time, requires some skill and a high level of decision making, especially in small building and rehabilitation work. The $9.50 (in some cases more) hourly wage may be a major satisfier, especially when compared to $5.50 an hour on assembly lines. Some negative aspects, however, are weather and sporadic employment. In addition, some jobs, like covering pipe with asbestos, are extremely injurious to health (many of my old coworkers may now be dying or dead of cancer as a direct result of their jobs), and the accident rate in the construction industry remains one of the highest of all industries in the country. However, the socializing or schmoozing is abundant, and buildings still rise.

# Coal Miner and Farmhand

One of the first radical activities I ever participated in as a kid was collecting food for the striking Harlan County coal miners who, father said, were being starved out by the mine owners. I was still in public school, and I remember asking the kids and people that I knew in the neighborhood to give a can of food for the coal miners who were "fighting the bosses." It was the depression, and I remember being quite embarrassed asking people to give up food that they needed so badly for themselves, but I was proud to be helping my early "cowboy" heroes, the coal miners. My father, with the help of Arturo Giovanetti, his Italian anarchist friend, had convinced me as a child that coal miners were not only the most important people in our society but the most inhumanly exploited as well. What surprised me in my food-for-the-striking-miners campaign was the generous response of people who were themselves so hard up, yet quite willing to help some unknown coal miners in Kentucky. I have seen that kind of working class fraternity demonstrated many, many times. Within a few days I had collected a large carton of canned goods and was so full of pride that I pleaded with my father to let me go with the truck that was to deliver the food.

Other places would become number one radical targets at different times, but just saying Harlan County to father gave me goose pimples. This was tough class war country, and if you wanted to fight in it, Harlan County was the place to go. Well, Papa said no, that was impossible, I was too young yet, but even so, I did not relinquish that dream of becoming a coal miner for some years. A common radical pastime in the thirties was the street corner meeting, and this was where I learned to speak and argue. At one such meeting I met a fellow, Lou Finelli, who said he was from Scranton, Pennsylvania, and had once been a coal miner. I quickly grabbed him, pulled him into the local delicatessen, and said to him, "Listen, Lou, I wanna job as a coal miner. How do I get it?"

"Well," he said, "to begin with, you gotta be nuts. Why the hell would anybody in his right mind wanna go down in those hellholes?" I had no idea what he was talking about. Coal miners were my heroes, "the most important members of society." How could he say such things? Lou was sympathetic to my radical politics, but could not connect at all to my desire to be a coal miner.

We talked away half the night. I guess I wore him down, because finally he said, "OK, you're nuts. That's your problem. But here's the address of my aunt and uncle, who live near Scranton, Pennsylvania. They have thirteen kids and seven of the nine boys are coal miners. They'll help you get a job if there are any, which they ain't."

I never heard a word he said. I was flying. Here was my big chance to be a coal miner. Once I got my hands on all that dynamite, by God, I would blow up the world.

It was spring, the weather was fine, and within a week, I was on a bus to Scranton. The ride was long and grinding as the old white bus, with the driver forever shifting gears, lurched its way from town to town until finally it arrived with a big turn into the tiny bus terminal in Scranton. I was the first off, saw a shoeshine kid, grabbed him, and asked for directions to the nearest mine. According to my shoeshine friend it was not too far. I started walking. Still elated over the prospects of becoming a miner hero, I ignored the drabness of the town, the row upon row of company houses, the coal dust that lay over the place, and the miners coming home carrying their metal lunch buckets, covered with coal and fatigue. The way they walked they seemed so done-in that I began to wonder if I had made a mistake in coming to Scranton instead of going to Harlan, Kentucky. They sure didn't look like no heroes; they just looked worn out. Oh well, I thought, it's the end of the day.

I watched one man turn in his gate. His wife, a big buxom

woman, said, "Come on back here, and I'll scrub you down." The man, all six foot of him, just nodded. Looking over the fences around endless rows of little peaked-roof houses, I watched as he undressed to his shorts, and as he slumped down on a small milking stool, he appeared to become small. His white body and black face and hands just hung there as she began to scrub him with a brush. As I watched I found I was crying for that beat-out coal miner overwhelmed by that big woman's love. It looked as if she was trying to brush the life back into him. Then she poured buckets of water over his head and he began to laugh as he began to see the light. He seemed to stop peering into space.

I found the Collinaris' house and went through the gate. A youngish woman answered my knock, and I quickly explained who had sent me, asking if I could see John. She seemed embarrassed in front of me. Was it because I was a city slicker? Many times in small towns in years to come I would encounter working class women who seemed vaguely threatened by big-city sin.

I moved toward the door, hoping she would invite me in. Instead she sort of blocked my way and suggested, "Why don't you just sit out here on the porch until John comes home. It's such a lovely evening anyhow." Somewhat disappointed at the lack of welcome, I sat on the porch, waiting in the cool mountain air, listening to the creak and clang of the mine hoists on their gallows frames dumping the coal into tram cars on their way to the colliers.

As I sat there waiting, a pickup truck pulled up and a big, six-foot-two guy jumped out with his tin lunch bucket. My presence seemed to surprise him because he stared out at me from what seemed to be enormous white eyes popping out of his black face. I introduced myself sort of cheerfully, which he did not seem to appreciate at all, and I recited who had sent me. He finally said in a sort of flat monotone, "There ain't no work in the mines and you shouldn't have come here."

John started in the door. The meeting was over as far as he was concerned. With the screen door half-open I pleaded, saying that I would do anything to get a job in the mines. "OK, go to D&H

tomorrow, see Smithers, and tell him I sent you. Ask him for a mule boy's job."

I hadn't the slightest idea what the hell he meant by a mule boy. I wanted to be a miner. He was already in the house with me standing outside. I added hastily, "What happens if I don't get the job?"

He looked me straight in the face through the screen door and said, "Then you're like all the rest of the folks around here; flat on your ass. What the fuck did you come here for? Everyone around here is leavin', lookin' for jobs, and you're comin'; you gotta be a crazy kid."

I was lost for a reply. Christ, how could I explain to him about Harlan County and miners as heroes and all that? Then he would be sure I was nuts. I just said, "Look, I can't go back to the city without some kind of job. People will think I was just a bust." By now I was beginning to have some real doubts about my career as a miner. In a last-minute plea I said, "Don't you have any other suggestions if the mine thing doesn't work out?"

John was becoming impatient. I said, "Why don't I come back later," hoping he might invite me in, which he did not. He agreed that that was a good idea. I left my bag on the porch and walked back onto the unpaved dirt street, trying to figure out what to do. I decided to return to the bus station, find that shoeshine kid, and ask him about mule boys.

"Mule boys," he said, "are kids who lead the mules pulling the coal cars in the mines. Now some mines got engines, and they don't use mules no more, but you gotta lead the mules, 'cause they are bat-blind and can't see nothin', 'cause they live in the mines and the darkness blinds 'em. Now a mule boy also gotta feed and take care of his mules. If the mules get sick or get sores, you gotta clean 'em up and put salve on their sores."

I asked him how could you get to be a mule boy. He said, "You gotta know someone who works there and know the bosses." He looked up at me real funny and said, "You really wanna go to work in those mines, dontcha? You must be nuts comin' from New York to a place like this."

"Well," I said, "you see, I'm a writer, and I want to write about the mines." He just laughed, twirled his finger on the side of his head, indicating I was crazy, and walked off.

I went back to John's house, saying that I was just here to pick up my bag. I quickly thanked him for everything. I guess he had eaten because he seemed more relaxed now. He said, "Look, go over to D&H tomorrow, see Smithers, and if he don't have nothin' for you, go out to my mom and dad's place in Factoryville. They got a 400-acre truck and dairy farm; around this time they can always use help. Just take the road to Nicholson. If you go under the big concrete railroad bridge, you went too far and should go back. That railroad bridge is the biggest poured concrete structure in the world. Buried in the concrete are two niggers that they could never get out once they started pouring her. When you get to the house, tell my mother I sent you." I sure felt better. Just in case things didn't go well at D&H, at least I could work at something without going back to New York as a complete bust.

I slept in the YMCA that night, rose bright and eager the next morning to see Smithers at the D&H Coal Company. I went in the front office where a young lady told me to have a seat and that she would get in touch with him. I must have waited an hour or so before she told me to go out into the yard and cross it to the little office inside the second shack on the left. Once in the yard I saw the huge gallows frames hoisting, squeaking, and rumbling their endless stream of coal onto conveyers and trams. Wow, this was exciting. I had a hard time imagining myself being part of this earth-shaking job.

Smithers was an older man, half bald, with huge stooping shoulders, and hands that gave him away as someone who had spent most of his life doing hard physical labor. He looked at me over his glasses and just said, "Yeah?" Expecting more, I stumbled into telling about who had sent me; a name with which he was unfamiliar, or if he knew it, he gave no sign of knowing. In my excitement over watching the coal-hoisting machines, I forgot all about mule boys and just busted out with, "I wanna be a coal miner."

There was a long silence as he sat looking out the dust-covered window. I had the feeling he was reviewing what he might say. He turned from looking nowhere to looking at me and said, "You ever been in a mine, kid?" He did not wait, for he seemed to know the answer.

Not knowing if I should lie or not, I hesitated. He stood up and said, "Come on, I'm gonna show you what the inside of the earth's asshole looks like. Maybe you can tell your friend John that he's crazy for sending you here. It would be better to send you to the crazy house."

As we walked across the yard he was a couple of annoyed strides ahead of me. He said, "We're going in the 'drys' for some old clothes." We went into a large, tin, garagelike building. The entire inside was covered with clothes hanging from the ceiling, and for each set there was a rope and pulley. He looked around at what appeared to be hundreds of washline cords, finally unhooked two lines, let the clothes drop, and said, "Now, get into these."

I kind of followed him as he put on coveralls, boots, and a helmet. We then walked out into the yard again to another building he called the lamp house where he asked Mike to give us a couple lamps. Mike pulled two lamps off a shelf and said they were all charged to go. Smithers gave me quick instructions on how to use the carbide lamp and ended with, "If you let it go out, you might wander around down there in the dark forever."

With the boots, coveralls, helmet, lamp, and belt, I was in my heroes' costume. I felt as though I was about to meet the oracle at Delphi, for somehow a fantasy seemed to be becoming real. I was so excited that I began not to hear what Smithers was saying.

Complete in miners' regalia we walked across the yard, past the huge tipple to the hoist head, where he grabbed a cord and gave it a series of pulls that rang a bell telling the hoistman we wanted to go to the three-hundred-foot level. We waited for a long time. Finally three or four other men came to the gate and asked Smithers, "Where the hell you goin'? You sure ain't gonna blast rock."

"No," he said, "I have a new miner here who is goin' to take a tour of our lovely mine. Imagine that dumb shithead Collinari sendin' me this poor kid here to work in the mines, who was never farther down than his cellar."

They all laughed and one of them asked, "Which Collinari?"

"Who else would be so dumb but John."

Without thinking I asked, "How many are there?" Instantly I knew I had made a mistake. If I was a friend and all that, how come I did not know how many there were. I tried to cover by adding that I wondered how many work in this mine. It was a goof, but one of the men said, "I guess about seven in this one, and two in Diamond Number Four." My God, I thought to myself, imagine the power of one family with nine coal miners in it.

Suddenly the "cage," an elevator made of four sections of fence wire, arrived. The side we were waiting at flew up, and we stepped on. A bell sounded a couple of times, and as though someone had taken an ax and cut the cables, we were free-falling straight to hell into pitch blackness. My stomach was in my mouth as I hung onto the wire side for dear life, and all I could see were the flickering lamps of the men on the cage. As we were coming to a stop, my knees began to buckle and Smithers grabbed me to keep me standing.

I was feeling wobbly and sick as we stepped into a darkness I had never known—it was as if I had been dropped into a can of black paint. Smithers said, "Turn your light up and follow me." Christ, I didn't think it would be this dark. Now I was scared. Smithers kept saying, "Keep your head down," which I tried to do because my hard hat kept scraping the roof.

As we walked I became aware that we were sloshing along in at least six inches of water, and I realized my eyes were becoming accustomed to the dark. On the walls of the tunnels there were endless signs with numbers and arrows pointing to different work areas. Suddenly a whistle blew; Smithers, who had been silent for some time, pushed me against the tunnel wall, and a huge blast seemed to creak all the timbers holding the place up. There was a terrible stench of sewer gas as clouds of dust bellowed through the mine, reducing our beams of light to a few feet in front of us.

I kept peering into the darkness, looking for signs of miners at work. I knew from their sounds they were there, but where? Finally, after stooping down more and more to where we were walking bent in half, there was a roaring noise of rock drills and all I could see were many flickering lamps darting about. Smithers took my arm, indicating we should stop in this working area.

About twenty men were drilling, timbering, and mucking coal. The noise of the rock drills made communicating by voice impossible. Smithers gave a sign, and the men stopped the drills. They pointed their lamps and, recognizing Smithers, greeted him with, "How the fuck did you get down here? What happened? You get lost on the way to the shit house?" He acknowledged them but somehow did not join in the banter, saying, "This young man here wants to be a coal miner."

I couldn't see expressions on people's faces down there. Everyone looked like Al Jolson doing Mammy. They then turned so that their head lamps shone on me, and one miner said, "Where you from, kid?" "New York." It somehow seemed to be a very funny joke and everyone laughed. "Give 'im a shovel and let 'im muck for a while. We'll see what he wants to be."

I was handed what seemed to be the biggest shovel I ever saw. I pushed it into a pile of huge chunks of coal and not seeing the coal car with the old mule in front of it, asked where to put it. The men laughed, "Carry it upstairs to Minnie Bell's whorehouse, and maybe you can get a piece of ass for it."

They laughed at the poor city slicker who didn't know how much fun he could give a group of coal miners. Well, I lifted the shovel of coal to put it in the car; the shovel hit the roof and the coal flew, mostly all over me. More roars of laughter. Well, by now, I was laughing too, and Smithers said, "OK, you're cured. Now go get yourself some fancy-pants job in an office and you won't get your dumb head blown off."

I sensed that the men underground loved our visit so much they wished that we would stay a little longer. One after another they coaxed, "Let me put 'im on the drill, let 'im set the charge, let 'im put up a timber." They had an absolute delight in making it pretty clear that the city slicker didn't know anything.

As we sloshed away, someone shouted, "Take him up and get him laid. Then he'll know where to shovel this shit." And another yelled, "Hope he knows more about where to stick his dick than he does about muckin' coal." The place rolled with laughter. I knew that I was the joke for the day and somehow did not mind it that much. Many times I was to see men find ways to laugh while working in hell.

The miners I visited that day, like many I would meet much later as a union representative, shared a communal tie that I have seldom seen in any other group of workers. How adversity welds people together! Such ties grow out of need at work, but in the case of miners, they are also part of a tribal pride that results from facing death together every working day.

Smithers and I went back to the "drys," cleaned up, hoisted the coveralls back up on the ceiling, checked in our helmets and carbide lamps; my mining career was over. Smithers now put his arm on my shoulder and said, "OK kid, you satisfied now? You don't want no part of these mines." I hesitated, but he did not wait. He said, "I hope you can find some nice clean place to work where you won't get your balls blown off like in these goddamned coal mines." That was it. There was no more to say. I was a little sad but still elated by the trip into the mine.

"Get yourself a job in a nice clean place." How often I would hear that phrase repeated over and over again. I now believe what most workers want is a job in a nice clean place. Could this be why, when full employment gives a choice, as in some European countries like Sweden or Germany, people seem to prefer not to do manual work? Is it because most manual workplaces are not nice, clean, comfortable, tidy, or air-conditioned? And yet, miners have such an intense capacity for laughter, living, and loving. In contrast, people in nice clean offices often do not seem to know about life; maybe this is because they don't know what people who work in the earth know about death.

I never did get to work in the mines, but I had a brief and wonderful association with miners as a representative of the Mine, Mill and Smelter Workers on the East Coast and in Montana. It was in Montana that I got to know hard-rock miners as one of the most intense bunch of lively people I would ever encounter. The relationship with that group of men made all subsequent ones seem pale in comparison. Well, it was also a crusade, a major campaign to save a union, which creates a tremendous amount of life energy—but more about that later.

I felt let down by my very abrupt career as a coal miner, but could not see any way to reopen the subject. I thanked Smithers, took my bag, asked for directions to Factoryville, and thumbed a ride on a small dump truck. The driver asked where I was going and said he would drop me there, adding that the family I sought "was all damn hard-working guineas."

As we bumped along in the cab of the truck, I had a funny feeling about the mine that made me a little glad that I didn't get the job. I recalled how my eyes hurt as the cage emerged into the light, and I thought how lousy it must be to have to become accustomed to daylight every day.

The driver asked, "You're not from around here, are you?"

Startled and fearful that my identity was being revealed, I said, "How do you know?"

"Well, as soon as you opened your mouth, I could tell you weren't from Wilkes Barre-Scranton, 'cause folks 'round here don't talk like you."

"Like what?" I asked.

"Well, kind of hard. Like you're always pushin' somethin', not just conversationing. What you gonna do here?"

"Well, I hope to work on the farm."

"I guess they can always use some help, with all the boys working in the mines and the damn farm mostly shalestone. You know anything about shalestone?"

"No," I said.

"Well, it's the goddamnest stuff. You can pick a field clean as a baby's ass of shalestone by Friday, and you know what? On Monday it'll look like it rained shalestone all weekend. Just don't know where it comes from, but it just keeps comin' up."

The truck started slowing down in front of a big white farmhouse set back a couple hundred feet off the road. Huge shade trees and several large and small barns surrounded the main house. There seemed to be lots of things happening right around the house with kids and animals moving about and a group of people around a makeshift stall with the biggest damn horse I had ever seen in it.

I walked up to the house, knocked on the front door, then pressed a button. Nothing happened. I was unsure and hesitated, not wanting to walk in the yard with all those men around that huge horse. Besides, I wanted to talk to the mother first because I felt she would be the most sympathetic. A boy about twelve years old kind of spotted me, came over, and asked, "What you want?"

I asked, "Where is your mother?"

"She's in the milk house. I'll go get her."

"No, I'll wait until she's finished."

The kid never heard me. He was off and running. The mother emerged from one of the barns, wiping her hands on the black apron that she wore over her black dress. Her hair was gray and tightly pulled back. She was about five foot four, wore steel-rimmed glasses, and looked utterly exhausted. She did not seem at all friendly as she came up to me, simply matter-of-fact. "What do you want? Who sent you?"

I explained as quickly as possible that I could work hard, do anything, and needed a job real bad. She never looked at me, just continued in her monotone voice, "You can stay until the fall, your room, board, and six dollars a week. Did you ever do farm work?" How to answer that without lying! In the depression years there was no limit to what was considered ethical in order to get a job, so you just lied. "Did you ever do farm work?" The answer was "Yes, of course I have," anxiously hoping she would not pursue my answer with any further questions. Luckily she did not.

The twelve-year-old kid sort of standing against the porch railing was taking in the whole scene. His mother said, "Patsy, take him up and show him the room, then let him help with the afternoon milking. Then after that we'll have dinner."

Patsy led the way up the narrow wooden stairs of the old farmhouse. The house smelled of old, peeling wallpaper, cooking oil, garlic, roasts, and old dirty clothes. In the second floor hall there seemed to be an endless number of doors, almost all of them open.

As we passed, all I could see were unmade beds. We went into a tiny room at the end of the hall that had yellow, peeling wallpaper and just enough space to walk between the bed and the wall. There was a window that looked out on the fields in back of the house and a bed high enough so that you could lie there and see out over the pastures.

Patsy had me worried. He was a kid who had a way of eyeing me with a certain skepticism that just made me uncomfortable. But he also had an almost endless curiosity about the big city, and that saved our relationship. "How big is the Woolworth Building? Is there really a place where you put a nickel in a slot and get a sandwich? I don't believe that."

Patsy made me feel like a celebrity. "Yes," I said with great authority, "there is such a place and it is called the Automat."

Patsy felt he was being conned. "That's impossible, 'cause how would the sandwich get back in the little box once you took it out." Now I expanded my story, explaining the mechanics of the Automat. His interest in my big-city stories was matched only by his skepticism about what I told him. He would almost always say, "Yeah—but I don't believe that."

I changed into some old clothes I had brought with me and started with Patsy for the barn. As we passed the group of men gathered around that giant horse tied up in some sort of half stall, Patsy explained that the horse hated being shoed, so the six or seven men were trying to hold him for the blacksmith to do his job.

Patsy was beginning to compete with me in telling about his place, the farm, as I told him about my place, the city. He said, "That horse doesn't like to be shoed no way. And, you know, he's so strong that he'll pull that whole damn stall and six men down with him if he wants to because he and his brother won the Pennsylvania State Fair championship for workhorses. They're Belgians, you know."

The men around the horse all looked at Patsy and me. No one said anything and no one was introduced. Nor was anyone formally introduced to me in all the weeks that I worked there. It was a shyness born of a leeriness about outsiders, and I was suspect as a stranger entering their home.

Patsy and I went into the barn, where two men had begun milking about seventy cows. Patsy gave me a bucket and said, "Put some soap and water in it, stay ahead of Mike over there, and wash the cows' teats."

Not knowing what the hell he was talking about, I said, "Yes," filled the buckets, went over to the cow next to Mike, and looked at the udders. I took the rag, tried to squeeze between the cows locked in their stanchions, and began to wipe around the bag, kind of avoiding the udders.

Mike watched and without saying anything came over, gave one of the cows a whack, yelled, "Get over there you," and with that just gave the cow a shove.

He took the rag from my hand, soaked it in the bucket, began to scrub the udders, bag and all. Then he handed it to me, saying, "These ain't no virgins, kiddo, scrub 'em, don't tickle 'em." I did, and I found the udders to be the sexiest damn things, so warm and soft. With that nice milk dripping from them, I began to wish I had a bunch of nice warm penises like those udders.

Mike came up behind me and put the milking machine on the udders after I'd washed and scrubbed. In the course of this I was getting my shoes full of cowshit, which somehow I didn't seem to mind. The smell of the milk, the oats, the manure, and the feel of the cows kept me in a perpetual state of excitement. I was just getting a little ahead of Mike with my wash and scrub when he said, "Hey, kid, come over here now and milk these cows dry."

It turned out that the machine with all its fifthting and fufthting did not dry out all the milk from the udder. It was necessary to dry the cows out by hand. I watched as Mike dried a few cows. He proceeded to squeeze the udders, and milk came out until it was dry. Then I tried, but nothing happened. I squeezed harder and harder until I was feeling sorry for the poor cow, who turned her head and looked at me with a great air of incredulity.

Mike came over and, watching me for a minute, said, "You don't know nothin' about cows." Pushing me aside almost as he had shoved the cows, he sat down on the milking stool and said, "You got to squeeze and pull at the same time." The cow seemed to be stomping around a lot so Mike looked at her udders and said, "Let me see your hands."

I pushed them out palms up. He turned them over, looked at my nails, saying, "This ain't no beauty parlor. Go cut your fancy New York fingernails before you have every cow's teats in this barn so raw we won't be able to touch 'em without the cow stompin' your feet off. Damn, dumb kid, think you're in a French whorehouse instead of a cow barn?"

I was scared again, sure I would be fired. Christ, I thought, I wasn't going to make it, even as a farmhand. Now, where could I find scissors? I didn't dare ask Mike. Where the hell was Patsy? Luckily, I found Patsy in the milk room pouring milk from the buckets into milk cans.

I was hardly in the room when he yelled, "What you doin' comin' in the milk room with all that shit on your feet!" More panic. I backed out and stood at the door, asking him if there were any scissors around that I could cut my nails with. He thought for a while then said, "Yeah, over in the feed room, near the bran sacks."

I found the feed room, where the scissors turned out to be tin shears. I clipped off my fingernails and rushed back to the barn only to see that they were almost finished. I put my stool under one of the last cows, tried again, and managed to get out a few drops of milk. Though I had only been trying this hand-milking on a few cows, I felt my fingers would drop off if I had to do this twice a day with seventy-two cows. I understood why someone, experiencing what a finger-breaking labor this was, had invented the milking machine.

We were pretty well through milking and I was relieved until Mike said, "Start opening the stanchions and let 'em out." I figured out pretty quick how to open the stanchions, but I was afraid of the cows' horns. Some would whip their heads as I opened the latch, and so I had to move back. As I let them out, some of them just stood there gazing at me and bumping into one another. Frustrated, I thought, goddamned dumb cows, don't even know what to do.

Mike came over, picked up a broom and whacked their backs. "Get 'em out of here," he yelled at me.

I took the broom, and half-scared, I tapped them saying, "Out, out." Nothing; they just stared at me without budging.

A voice from the far end of the barn yelled, "Whack 'em, god-damnit." Without thinking, I whacked the first cow nearby. She lurched for the door and to my surprise, out they went. By God it worked! I went around that barn with the broom, whacking cows and feeling more like a matador than a farmhand. There is a great sense of power in making big animals do what you want, especially since you are aware of the danger that lurks in those horns. One swing of her head in your guts and you're as wide open as a side of beef in the local butcher shop.

Once the cows were gone, Mike, Patsy, and another man began to push out the huge amounts of manure. We cleaned down the whole barn with hoses and then washed ourselves in a long trough. As we washed, nobody talked. The work seemed to be too tedious to allow for conversation, or maybe they were all sick of being married to these seventy-two head of cows to be milked twice a day, 365 days a year.

As they drifted toward the house I followed them. It was a warm, lovely evening and everyone seemed to be moving slowly. The big Belgian was out of the shoeing stall in a nearby pasture with his brother. The cows were eating their way out to a distant field. The smell of hay, animals, and sweet manure filled the air. I felt good about the place but strange about the work. It was the end of my first day as a farmhand.

I ate dinner that night around a big oval table with about twelve people: seven sons who came home from the mines, two daughters who ran back and forth to the kitchen, two hands in addition to myself, a baby who scurried around the floor and was fed off the table together with two dogs. The sons who worked in the mines talked about how the company was trying to chisel them on their tonnage.

Mrs. Collinari introduced me as, "He's from New York," and told me where to sit. There was some snickering, some embarrassment, and then the men wanted to know if the girls in New York "are really hot." I said I didn't know, and everyone laughed. I said little or nothing, feeling too embarrassed. I was starving, so the dinner was doubly delicious with lots of hearty food passed endlessly around the table, everyone eating voraciously.

After dinner the women went to the kitchen as the men drifted off in the four pickup trucks parked in the driveway. I was dying to go with the fellows, but they never suggested it, and I was too shy to ask them, so I guess they figured I was still a kid.

I was left at home with the younger kids, mama, and papa. Nobody seemed interested in conversation, so I went to my room, got a book, and went out on the porch to read. I found I could not concentrate on the print. I just sat there taking in the smells, the evening bird songs, and the house across the road.

I was tired and could have nodded off to sleep. However, my first day's excitement was still upon me. There is something about intense physical work, besides the fatigue, that makes reading hard. I think it has to do with the different nature of the two activities, one a live, multidimensional experience and the other an intellectualizing of experience through little black printed symbols called words. The symbols are quite pale in contrast to a barnful of cows or the blasting of coal out of a mine face. I was unable to get into the books I had brought along.

Across the road, a girl moved around the porch. I could not see her eyes but I sensed her looking at me. She was a big girl and bursting from her blouse. I made believe I was looking at my book, but it didn't work. The kids were playing catch in the back, so I joined them. About nine o'clock the unsmiling, exhausted Mrs. Collinari said, "We get up at five to milk, so you better get plenty of sleep. Good night." She went into the house while we continued to play catch.

I went to bed wondering what I would be doing the next day. It seemed I had been sleeping but a short time when I heard the alarm ringing and the whole house coming to life. When I went downstairs expecting breakfast, people were heading toward the barn.

Patsy, still irritated with me, said, "Come on. First we milk, then we have breakfast." One of the girls, with the aid of a collie dog, was bringing in the cows. I watched the dog work in absolute awe. It was as though Lassie of the movies had suddenly come real. The dog kept moving in wider circles around the herd, barking and nipping at the cows' legs. Though all tangled in each other's legs and teeth, neither the cows nor dog ever seemed to get hurt. I loved watching that dog working, for he seemed to enjoy thoroughly his routine task as it was repeated over and over, each time done as if it were a brand-new discovery. It was one of those untamed farm experiences that city kids are deprived of.

As I watched the dog working, one of the hands asked me what I was looking at. When I told him, he could not understand how that was interesting. I began to feel that the people working around the farm had as little interest in what they were doing as the cows coming to the barn, where some just seemed to stand in the big doorway waiting to be told where to go. Sure enough, the whacking started again. I just let them go to whatever stanchion they chose, but that quickly earned me a "Goddamnit, you just don't know nothin' about nothin'! How the hell are we gonna keep records of what these cows are giving if we don't know who is in what stall?"

I thought all the cows sort of looked alike but I began to realize that these farm kids and hands knew every one of the seventy-two cows and what stanchion they belonged in. They showed me a brass tag in each cow's ear that had a name and a number so you could check to make sure, but Patsy said, "If you gotta do that, you'll get stuck with one of those horns sure as shootin'." Well, with plenty of whacking, pushing, yelling, and shoving we finally had everyone where they belonged, and we then proceeded to feed, wash, and milk them. In spite of directing some cows to the wrong stanchion, I was beginning to feel comfortable working in the barn, for I was learning my way around and I liked the smell, the feel, the magic of the milk coming out of the cow.

We finished milking and went to breakfast, which was like dinner: pork chops and tomatoes. The kids (with whom I seemed to have been included) and I had cold cereal. The sons laughed at me. "It's a good thing you don't work in the mines, you'd never make it on that stuff."

The miners left in their pickup trucks, each with his lunch bucket that somehow mama had managed to pack while we were milking. As they were leaving, she crossed herself, kissed each one, and almost inaudibly in Italian said a small prayer for each of them. This ceremony was repeated every morning, and the miners believed in it as much as mama did.

After we had finished breakfast, Mrs. Collinari, who had hardly spoken to me since I had arrived, said, "Take the brothers and plow that upper forty." The instruction was given in such a way as to suggest that any fool, except me, would know what it meant. I did not dare ask who or what are the brothers and where are the upper forties.

I said nothing until we left the table, and then I caught up with Patsy to ask him where the brothers were. "In the barn, where do you think?"

I went to the barn; of course, I remembered, the brothers were those two mammoth Belgian horses. Now as I stood behind them they seemed to be the biggest animals I had ever seen.

Patsy said, "The bridle's on the wall and the plow's outside." Having hung around the milk-wagon horses in the city, I had a general idea that the bridle went over the horse's head, but beyond that I did not know much. I took the bridle and tried to get in the stall next to the horse. I was scared that if he ever moved against the stall I would be crushed. I finally got to the front of the horse, but every time I lifted the bridle to put it over his head, he would buck his head and the bridle would end up on the floor.

Patsy was sitting across from the stall watching me all the time. By now I was getting mad at his obvious delight in my stupidity, and that little sonofabitch finally said, "You don't know nothin' about horses, and you don't know nothin' about Automats."

I burst out with "I'll give you a quarter if you help me get these goddamn horses on the plow."

"OK," he said, and all four foot five of him strutted over to the stall. "Get outa my way," he commanded as he walked into the stall, unhooked the rope, whacked the horse's rump and yelled, "Back up, back up." The horse backed out of the stall into the open barn space. Patsy said, "Here's where you bridle up a horse—not in the stall, stupid."

He walked back and forth, taking straps off the wall, throwing straps over and under the horse. All the time he kept saying, "You better learn this, 'cause I ain't gonna do your work."

I was trying to concentrate on all the different straps. Luckily, there were two horses to do because I would never have got it from the first one. We finally finished and Patsy took the reins, saying giddyap as those two giant rumps moved slowly out of the barn.

Outside, Patsy hooked the plow to the bridle line, showing me how to move the blade up and down. He pointed to a field up a hill. "That's the upper forty beyond the barn, past the two pastures."

Greatly relieved, I quickly paid him his quarter. He looked at it, then at me, and said, "You're OK. You keep your word."

I said giddyap and walked proudly behind those two huge horses' rumps. I breathed another sigh of relief: I had survived another crisis. After going through a variety of pasture gates, most tied up with pieces of wire, I came to the upper forty. I lowered the blade as Patsy had showed me and said, "Giddyap." Wow, the horses started pulling. Was I surprised! The plow blade cut deep into the earth, growling against rocks. The brothers seemed to be simply taking a walk, but their power so overwhelmed me I found myself singing at the top of my lungs an old union song, "Hold the Fort, For We Are Coming." The brothers kept looking back at me as though they were confused, thinking that the song was some kind of a new command. I continued to sing with a little less command in my voice.

We plowed to the end of the field, where the horses stopped, looking back at me for instructions. Of course, I thought, I have to give them direction with the reins. I let go of the plow handles and pulled the reins for the brothers to go to the right. They did, but quicker than I could get my hands back on the plow. Over it went, twisting all the straps as it dragged along on its side. I yelled, "Whoa, whoa." Thank God that worked and the brothers stopped.

What a mess! What was I gonna do with this tangle of straps? I began to unhook one strap at a time, trying to straighten them out. The damn horses kept bobbing their heads and whisking their tails, trying to keep the flies away, all of which just added to my confusion. Things were getting worse, for together with my growing panic came swarms of bees buzzing around. The sun had come up hot, and as I looked toward the barn I happily noticed that my savior, Patsy, was on his way.

He arrived with a bag and dropped it on the ground, saying, "That's your lunch. There's water over there," pointing to a hollow. Then he looked at the condition of the plow, looked at me with his usual snottiness, and announced, "You don't know nothin' about plowin'."

He said he would show me this one last thing and that was it. He obviously had been watching me from somewhere, because he said, "Jesus, dontcha know nothin'? You can't hold the plow and the reins both, so put the reins around your shoulder. When you wanna turn the horses, turn yourself the way you wanna go, but keep the reins tight so they always know you're there. They gotta know you're there." Then he added with total contempt, "Listen, those are the smartest horses in Pennsylvania, so don't you go blame them if you don't know what you're doin'." I had not said a word about the brothers. Patsy unhooked each leather line, untangled and rehooked them. He said, "OK, you can try again. But you better do it or mama's gonna be mad."

I learned to plow. For a few days I liked it because the brothers and I seemed to become friends. I thought this because when we were near the stream in the hollow, I would let them drink and they would turn to look at me, shaking their heads, which seemed to me to be a thank you.

I was behind that plow for a few weeks that now seemed like forever as the soreness in my ankles increased from walking over the roughly plowed earth without being able to choose where I could step. I had to just keep up with the horses. I got to know the brothers mostly from their huge rumps. After a few days, I began to be able to tell just when they were getting ready to shit. The huge tail would be continuously swishing flies away, then it would lift just a little, exposing his anus. Then there were a few small farts. Sometimes one of them would fart and turn his head to look back at me as though to see what was happening. I would yell, "Beautiful, do it again!" He would buck his head. Then, little by little, the tail would go up, the anus would undulate awhile, and then those huge beautiful shit balls would just roll out one after the other. As we continued plowing I began to love these horses, and I thought they were the only creatures I knew that were majestic even when shitting. There was something about walking behind those giant behinds that gave me a great sense of power. I felt like the master of the earth.

Pissing was something else again. The penis would start to emerge, long and languorous. It would grow longer and longer. They would both stop when either of them had to piss, the other waiting until the pissing one had finished. Now there's real friendship, I thought. Then we would go on plowing, but the penis would hang out there for a while airing itself. Sometimes I would join the brothers in a piss; even today, I still enjoy an outside leak compared to antiseptic toilets.

Watching that huge penis, I would fantasize on how it would be to see one of those horses fucking a mare. Wow! Work often includes time for sexual fantasy, but here was a very live reality that I found very stimulating indeed, even though I was physically tired. In contrast, working in an office can be as antiseptic as iodine, and most factories are so mechanical as to destroy sensual experience, though not necessarily sexual fantasies.

After a few weeks, work on the farm seemed to be getting quite routine. I plowed, helped with the milking, cleaned the barn, pitched hay, and sat around at night with the kids, since the older men never bothered much with me except to make remarks periodically about the "big city slicker" who "reads books but don't know a horse's ass from a knothole." I had brought along some books that I would look at once in a while, though I never got into much reading. It was one of these books that I had not read which would abruptly end my job as a farmhand. However, before leaving this job I was to learn something about stoop labor that I never forgot.

One morning at breakfast when I was somewhat uncertain about my work assignment for the day, mama announced with some defiance, "Today we pick beans." From the moans and looks on the kids' faces I knew this was going to be bad, and one of the coal miners commented that he'd "rather be in the mines than do that."

Papa Collinari, who never spoke, announced, "I'm goin' to town."

Mama said, "That's right, all you big tough men leave the hard jobs to me and the kids. Nice bunch of men you are."

I did not like being part of the kids and mama's bean-picking brigade, but that is where I was put. I was given a big hat, told to keep it on because we would be in the hot sun all day and to go with the kids to start picking.

As we walked to the barn to get the bushels, Patsy was hitching one of the brothers to a wagon. He looked at me sort of funny, a twelve-year-old wise guy, giggling and saying, "The Polack's daughter Margaret from across the road is going to work beans with us today for twenty-five cents a bushel, so you and her can work together on each side of the row." He skipped off giggling while he finished hitching the Belgians to the buckboard. I was excited by the thought of Margaret, remembering my sight of her from the porch. Margaret arrived, shy and kind of big, and when we all climbed in the wagon, mama gave Margaret and me a look that said she knew that we had evil thoughts on our minds. Off we went in the wagon in what started out to seem like a picnic but turned out to be a day of various tortures.

As we rode in the wagon, Margaret and I surreptitiously stole glances at each other. We finally arrived at the bean field. I had seen a bean patch, but never acres of it. I thought, my God, we couldn't pick this in a year. The wagon was unloaded. Bushels were distributed and mama assigned us our rows and off we went. We started picking beans, and I thought, Jesus, this is easy. The sun was hot, the bugs were all over us. My first desire was to peel off clothes, but I was learning to watch what farm people do and everyone seemed to be covering up , so I decided that it would be best for me to do the same.

Margaret was on the other side of the row, and slowly we began to talk as we picked. Her blouse was open enough for me to see her large breasts squeezed into her bra. Our conversation was all about the city. That made me feel important as I talked about the tall buildings, the many movie theaters, the subway. "Can you really walk inside the head of the Statue of Liberty?" she asked.

"In the head?" I said. "Why, you can go right up the arm."

"Wow," she replied, "that's amazin'."

Most of the day in the bean patch I worked with a hard-on, which was fine because it kept me from taking notice of the condition of my back until later that night, when I thought I would die from the pains as I tried straightening up.

As we picked, I talked with Margaret a lot about books and things I had read. We were both being excited by each other. Unfortunately there was mama's ever-watchful eye, so we knew we would have to meet somewhere alone. I wondered why mama let us work together. Was she tempting me or was she just being good to both of us? Or was she about to show her little daughters the evils of city men? I finally suggested to Margaret that we meet after dinner at the swimming hole near Nicholson Bridge, where we could read some of the books together that I had brought. She was terribly embarrassed and her big wide face turned red, but she nodded her assent. I was wishing I could go back to plowing before my meeting with her so I wouldn't be so stooped over when we met.

The swimming hole was about a half mile from the house, down an embankment. It was late in the evening when we met, and I felt so strange, half-stooped over from the bean picking. We took a quick swim, cooled off, dressed, and went for a walk under the huge arches of the Nicholson Railroad Bridge. Margaret was a big girl, not fat, just big all over, and she seemed to be busting out of everything. We finally found a place where we sat down to read the books I had brought along. In the middle of all the frenetic excitement of our rendezvous, my back throbbed as though I had been hit with a sledgehammer.

We looked at book covers, thumbed pages, and stared at each other in wonderment. We finally kissed. It was so exciting I didn't know what was happening, and I think I came in my pants. I thought we were going to go all the way when Margaret announced, "You can touch me anywhere from the top of my head to my belly button and from my feet to a little above my knees, but that's all. So if you got any other ideas, I'm not that kind of girl."

At the time that seemed like plenty of room to work in, so I grabbed her tits. We kissed and rubbed each other under that Erie railroad bridge as the long lines of freight trains rumbled above us. We both were out of breath and in such a sweat that my pants felt like I had pissed on myself.

It was almost dark now. The mosquitoes were eating us up. As Margaret got up from the ground, she began to straighten herself out, put her tits back in her bra, and comb her hair. She was feeling herself around her crotch when she said, "Oh my God, you stuck that thing in me, didn't you? What am I going to do?"

I assured her I had not, but she said, "Well, why am I all wet down there?"

I asked if I could feel. She said absolutely not, as I had done enough damage already. "I should have known that's all you were after." I tried to explain to her how girls get wet when they just kiss or pet, but she absolutely didn't believe me. She calmed down as we talked, finally asking me if she could borrow one of the books I had brought, Faulkner's *Sanctuary*, which I had not read. I said she could, figuring it would be a good way to get together again when she wanted to return it.

We walked back up the road together. It was dark now. The crickets were chirping and we were holding hands. I went up to my room, since the house was dark.

As the excitement over Margaret died down, the pain in my back increased. All through that sleepless night I thought if I had to continue bean picking I would quit. I even thought that I would have quit that afternoon when the sun was broiling me if it had not been for Margaret's presence in the bean field. Maybe that was why mama teamed me with Margaret. It was an extreme example of the power of socializing at work that probably keeps many people interested in crummy jobs. Another example of the schmooze factor.

The next morning I went looking for Patsy and found him in back of the house by himself, hitting a ball against the side. I asked him, "How long will the bean pickin' go on; my back's broken."

"Oh just a few days," he said, "and then we'll start choppin' corn. That ain't hard, because the machine does the work."

He looked at me, saying, "Why don't you give up farmin' before you get like my father. He don't even talk no more; he's so tired. Even minin's better 'n farming, ask my brothers. At least you can go get drunk every night, and you don't have to worry about milkin' them damn cows every day." Patsy surprised me because I had not suspected he knew that much about what was going on.

I went to the barn and all I could think about was how I was going to make it with Margaret. All the smells, tits, penises surrounding me were now just adding to my horniness over Margaret. So I began to fantasize about going to Scranton to get laid before long, or I would surely rape Margaret.

I had been working at the farm about six weeks when I was told there would be a party Saturday night, and if I helped serve the beer I could come. I gladly agreed to do that, figuring there might be a chance to make out with Margaret. I thought how I would feed her lots of beer, then ask her to go for a walk where we could sneak up into the hayloft. Oh my God, what a time. In my excitement over Margaret I was almost forgetting about the work.

Saturday came and we set up the beer coolers on the porch. A huge barbecue was started in the afternoon. By dusk people began arriving in pickup trucks, and the drinking and eating got underway immediately. Those who came were mostly Italian farmers, many of whom, I learned from the conversation, had sons working in the mines.

A wind-up phonograph was brought out to the yard. Records were played and people began to dance—the kind of dancing farmers and miners seem to do, with lots of hops, big stepping, and sweeping movements that made you want to keep out of their way. I kept looking for Margaret to show, but she never did. Instead, with the party a couple of hours old, I was talking with Patsy about the subway, when one of the Collinari sons, Louis, came over to me behind the beer spigot and said, "You better get the hell outa here. The dumb Polack from across the road is looking for you with his shotgun."

Frightened, very confused, I said, "For what? I didn't do nothin'."

Louis was quite emphatic in his reply. "Well, that ain't what he says, and he's nuts. Besides he's been drinkin' and when he drinks he really gets crazy and strong as our Belgian brothers, and we don't want no fightin'. He's over there [nodding toward Margaret's house] workin' himself up to killin' you. He's already beat the shit out of Margaret. If he sees you, he'll blow your head off with that cannon of his."

I was very troubled. What the hell did Margaret tell him? She would not have said I fucked her when I didn't. I said to Louis, "Look, we just kissed a few times. Honest that's all we did."

"Oh no it's not," he said. "One of Margaret's brothers found that dirty book you gave her to read with the guy watchin' his wife being fucked by some other guy with a corncob. Why didn't you tell us you had dirty books?"

Wow, I was not at all ready for this. I said, "I never read that book, and I didn't even know what was in it."

Louis just looked at me, obviously not believing a word of what I said, and automatically said, "I'll tell mama you're leavin' and I'll get you your money and drive you to Scranton, 'cause this is Saturday, and as the Polack keeps drinkin', the crazier he'll get. We don't wanna have to fight him, 'cause it takes half my brothers to hold him down when he gets crazy. Get your stuff, and I'll meet you by the garage."

I was sad to leave the party, the farm, and Patsy, but I just could not find grounds on which to argue. I packed quickly, throwing my stuff in the bag, and went down to find Patsy. I told him I had to leave suddenly. He was a little sorry, I could tell from the way he looked down at his shoes, and he said, "Yeah, the Polack's lookin' for you, 'cause you did somethin' bad to his daughter." Goddamn, I was so frustrated. How could I leave without explaining all that had happened to somebody around here? I went to talk to mama, figuring she might understand. As I approached, she just looked at me kind of mean.

I heard the horn from the garage. I just reached in my pocket, found a quarter, gave it to Patsy, and said, "You're a great kid; you were a real friend. If you ever come to New York, I'll show you the restaurant where you can get a sandwich out of a little box, OK?" He nodded, and I left.

I climbed into the pickup. Louis handed me my pay and I put it in my shirt pocket. "Count it," he said. "I don't have to," I said. "It don't make any difference now." We were off to Scranton.

As we bounced along in the pickup, after a period of silence he said, "You should have never fucked that girl. She's got big tits and a big mouth. If you wanted to get laid, you shoulda come with us; there's lots of whores in Scranton, and for two bucks you could get everything. You didn't have to go fuckin' some dumb Polack farm girl. All you city guys are alike."

I tried to break in, but he kept right on saying, "That's the trouble with you city slickers. You think all farm people are dumb, but we know what you're thinkin' when you're lookin' at a girl like Margaret. How can you fuck her, that's all."

I managed to say I was sorry but he was mistaken, but I quickly realized that everyone in the Collinari family, except maybe Patsy, thought I was just a city slicker who came to seduce their daughters just like in those old traveling salesman jokes.

Family farming was hard, tough, physical labor that seemed to leave little or no energy for anything else. Years later I went back and visited the Collinari's farm. The horses and cows were gone. They told me they had had to give up the cows because it didn't pay anymore, and besides, the kids had all left and there was no one left to get up every morning at five o'clock to milk them. I said to Mr. Collinari, "I see you have a tractor now."

"Everyone does," he replied. "Horses are too expensive. A tractor you feed only when you use it, not so with a horse. He eats all the time.''

"Where are your sons?" I asked.

"All gone. Some in Pittsburgh, some down South. All gone, but I'm glad they got out of the mines. Only one of them was killed in a mine accident, John. You didn't meet him; he lived in Scranton." Well, of course, I had but I was unable to relate the whole story of trying to get a job in the mines.

I felt real bad. It all seemed so sad, and I left it at that. Farming had been for me a lovely, sensuous experience. But as a continuous way of life, farming seems extremely hard. One becomes an extension of the soil, the rain, the weather, in a unity with nature that seems so pastoral for the moment; but over time it makes you its slave.

I have often thought that according to Marx's concept of alienation, farmers should be the most unalienated people, since they indeed have a oneness with nature and a control over their means of production. Now I wonder if the oneness does not make the farmer an employee of nature with God as his exploiter. The Collinari family had to live with all the vicissitudes of drought, floods, bugs, plant and animal infections, and an unpredictable market. No wonder pastoral man was so determined to conquer nature, as Mr. Collinari was trying to do with his tractor.

# Packard Motor Car

Packard, with its slogan, "Ask the Man Who Owns One," was a make-ready as well as a service shop on Manhattan's West 54th Street. I was interviewed for the job of make-ready man. The personnel interviewer told me that while I would be started on simple things such as putting on wheels and installing radios, heaters, and trim, there would be a real opportunity to learn and get ahead if I wanted to. "Packard is a great company," he said. "What you do and where you go is up to you." I felt scared of that "it's up to you" stuff. It only increased my anxiety over whether I could do the job. The important thing was I got the job. He advised me what tools to get. These consisted of a basic set of socket wrenches, screw drivers, pliers and drive punches. Though they were fairly expensive, I was glad to get them because they made me feel like a real mechanic. He also gave me two pairs of coveralls and said, "You are responsible for keeping these clean and maintaining them. If you lose them, we take it out of your pay." He had me fill out all the necessary papers and told me to report on Monday at 8 A.M. to Fred Svenden, the foreman, and "He'll tell you what to do and explain the piece-rate time standard to you."

On the designated Monday I arrived almost an hour early because I overestimated how long the subway would take to get me there. I found the employees' entrance and the time clock, searched for a card with my name on it, and punched myself in. The men were drifting in, some with their coffee and the *Daily Mirror* or *News*. They seemed to drift off to their own work areas, many just keeping to themselves, drinking coffee and reading the paper.

At eight o'clock the bell sounded. Everyone started to work. In a little while there was a strong smell of exhaust fumes, gasoline, and new car paint, an odor that to this day sends me right back to Packard. With some assistance I found Fred Svenden's office and told him who I was. He was a clean, crew-cut man, all business, who always had a bunch of shop work orders in his hands. I tried to tell him that I was glad to get the job, but he never gave me a chance. He simply was not interested in conversation, only work orders. Even though Packards were being built on assembly lines in 1937, many of the final customer-chosen items were installed at this shop.

The plant was similar in appearance to the furniture factory except that it gave an impression of much more open space. It had large elevators as well as a ramp, both of which could accommodate automobiles. In some work areas the cars were just lined up, and in others each mechanic was assigned his own space where he kept his tools on a workbench.

This was my first experience with being paid a piecework rate instead of an hourly wage. Svenden explained how each job to be done had a fixed piece rate as well as a set time period for doing the work. "For instance," he said, "you might be allowed six dollars and three hours to do a brake job. If you beat the time, you can pick up another job—if there is any, of course—and make more money." That all sounded so wonderful, as though if I worked fast I could get rich. Except he forgot to say that if I ran into trouble and went over the time allowed, that was my tough luck.

Svenden showed me how to read the shop orders, took me over to a line of new cars, and said, "OK, Schrank, start putting wheels and trim on these cars and then Carl over there will show you how to install radios and adjust brakes." Wheels and trim were an hourly rate of about 80 cents, radios were on piece rate of about $5.50.

I tried making friends with some of the guys around me, but without much luck. I began to feel as though the men who worked there behaved more like prima donnas than auto mechanics. Packard was a "classy automobile," and the men worked with an air of individuality as though each one was tending his own business by beating the piece-rate time standard.

The mechanics worked very much alone, relying little on anyone for help in the specific work tasks they were doing. In contrast to working cooperatively, piecework tends to encourage going it alone in a sort of individual entrepreneurship.

In all the factories I knew, you would punch in and out on arrival and departure. In the auto shop, the clock took charge of my life because I had to punch in on every job for which I was permitted a fixed amount of time, and then punch out when the job was finished. Everything would seem to be going along fine until something went wrong, and then in proportion to my trouble the panic would start to grow. The piece-rate system placed the full responsibility for the work on the mechanic.

I was in a state of panic one day; I was installing a special carburetor on a V-12 Packard engine when a stud snapped. There were few V-12 engines built, so that working around one was probably such an exciting experience that I did not know my own strength and busted the bolt. There were a lot of different ways to extract a broken stud, and as I tried each one and failed I was becoming more and more frightened. Not knowing what to do, I was starting to get desperate. I began asking some of the guys around me for help, but got nothing but a sort of passive "No, I'm busy" answer. (I've forgotten to mention that it was Lou Gehrig's car.) I knew if the boss found out, I would not only catch holy hell but I would probably be canned.

I finally went to one of the other floors and found little Henry Dormer, who seemed to look a little more sympathetic than the rest. I did not know him, nor had I any idea how he would react to my plea for help. But we were both Germans. (Wow, I had not used that one before!) I told him about my predicament with Lou Gehrig's car. He looked at me over his heavy-framed, greasy-lensed glasses and said, "Listen, kid, I'm busy. I can't be fixin' your fuck-ups. If I do that for you, everyone around here will be asking me to fix things for them, and who will do my work?"

He seemed to be getting some kind of satisfaction in what he was saying, as though he was glad I had messed up. Maybe that meant he had one less person to compete with. Prima donnas always seem preoccupied with their competition.

After scurrying around half the place and receiving no encouragement and really not wanting to lose this job, I struck on the idea of offering to pay one of the guys to rescue me, and one did. After work hours, pretending to work on my own 1929 Packard that I had acquired from the Manville Estate for sixty dollars (with all-leather interior), we fixed Gehrig's car, and I paid the "brother" five bucks.

The men who worked at Packard were far more fearful of the company than either the furniture workers or plumbers. As I would think about that, I came to feel that the piecework system was responsible for the fearfulness. It seemed as though each worker was running a little business of his own between himself and the boss, and the result was little or no sense of mutual interest or support. While the trade union influence of my IWW father was very much part of me, I think it was really the piecework system at Packard that evoked my first strong desire to unionize a place. I hated that piecework system and found myself in terror of not making rate or of cutting rate by undercutting the time. Either way, it was a nerve-racking experience that created a cutthroat competitive atmosphere. In some piecework operations I have observed formal or informal understandings made by the workers on how much is to be done, but even so there would be an endless manipulative game between workers and management to see who could beat the other.

During lunch time at Packard a few of the men would eat together. I found myself seeking out people I could talk to about the piece-rate system. Joining different groups, I was not given much of a reception and found it difficult to make friends or to get much of a conversation started. Most of the mechanics were preoccupied with the work, which meant that I could talk carburetors or compression ratios but not much else.

It began to dawn on me that at Packard not only did the company love the piecework system, but so did the employees. This was because piecework is a highly individualized system of employer-worker relations. Years later a friend at Remington Rand would call it "hofome fuyu," a Chinese screwing, which translated meant, "Hooray for me and fuck you."

Svenden called me to his office one day to lay me out for having "dirtied up the interior of Mrs. Holden's car." Before I could open my mouth he said, "If it happens again, you're through," and walked out—end of conversation. I tried talking to Mike Antonelli, one of the best mechanics and, I thought, one of the more sympathetic people around the place. He was leaning over an engine as I told him what happened. He never stopped working, did not look up, just said, "That's the way it is, kid, tough luck."

Most of the foremen were like Svenden. It seemed that most of the supervisors at Packard, as well as at other auto plants I would come in contact with, had this thing about being kind of cold, as a demonstration of how tough they were. They would love to lay you out in public for any chicken-shit reason. In industries where brawn is a prerequisite for survival, being tough and mean is traditional. Though many no longer actually require it, like the steel industry, the past lingers on as a sort of cultural heritage. Because the management style of an industry is tradition-related, the rugged individualism of the founders of the automobile industry tends to permeate its manufacturing plants. Many of the founders of the auto companies started out as inventors working in their backyards. They became the self-made men of the automobile, best exemplified by Henry Ford. When I was an auto worker, the mass assembly production of cars was only twenty years old, with assembly lines quite primitive compared to now.

Bill Williams was typical of the creative auto mechanics who had grown up with the industry and felt very much part of its development. When I worked on my '29 Packard during lunch, and at times after work, Bill Williams loved to advise me on that big, straight, light engine. He would come by, saying, "Whaddya tryin' to do with her?"

"Well, I'm trying to improve the compression," I replied.

"Why don't you bring the head up the machine shop and have it cut down?" There were others who, like Bill, would come up and talk with me when I was working on my own car but would be indifferent to what I was doing if I was "clocked in" on a customer's job. Some of the men I worked with at Packard considered themselves true craftsmen because they had built custom-made automobiles from components and raw materials to the finished product.

Like Bill Williams, they had a fiercely independent quality. Even in the depression, they seemed to be more independent in spirit than unskilled production workers. The "independence" could come from a feeling that having a skill gives one control over machines, which breeds an air of confidence that can be very impressive to personnel interviewers. I have seen unemployed workers feeling down on their luck whose psyches hang on to their skills as if it were the very source of their life's energy. In contrast, unskilled workers seem to have much less sense of who they are and so tend to be more vulnerable when they are unemployed.

Many of the early skilled automobile craftsmen like Bill Williams became the plant-level supervisors who brought with them a roaring contempt for any lack of confidence or skill. This type of supervision at Packard created an excessive amount of anxiety, which frightened me into lots of smoking and hanging out in the toilets. There were always plenty of other guys doing the same thing, for work life at Packard seemed pretty unhappy.

My unhappiness in the auto shop was about to transform itself into action when I found myself one evening in the United Automobile Workers Local 259 union hall. The hall was a dirty little manufacturing-type loft building. Most of the loft space was left open for meetings, except for a partition in the rear of the hall that was an office with a small window like a bank teller's. There were men sitting around in small groups on folding chairs playing cards, talking, or reading. I was scared because I knew if "the company" learned of my whereabouts that evening I would be out of a job the next morning. My fear made me hesitate to talk to anyone, so I just hung around for some time watching what was going on. A few people seemed to be going in and out of the back office, and I finally found enough courage to speak with one of them.

"I work at Packard, and I would like to get the union in there, 'cause we sure need it."

He was a short, dark-haired, stocky man wearing a work shirt. He looked like an auto mechanic and stared at me for a minute as though very surprised by my statement, then shot his hand out to shake mine and introduced himself as Michael Sienna, the local union secretary. "Come on in the office so we can talk. By the way, does anyone know you're here?"

"I don't think so."

"That's good. Keep it that way."

Mike handed me an application card, asked me to fill it out and pay the five-dollar initiation fee. "If you can't pay it all today, you can pay it off later. The dues are seventy-five cents a month." That seemed like a lot of money, especially since I was putting my job on the line. But I filled out the application and paid part of the initiation fee. Mike asked me if I had any organizing experience, to which I said no. "OK, wait here a minute while I go get some guys for you to talk with."

Mike introduced me to a group of about three or four men he had gathered around one of the tables. As we sat around he explained that "this kid here is working at Packard and he would like to organize the place but needs some help. So let's help him." The men around the table began to fire questions at me.

"How many people work there?"

"Couple of hundred, I think."

"Can you get an exact count?"

"Why is that important?" I asked.

One of them explained, "If we go for a Labor Board election, we need a majority of the men signed up before we can get a vote." They all kept stressing to me, "Don't get yourself fired now. We need you on the inside. That is where you can be most effective as an organizer. When we try to organize from outside the plant, the company has the advantage of making us appear as some kind of radical troublemaker outsiders or foreigners."

They gave me a bunch of authorization cards asking for an election and told me to be very careful not to be caught trying to sign men up, as I would surely be fired. Mike warned, "Be careful who you ask to sign a card. The company has finks all over and you can never tell." I felt very exhilarated as I left the union hall to go home. My mission was clear; I had to sign up a majority of men at Packard, get an election, win it, and the union would make it a great place to work. That's what I was thinking late that night as I rode the empty subway train home.

Mike had also suggested I try to get some men at the plant to form an organizing committee that could help with signing people up. "But, make sure you can trust them," he said, almost as his final shot. As I sat in the empty subway car, I began to think of people I could possibly trust. I kept asking myself, How can I tell? How can I know for sure? Can I tell from the paper they read? How about nationality or religion or age? The more I thought about it the less sure I was about whom I could trust.

By the next morning I was so nervous over my new role of union organizer that in place of my brown paper lunch bag I took a bag of dirty socks that was lying around in the kitchen. I bought my lunch from the hot dog wagon, looked for some men I could eat with and, I hoped, feel out about the union.

Each day I would look for new groups of men to have lunch with in the hope of engaging them in a discussion about a union. In a few weeks or months I began to give out the authorization cards to individual men whom I thought I could trust. During the same period I was at the union hall two or three nights a week, getting to know many of the other local officials and becoming real friends with Mike Sienna.

Becoming part of the union bunch was fun. I was beginning to feel like I belonged. We were a chosen group who "knew how the workers could make a paradise for themselves through organizing." My childhood exposure to anarchists and socialists was being reawakened by our endless singing of "Solidarity Forever," a union classic sung to the tune of "Battle Hymn of the Republic." I was rapidly becoming a zealous crusader and correspondingly more daring, in spite of what Mike was telling me about being careful.

As my mentors would later point out to me, I did not do well. One day I arrived at the plant only to be told that I was transferred to the Bronx Packard Shop on the other side of the zoo from where I lived. I was shocked at how fast the company had learned about my union activities, but when I called Mike Sienna at the UAW and told him what had happened, I secretly expected him to be able to do something about my transfer. Instead he said, "Goddamnit, Bob, we told you to be careful. OK, don't worry. We will start to leaflet the 54th Street plant from the outside."

As I began to check with some of the 54th Street people, they told me that they had heard that someone overheard me talking union in the toilets or during lunch time and saying some bad things about the company. (Packard was extremely sensitive to criticism. Their paranoia was such that my transfer was really more a reaction to my criticisms than to my unionizing efforts.) I was immediately identified as a "troublemaker" or an "agitator"; the latter was considered worse than the former. A troublemaker may just be a crank, while an agitator may be a radical ideologue.

After my transfer, Mike and other UAW organizers told me I was moving much too fast at the Bronx shop and that I should slow down. One day in a discussion with Mike he asked me what my major organizing issue was. I told him I was trying to sell the union on the basis of "job security." "Well," he said, "is that what the workers want or is that what you want?" I told him I did not know. "Well, you better find out." How could I if I could not talk union to them? I was becoming very frustrated and impatient with union organizing.

Mike put his arm on my shoulder and quietly said, "Keep looking for issues that the workers will respond to. Keep signing guys up for the union. In the meantime, sit tight. Take it easy."

I did not seem to be able to develop any issues that the workers responded to, so I made the elimination of the piecework system the center of my efforts. I thought it was a great idea and began to talk it up during lunch and coffee breaks. I had become enthusiastic and optimistic again, but then Mike pressed me on how many of the fifty or sixty workers in Packard Bronx had signed authorization cards. I had to acknowledge only about twelve had. Few, if any, of the workers supported the elimination of piecework because most of the men liked the entrepreneurial character of a system that encouraged their endless little deals with the supervisors.

These little private deals were agreements that a mechanic might make to do a job in less time than the given rate, in return for which he would be given certain "good jobs." I was being dealt a lot of shit jobs, since the company had it in for me and was clearly trying to get me out. I kept complaining to Mike that the workers under the piecework system were behaving like a bunch of sniveling dogs, each one vying with the other to catch the best piece-rate bone.

"Mike, these guys have become totally self-centered, cold, and indifferent to their fellow workers. They're as unsociable a lot as I've ever met. There's no shop floor camaraderie, no nothing!"

Mike laughed. "What happened to your workers' paradise?"

"Not with this gang!" I replied without thinking.

He explained how there were unionized plants that continued the piecework system and had made the setting of rates part of the bargaining process. I thought that this was obviously an improvement, but I still had a real bias against piecework, because it created such tension between the worker and the task, as well as competition among the workers themselves.

I would periodically retreat from my unionizing work, and then when I was mad about something that would happen in the plant it would flare up again. The company by this time had me well tagged as a "labor agitator" and the game of hunter and hunted was on. The foreman in the Bronx plant now started to give me the crummiest jobs in the place. Most of the men working there seemed to sense what was going on, for a strange phenomenon occurred. Because I was marked as being hunted by the company, people began to shun me as though I had the yellow fever. I don't know if it was something in my behavior, but the wolf pack element in the men seemed to sniff a kill in the wind. Fewer and fewer men talked to me or to each other, as when the feeling of some evil thing hanging in the air causes people to hide from each other.

The rope was pulled one cold Monday morning. I was called into the office by a shifty-eyed manager who looked all over the room but never at me and announced to the corner of the ceiling, "Schrank, you ruined a $500 engine from one of Tommy Manville's limousines by sending it out without crankcase oil in it. Pick up your pay. You're through."

My blood ran cold. I thought I would faint. I never expected to be fired quite this way. There was something so final about it all. I stood there feeling absolutely powerless. A million thoughts raced through my head: What will the workers do when they hear about this? What'll the union do? How will I get another job? What should I do right now? I pleaded with the manager, saying, "Look, that's impossible. I would never have done such a stupid thing. I will replace the engine. I'll pay for it or anything else they claim I ruined." I felt as though I was in a prison cell pleading with the warden for a stay of execution. It was of no avail. I tried to convince him, pleading with him for another chance, but it soon became clear that he had no intention of engaging in a discussion with me. He had already called the security guard, who stood there with his hands on his gun belt like a prison guard and said, "Let's go."

As we walked out of the manager's office into the shop, I asked the guard if I could walk around the plant to say good-bye to some of the men; I was hoping that I might get some spontaneous action on their part. He was ice-cold to the idea, just shook his head saying, "Get your stuff and let's go."

As we went through the plant to the locker room, the men looked up to see me walking with the security guard. They knew what had happened. A few shook their heads a little, but that was about it. The rebellion I had hoped for never flickered. I picked up my tools, changed my clothes, rolled up my overalls, and before I could understand what was happening, I was standing out in the street with my junk. Though I knew I had been framed by the company and was convinced that everyone in the plant knew it, I saw that nothing could be done. The place was permeated with fear.

I took my stuff home and called up Mike Sienna at the union. He suggested that I go to the plant at quitting time to talk to the men as they came out. I went back to the plant, eager to talk with the men about how I had been framed by the company, but most of them ran past, making sure they were not seen talking to me. One or two surreptitiously said a couple of words to me as if I were now an evil thing. Ashamed of their own behavior, they did not want to be confronted with taking a stand.

That night, feeling despondent, I went straight to the union hall. Upon arrival I was welcomed as a hero with Mike's greeting, "Well, the bastards got you. Don't worry, this fight's just begun." He put his arm around me and we walked through the union hall. He told the men hanging around there what had happened to me, how I was framed by the company. "The workers were scared so shitless they just sat there and did nothing," he said, adding, "What an educational job we've got ahead of us to make men out of cockroaches." We went in the back office to talk with other officials of the local. I was sure feeling better now with all the attention and support I was getting. After considerable discussion it was decided to file an unfair labor practice charge against the company, claiming I was fired for my union activity and not the ruined engine.

I met with the lawyer for the local, who asked me to try and get some of the workers at Packard to testify on my behalf either in person or by deposition. *Schrank vs. Packard Motor Car Company* became case No. 1 before the New York State Labor Relations Board. We lost the case, mainly because I could not get any one of the men I had worked with in the shop to testify for me. But in the years to come Packard would eventually be unionized, and little by little the workers' behavior would change when they no longer found it necessary to slink around the plant in fear of each other and the boss.

At that time Packard was a particularly bad place to work because there was no sense of community among the workers. Many students of workplace problems do not know or understand much of how blue-collar workers create a community at the workplace. Looked at from this viewpoint, the difference between the furniture factory, the plumbing shop, and the auto plant was startling. The first two had highly developed informal systems that regulated work flow, assured mutual support, and generally created a spirit of togetherness. At Packard the informal work group that is the key element in determining the nature of the workplace created a highly competitive, uncooperative system of individualized piecework. While I would like to blame that cutthroat attitude on the piece-rate system, I frankly cannot be sure. I have seen a well-integrated, highly supportive work group take a hellhole of a workplace, like a cast iron foundry or a coal mine, and turn it into a most positive living experience. The joking and laughter of miners is one of those unforgettable lessons in human courage that always comes to mind when I hear behavioral scientists speak of "humanizing the workplace."

Stan Weir, in writing about the workplace as a community in *Rank and File*, makes the observation that

The greatest enemies the [work] groups have are unemployment or any change in the technology that destroys the group's life continuity, internal relationships and group-culture. Industries that don't have these groups, like teamsters who drive alone on a truck, are at a natural disadvantage.

Each day people seek new solutions to oppressiveness. A workplace isn't a collection of individuals so much as a collection of informal groups. Until you recognize that, you're not really into utilizing the power of people in the workplace.

In much of the literature on improving the quality of working life, the issue of how informal groups operate at the workplace gets little if any attention. My hunch is that at least some behavioral scientists as well as industrial engineers are unaware of the influence of the informal work group. Or they may perceive it as an obstacle to increased productivity and control, thus failing to recognize its importance. Workers generally seem to have a need to belong to a community of their own, independent of management, as a way of dealing with daily trials and tribulations. For instance, there was worker participation in decisions at Packard as they affected each individual's work tasks, but there was no participation of the group in that process. The result was a "privatism," an "I make my own deal" attitude that permeated that workplace, resulting in fearfulness, paranoia, and the absence of a positive community spirit.

How employees can participate in decision making is an underlying issue that periodically surfaces in union bargaining as well as in the literature on workplace problems. Maslow speaks of the higher need of individuals to be autonomous and creative, and Herzberg speaks of making the task itself an interest-creating challenge. It was my experience at Packard that started me thinking about how worker participation in decision making develops in a plant.

To the democratic mind, participation is a much-desired ingredient for the functioning of society and its institutions. At the point of production, decision making is at its lowest level, since all design and manufacturing issues are settled long before they reach that stage. To participate in decisions that affect the organization beyond the point of production requires a broad knowledge of the organization that most people have no access to. In the work setting, because of the way responsibility is divided, with each person tending to be an expert in a particular task or responsibility, the problem of defining participation becomes quite difficult. The difficulties are particularly acute in institutions employing large numbers where very few, if any, persons have some idea of what goes on in the whole organization.

Some behavioral scientists who speak of participation in decision making are referring primarily to a small area within a person's task assignment. In manufacturing this is limited, due to engineering schedules for all tasks. Workers in service industries (like the repair mechanics at Packard) are permitted a wider latitude in decision making than manufacture workers, but some service workers are limited to a replacement function, which offers less scope than a repair operation. I am arguing that the possibilities for participation in decision making may be somewhat determined by the type of work being done, with some occupations lending themselves more to a participative model than others.

Most manufacturing plants do not lend themselves to the democratic model of worker participation in decision making, particularly if the finished product has a large number of parts or subassemblies (like the automobile) that require considerable overall planning. Participation is much more feasible in continuous-process operations such as oil refineries, food processing, or chemical plants, which can be highly automated, where the major work task is equipment adjustment and maintenance for product control. While the area of decision making here too is limited, there is a much greater potential for decentralizing control than in unit manufacture.

Finally, a most important element in determining the level of worker participation in decision making is the management style. The style can be punitive, controlled, or tightly supervised; and conversely it can be open, rewarding, and autonomous. Whichever it is can be a determinant of how workers participate in having some input about how the work itself is organized.

All of the discussion about worker participation needs to be predicated on an assumption that there is job security. There can be no meaningful participation by workers without security. While the level of fearfulness may go up or down depending on a management's style, without some sense of job security there cannot be any democratic participation. With the exception of those who really want to go it alone, it may turn out that the nature and degree of participation by workers in decision making may be directly correlated to levels of security and fearfulness. The abject submissiveness of the workers at the Packard plant grew out of a lack of any feelings of solidarity or security on the part of these workers.

The UAW local asked me to do some organizing work in unorganized plants. I was about to get my first lesson in learning how to survive clandestine, subversive union drives. My experience at Packard had created a cunning sense of who could be trusted. I would come to develop a sixth sense that helped to detect potential stool pigeons, who when squeezed, threatened, and finally cajoled by the company with some payoff would do just about anything they were asked. When confronted, their explanation usually started with something like, "You know I got a wife and a couple kids I gotta think about." I heard that explanation so many times that my response became an automatic, "Don't tell me about your wife and kids. Just tell me about what you are doing."

The three big automobile manufacturers had not yet been organized. I was sent out to the Ford plant in Weehawken, New Jersey, the Chevrolet plant in Tarrytown, New York, and the Bell

Aircraft plant in Buffalo to distribute leaflets at plant gates, to visit workers in their homes, and to spend a lot of time hanging around union halls. That turned out to be the beginning of an apprenticeship in union leadership. Some years later it would have a real payoff for me. (Hanging around is a more directed activity than just schmoozing. A major activity in a union organizer's life is trying to convince workers to sign up. This means "hanging around" places where workers gather, and it becomes a daily activity.)

I learned about how unions operate and how workers are organized through on-the-job training as an organizer with Mike Sienna as my teacher. "You have to approach an organizing effort as if you were fighting a small war. Learn what the major issues and gripes are in the plant by listening to what the workers have to say and asking them questions. Listen, just listen," Mike would tell me. Then he would look me straight in the face and say, "Study the company, your enemy, know its turf, how it is laid out financially, physically, and its relation to the community. Then get to know your workers, where they are from, what nationality, what is the role of the church, the fraternal groups, their politics, and their lifestyles." After a few beers at the bar in Tarrytown, Mike would really warm up to his subject.

"Agitation," he would say with great emphasis, "is the ability to sense an important issue, dramatize it, and move it into action." Mike would look at me for a moment and then say, "Some people are natural-born agitators. I think you are one." At the time I was unsure what he meant, but I would be startled at times by the response I would get at an organizing rally or a union meeting when I would make a suggestion that then turned into an immediate action. It was as though I as an individual had nothing to do with what was happening.

I remember being sent to an Isbrandsen Line pier in Brooklyn. Standing on an old crate during lunch hour, I made an impassioned plea to the longshoremen to support a sailors' strike by refusing to load the ship tied up at the dock. To my absolute amazement they did just that. I stayed up all that night wondering how I did that.

Though I never quite knew, I was to do it many times and it always was a bit scary.

Agitating became fun because it usually tended to create some action that was not always predictable. More conservative people were annoyed with an agitational tone as being "too emotional" and without enough "reason." I would often try a cooler, more reasoned style, only to find that it did not energize people into action. It was as though a release of psychic energy was required in order to create some movement, make something happen, get things off dead center. Agitation might have been the catalyst that released the psychic energy stored in the anger, resentment, and frustration that comes from being exploited or oppressed.

My apprenticeship as a union organizer was a period in which I learned that working with people was in some ways more satisfying than making things in a factory. There was no comparison to the routine drudgery of a factory. Time passed so quickly in learning, schmoozing, and socializing that all merged into a most rewarding work experience. Because most communication among workers tends to be face-to-face, there is not much trust in the written word. Blue-collar workers seem to prefer to react in a direct, person-to-person way rather than through the medium of writing. As a result, I find workers' responses to people much more visceral and direct than those of intellectuals. This creates a real communications barrier between workers and intellectuals, making it difficult for the viscerals to talk with the cerebrals or the other way around.

While working for the UAW local was fun, I found something new beginning to bother me. It had to do with my not being a skilled worker. I did not feel as though I was respected by other workers, nor could I be an effective union leader without some craft skills. I had grown up in a world of admiration for the craftsman. I suffered a paranoid fear that workers might accuse me of being an official union pork chopper because I could not do anything better. Becoming a craftsman was the route to becoming a real union leader, which was secretly what I wanted.

My sudden job dissatisfaction with union organizing came about because I smelt an opportunity to do something exciting, challenging, and interesting. It was an instance of job dissatisfaction acting as the push needed to force me to look at what I wanted to do with my life. An opportunity to work as a machinist's helper in a powerhouse substation came up, and I took it.

# Machinist

My career as a machinist began in a powerhouse substation in which electricity was still being generated by four old reciprocating-type steam engines and two newer-type steam turbines. There were six huge coal-fired boilers tended by firemen and coal passers in an around-the-clock operation. I worked as a helper in the machine shop that built and maintained equipment for a number of these small electricity-generating substations.

I was interviewed for the job by Johnny Anderson, a tall, thin Scandinavian man with little or no hair on his face and a blond forelock that continually fell over his eyes as he spoke. When he hired me, he said that I would start out in "stores," as the stockroom was called, work through wiper, oiler, and then "If you make it OK we'll give you a chance in the machine shop." Many of the men who worked in power stations had come off ships, and their language sometimes made me feel as though I were at sea: We shaped up, did a watch, went to the head, and were forever watchful for emergencies. While I was working in "stores," Johnny suggested that I get one of the machinists to show me how to rebuild a roomful of every conceivable type of old steam and water valve. I stood there looking at this small mountain of valves, convinced that my life's work had been cut out for me.

One of the machinists, Karl, showed me how to rebuild every part of each valve, one at a time. At the beginning, completing each valve proved to be a real challenge because of their great variety, and I worked hard to learn all I could about them. But once I had mastered the techniques of rebuilding valves, the work became tedious and I found my objectives began to shift from learning to do the task to thinking about how to get it done more simply and quickly. The tedium grew as I kept rebuilding valves, and the days rolled into weeks and months. My work became known around the place as "the valve project" and I found myself thinking a lot about how I could get rid of it. I had not made any real friends, since "stores" was an isolated work area where people came just to pick up requisitioned parts or tools.

Somewhat reluctantly I asked one of the machinists, "Minnesota," what he would think if I developed a production technique that would process a couple dozen valves at a time instead of custom-rebuilding each valve. This would not only increase my productivity but it would also make the work much easier. Minnesota, a Finn who had lived most of his life in Duluth and who would eventually become my journeyman teacher, thought for a moment and agreed. "Just tell them it will save time, which to them is the same as money, and they'll let you dance."

Why make the work easier? Because it meant considerably less concentration on something I now had mastered. Besides, I would have more time to roam around the power station and schmooze with the other men. Minnesota helped me to separate the hundreds of valves by size and type. We then made some arbitrary decisions on which part of each valve to replace and which to remachine. Instead of individually rebuilding each valve, the work now became a series of production runs. First operation, cut all new seats; second, install new stems; third, new discs, and so on. The work was now highly repetitive, and more efficient. To my surprise it gave me considerable satisfaction when the task was completed in a few months. I was very proud of being able to complete unpleasant work rapidly in order to get on to something else.

It was hard for me to believe how my productivity increased once I had gotten the valve-rebuilding production line in operation. My motivation had been to get rid of tedious work, but I was being cited by the boss for having saved him $x$ number of dollars. But hero or not I had had it with valve rebuilding, and I told Anderson I would be happy never to see another valve again in my life.

My reward for efficiently completing the valve-rebuilding project was my assignment to work with Minnesota. Johnny Anderson said, "Look, he's one of the best damn machinists I ever saw, but he is getting old and he drinks, so get in and help him. In a month you'll learn more from Minnesota than you would in school in a year." I was nervous, unsure if I would measure up to the legend of Minnesota.

Minnesota was either a heavy drinker or a "drunk," according to circumstances. He would be called a drunk only when his drinking made it impossible for him to function on the job. But Minnesota was a fine machinist. He was a man in his late fifties, of medium build, with a head of gray hair that fell over his steel-rimmed glasses. When he spoke to me he would look over the tops of these perpetually greasy glasses that sat on the end of his nose. When I looked in his eyes there always seemed to be a sadness present. It was that melancholia that I thought made him drink, yet when he did drink, it just seemed to make things worse. When Anderson assigned me to work with Minnesota, I was told by other men in the shop that my job was to "make sure that Minnesota did not get hurt." I was expected to cover for him when he was under the weather and could not make it. In a way I was proud of my new responsibility not only for the work but for Minnesota as well, and I assured everyone that I would do the right thing for him.

If there was any romance in the industrial revolution of the nineteenth century, it was with the steam engine, and no wonder! What a creation that was! My own real affection began one day when Minnesota announced to me, "Kid, did you notice Number 3 down in the powerhouse? Well, she's cooling, so we can work on her." "What will we do?" I asked. "We have to tear her down, check out each part, and see what's ailing her." Minnesota spoke of "her" with a kind of affection usually reserved for women.

Unlike today's machinery, most steam engines were not mass-produced. Rather they were custom-built, and working on them meant getting to know the uniqueness of each engine. As Minnesota explained it, "We will study her very carefully before we take her apart." He had already done this on Number 3, but we went through it again to show me how to diagnose a steam engine's guts for any replacements needed. "Then we will go ahead and make the new parts, based on our measurements of what is needed," he said. Minnesota started teaching me this process of knowing the engine by running it, taking indicator readings, and listening to its insides with the help of a mechanic's stethoscope, a steel rod with one end stuck in Minnesota's ear and the other end some place on the engine. "The key thing is to start out listening. Learn what the engine sounds like, then when she don't sound right, you hear it in your head," Minnesota said. Sometimes I would watch him when he was half bagged. He would be listening and mumbling in a slight accent, "Yah, yah, ve have to change da rocker arms. So come here, kid, und listen."

I would try with the iron rod stethoscope in my ear, but I could not hear what was wrong. When I told Minnesota he would say, "Go listen more to the good ones, and den you know the difference." I kept doing that quite regularly, and sure enough, like a doctor who learns to listen to the human heart, I learned to understand all the little rumbles and knocks in the guts of the engine. It was some of those little knocks that signaled worn bearings or rods. Minnesota also showed me how to study the steam engine indicator readings. That was a sort of basal metabolism chart of how efficiently the engine was converting steam to mechanical power. Minnesota would suggest a problem, look me straight in the face over his glasses, and say, "OK, what do you think, smart kid?" At first, anxious to please, I would always agree, until he began to trip me up with foolish suggestions. Then he would say, "Think for yourself, boy, otherwise you will be no good around these machines. Every one is different, so you gotta use your head."

After a series of decisions by Minnesota a diagnosis was usually agreed upon, which meant we would begin to disassemble the engine, first by putting up the necessary rigging to hoist and remove the parts, then carefully marking each part, since they were not interchangeable. We would then separate all the parts that needed to be replaced. Next, Minnesota would develop a new set of specs for the replacements, adjusting for wear. We might spend the next month in the machine shop making the parts. Each part had to be custom-made. The fact that we could not interchange parts on these engines required a level of craftsmanship that could assure a custom-made fit for each replacement part. I believe that this kind of true craftsmanship in the workplace has almost completely vanished. As I look back at it, I see how very lucky I was to work with Minnesota on rebuilding steam engines. It gave me my first and probably last chance to work with a real craftsman.

Minnesota worked closely with me in the machine shop, patiently helping in my machine setups, constantly checking and always encouraging me. "That's fine, kid," "You're doin' good, kid." "Measure, measure before you take another cut." Except when he was off on a drunken bender, he seemed eternally alert to what I was doing.

One day when I came into the machine shop, there was Minnesota running a cut on the big two-foot lathe with the twenty-foot bed. He was rocking back and forth like a metronome. I had been working on the powerhouse floor and had not seen him most of the day. It was now late afternoon and he had obviously been at the muscatel most of the afternoon. Scared he would fall into the lathe and get wound up in the chuck, I ran over to the machine, shut it off, and told him, "Now you sit down and tell me what to do and I'll do it." Mumbling, mumbling, "I am better drunk dan you sober." After some persuasion, supported by the other men in the shop, he agreed and said, "OK, you do it." Two of the men agreed to keep an eye out for the boss; if he showed, we would somehow get Minnesota back in front of the lathe and I would find something else to do.

That is how I began to learn my craft as a machinist, with Minnesota behind me, his steel-rimmed glasses on the end of his nose, his gray, thinning hair hanging in his face, mumbling his whiskey commands in my ear. As time went on, Minnesota's drinking seemed to get worse, as though his increased reliance on me gave him more time to hit the bottle. Together with some of the men in the shop we would try to have two machines set up. When the foreman showed, it would look like Minnesota was on one and I on the other. Sometimes Minnesota would just stand behind me expounding his philosophy about machines, saying, "Know the machine, so she will follow your wishes and not do what she wants. Make her do what you want, then you are the boss." Often he would stand behind me when I was running a lathe, a miller, or a grinder, commanding, "Take plenty. Take plenty. Don't be afraid of the machine. Are you a man? Then take a real he-man cut. Listen, kid, this is no virgin here. This old whore can take all you got, so give it to her!"

My God, how I wanted to please this old machinist who carried his tools in an old wooden shoe box and seemed to know all there was about machines. As time went on, I began to feel proud of what I was learning, and almost as an appreciation, I enjoyed protecting Minnesota. Minnesota reciprocated my support. One day I was turning an eight-inch-diameter bronze pump shaft on a lathe, and, following Minnesota's dictum of "take plenty," I ended up taking too much. Having discovered it about eight inches down the twelve-foot shaft, I shut down the machine in an ice-cold panic. I was sure if Johnny Anderson found out what had happened, my goose would be cooked. "Where is Minnesota?" He was nowhere to be seen.

I ran around the powerhouse, the boiler room, the huge, dark coal bunkers, yelling and pleading with the men, "Did you see Minnesota? Goddamn him, where is he?" No one had any idea where he was. I was desperate and could not find him anywhere. Finally one of the coal passers, Joe Peters, said, "I think you'll find him asleep behind Number 3 boiler." Sure enough, there was Minnesota coiled up like a big tomcat in winter next to a potbellied stove, fast asleep. I shook him, slapped him, pushed him but nothing happened. He was in a booze stupor and I was getting mad. I began to holler, "Minnesota, I followed your goddamned dumb fucking advice and took plenty, so now I got a twelve-foot, eight-inch-diameter bronze shaft ready for the scrap heap. If the boss finds out, I'm dead."

What happened then was like rubbing Aladdin's lamp. Suddenly he was sober. He jumped up, dusted himself off, and then said something I would never forget, "Listen, stupid, anyone can make a mistake. But we know the pros from the amateurs by how you figure out how to get out of the fuck-up. So stop cryin' like a little baby and let's go."

His ability to sober up astounded me. He came up to the lathe, turned it on, and said, "Keep the lathe running. That'll keep the boss away while we look for a piece of bronze to slip over your fuck-up."

I followed Minnesota to the stockroom, where he found the bronze. When the stores man asked him what it was for, he simply said, "I want to make an umbrella stand for the boss." He motioned to me to take the piece, told me to put it in a lathe and bore it out a few thousandths of an inch less than the undercut shaft. After the shift had left, we put it in the furnace to expand it and then slipped it over the undercut part of the bronze shaft. We were really hustling. When we finished it was around seven o'clock. Minnesota said, "OK, kid, now turn it and nobody will ever find out that shaft is really two pieces."

Wow, was I relieved! I wanted to hug that man. We were in the locker room, an old man and a young boy stripped to the waist, washing up in the big round Bradley washbasins, he on one side, me on the other. I looked up at him and said, "Minnesota, you saved my job. I want you to know I really appreciate that. I want to do something to show my indebtedness to you."

He looked at me, squinting without his glasses, saying, "It's nothing. Somebody did that for me lots of times. Always remember, kid, if we don't work together, everyone gets fucked. Now, buy me a drink and then we go home." This was not what I wanted to do for him. I sure hated buying him those drinks and leaving him staggering onto the bus to go home.

Minnesota's drinking kept getting worse. One of the last times I remember seeing him was on a cold Christmas morning when we were on duty at the powerhouse. An ice storm had covered the city. Minnesota was crossing the street to the powerhouse entrance carrying a brown paper bag (the wino's briefcase) when his legs just seemed to fly out from under him and his head smashed on the pavement with a resounding thump. I watched, horrified and sure he had fractured his skull. Unbelievably, as he went down, the bottle in the brown paper bag held high above his head had never touched the ground. I ran to him and helped him up. He had a silly grin and his only comment through the blood running down his face was, "Ve saved the bottle, yah."

It was heartbreaking for me to patch him up and take him home. His wife looked at him, then at me, and turned away, crying quietly. Minnesota showed up less and less. Finally he was let go. Johnny Anderson surprised me when he said, "Schrank, you haven't nearly finished your apprenticeship. I'll give you his job if you want it, but don't make any mistakes or you're out." I was concerned because I was not sure how the men would take it. Would they feel I had pushed Minnesota out? I went and bought a set of the *Machinists' Technical Library* and kept it in my locker. The men kidded me a lot about being a "book machinist," and they would say, "Well, kid, you're on your own now. No more Minnesota to fall back on. We'll see how good you are."

The powerhouse was my first experience with how a work community protects its "old-timers." I am sure it is not always true, yet it is hard for me to recall a workplace where the older men were not shielded and protected by the younger. This is one of those unwritten concerns of men and women for their fellows that tends to grow in work communities and can make tough workplaces like coal mines, foundries, and steel mills far more human than they might appear to a casual observer. The sense of community can only be experienced by being part of it. This is at least one reason that behavioral science studies of workplaces tend to be tales of horror. When people who work there read the studies, they might respond with, "Oh hell. It ain't that bad."

Minnesota knew that as a craftsman he was part of a dying breed. I often thought that this was at the heart of his drinking. The new machines with off-the-shelf replaceable parts began to surround him. He had spent most of his working life on steam engines. When he would be sent to work on a modern turbine or a diesel, or any piece of equipment in the powerhouse that simply required him to take out a part and replace it with another, he would hand me the wrench, saying, "Here, kid, you do it. What the hell they need me for to do this! Any monkey can learn to do it." He would give me the wrench or just drop it on the floor, then wave his arm at the work and go off drinking.

Like many foreign-born workers, Minnesota never really became part of America. He was often homesick and would talk about Finland's beautiful lakes and clear skies. I am not sure now whether all the kidding he got about being a "greenhorn" didn't bother him more than he would ever acknowledge. Part of our terrible melting pot stew is the digs we use to kid foreign-born workers about their foreignness. Those of us born here want to believe that somehow we are better than our foreign-born parents.

Unlike the furniture factory, the powerhouse is a service industry, which reduces the dangers of being laid off as a result of a poor product market. Therefore that was not a factor in getting the work finished as quickly as possible, as in the case of the valves. If there had been a layoff element in the powerhouse, I think other workers would have quickly cued me by suggesting that I "cut out the efficiency crap." Where the amount of work expected or agreed to is fixed, finishing early means more time to schmooze.

In the behavioral science literature there is some discussion about workers' desire to be autonomous, creative, and self-actualizing. Many of these concepts were developed by the psychologist, Abe Maslow, as a hierarchy of human needs. Maslow suggested that once people have satisfied their basic needs for food, shelter, clothing, safety, and security, they are freed to pursue a higher order of needs. But in their application of Maslow the behavioral scientists tend to forget an important set of needs that Maslow has termed "belonging needs." I have found that it is terribly important to feel part of a community in the workplace. This is something that the work itself can never provide us with. In the case of rebuilding valves, for instance, I became creative because the work as it was organized did not permit me enough schmoozing time, time to wander around the plant, visit and talk with people in other departments and not be stuck in one spot doing the same thing. We need to see workplaces as communities rather than just places where people go to carry out tasks for which they are paid.

Though the work itself is important to the workplace community, what is most neglected by those concerned with its problems is the nature of the human relationships: the rituals such as greetings on arrival, coffee breaks, lunch time, smoke breaks, teasing, in-jokes, and endless talk about almost everything are the important ways in which the community maintains itself. In organized plants the union creates a whole additional community of stewards and committeemen, with grievance procedures and other transactions. All these elements and many more rituals are the cement that holds the work community together.

Learning from the many "Minnesotas" I worked with, I became a machinist and later on a toolmaker. After I stopped working on steam engines, it began to dawn on me that I was becoming a skilled worker, but not a craftsman. The skilled worker receives instructions given in the language of blueprints that set forth in one-dimensional drawings the specifications for what is to be made. As I would study the extremely precise dimensions that read in the thousandths or ten-thousandths of an inch, I would yearn to be back with Minnesota, listening to the heart of a steam engine. The steam engine permitted the use of a caliper that was based solely on feel, but none of the fine measurements dictated by blueprints can be read without the most delicate instruments. The small leeway permitted the machinist or toolmaker is called the tolerance. Tolerances have been getting continuously smaller, "less tolerant," as equipment has improved and more efficiency is demanded. The new tolerances, requiring dial indicators, allow no use of feel whatsoever. A skilled machinist or toolmaker is permitted plus or minus one-thousandth or one ten-thousandth of an inch. This means the work is in an extremely tight straitjacket. People doing this work are forced to maintain high levels of concentration at all times in order to remain within the allowable tolerance.

A machinist can be creative to the extent that he might figure some better or easier way to perform a task, but it still must conform to the tolerance. He may be creative to the extent that engineering has not specified how a certain operation has to be accomplished. He has a lot of responsibility, but there is little or no opportunity to create something of his own design. Autonomy may exist to the extent that skilled workers are free to decide how to do a particular task, but the trend in many modern plants is for engineering to spell out in the minutest detail the way in which the work is to be done. This makes the machinist or toolmaker a most competent instruction follower but leaves little room for autonomy, creativity, or decision making.

Being a machinist or toolmaker requires a great deal more concentration on the work itself than a plumber or a factory machine operator, not only because of the tolerances but also because of the very many tools and pieces of equipment he may have to understand and know how to operate. But compared to the repetitive, thoughtless work of the furniture factory, I preferred the machine shop, though many men I worked with did not. A day in the machine shop would go fast, and at least some work was a challenge—if nothing else to hold to the tolerances. Over the years many factory workers would ask me, "What the hell you want all that responsibility for? I just stand by this machine, watch it, adjust it once in a while, load it, and I can think about anything I want. I don't have to worry about all those tools and tolerances." There may be more to that than most behavioral scientists know.

However, I found that one of the best things about being a machinist or a toolmaker was the freedom to move around, to schmooze. Often when a machine tool has been set up for an operation, there can be considerable time to schmooze with the guys around you—go get coffee, a Coke, or a smoke. And a considerable amount of time may get taken up in figuring out how to make the task easier.

I was still working at the powerhouse when the war in Europe was beginning to heat up, and the government was starting to recruit machinists for war production plants. It turned out that I had been lucky in working with Minnesota and unlucky that it had been such a short time. Now machinists were in real demand. I went to work in a machine shop that was doing subcontracts for the navy and air force. We made propeller shafts and couplings for Liberty ships, and did special engine work for the navy. The shop was old, with many of the machines driven by overhead belts. The machine tools were big—a forty-foot-long lathe and a Bullard boring mill capable of turning a ten-foot ring—all of which was known as "elephant equipment" and was in great demand. The pay was good and the foreman who interviewed me for the job said, "You can work all the overtime you want." Wow, I thought, I can get rich here. Time-and-a-half for overtime. The depression was over. The war was wonderful.

The company had a normal work force of about 25 men, mostly "old-timers," as they were called in the trade. This now swelled to about 200. Among the newcomers in the plant were many young machinists like me, and there was something about this group of "Young Turks" who had recently learned the trade that made us awfully aggressive.

I quickly made friends with Teddy the Greek. We would talk during coffee and lunch breaks about the lousy working conditions in the plant—bad lighting, lack of heat, poor ventilation, and so on. We were in demand now, we no longer worried about losing the job. One evening Teddy and I went to the machinists' union office in Yorkville, a tiny little place where a very old man sat behind a rolltop desk. We picked up authorization cards, asked a few questions, said we would be back with some new members. None of this seemed to interest the old fellow at all.

We Young Turks prided ourselves on how quickly we were able to unionize the plant. We became part of Local 402 of the International Association of Machinists, the IAM. The newly elected union shop committee was dominated by the Turks. Our aggressiveness, our new-found union camaraderie created a certain contempt for the older men who had worked so long without a union. We began to show some of these old-timers how not to work so hard by improving their setups, using newer cutting tools, and working more closely together.

This was quite a switch from my furniture factory days. I was learning the importance of having a job, making as much money as I could, and doing as little work as possible. Hourly pay rates were going up, yet more important was the overtime that enabled us to get some fat pay checks. All of this led to a new kind of security with a simultaneous decrease in my motivation to work hard. Max would have been proud of me, for the machining of the propeller shafts turned out to be a schmoozer's dream. The shafts were thirty to forty feet long and about eight inches in diameter. They had to be turned, tapered, and keyed, all of which could take two to three days to run. The Greek would say, "Now Schrank, the trick is to set up the machine so we have a minimum amount of adjustment." This meant not having to stand over the machine. One old-timer who chewed and spit tobacco all day, Earl Wintergreen, said, "You kids are crazy. These old machines won't do what you expect." We just laughed and said, "Earl, we are going to show you some ingenious sensing mechanisms that will shut off the machine or sound an alarm if and when something goes wrong." We spent an incredible amount of time and energy developing components that would permit us to leave the machine to work on its own without our presence. This was automation.

Why did we do it? We felt secure, so we wanted to be free to leave the machine, walk around, talk to our friends. On the swing or night shift our homemade automation permitted us to go out of the plant for a beer while a buddy kept an eye (or ear) on our "automated" machine, and on occasion we even went to a nearby movie.

The navy was in the process of building up America's fleet of Liberty ships to carry badly needed materials to our European allies. Contracts were on a cost-plus basis and the company was under constant pressure to increase production. The Vass Ice Machine Company had been a small job shop, limping along with some old elephant machines. It quickly turned to war production and began making bonanza profits. The Young Turks who had recently come to work understood this better than the old-timers. We were determined to get our share of the windfall. The pressure to produce was endless, so that no matter how much we were able to cut the production time, the company kept pressing for more. In the manufacturing business the pressure for more production goes on without relief. It was only when I left the production line and the pressure suddenly vanished that I became aware of its force.

There is a production game that is played between workers and their supervisors. The supervisor or foreman almost always wants the people he is responsible for to produce more. Most workers seem to know instinctively that "more production" either leads to the challenging game of "you want more but I don't want to work harder" or to a bottomless pit. The challenge of the game can prove to be the most interesting part of the job. Workers are ingenious at this game.

I was talking with the Greek about how the foreman was catching up with our production innovations. "Look," I said, "we are in a double bind if we do the work as easily and as quickly as possible, maybe just to increase our schmooze time. If the supervisor catches on and says we're real smart and incorporates our short-cuts, we end up doing more work for the same money. This requires that we hide our shortcut timesavers—and that will take our most creative effort." The Greek looked at me for a long time and then said, "Listen, the next time Ramirez is running far ahead of schedule, I am going to show you something you won't believe, Schrank."

A few weeks later on a summer night, the Greek came by and said, "Let's take a walk." We walked to the back end of the plant, out onto the loading platform. There I could not believe my eyes. I saw two guys burying a thirty-foot propeller shaft in the backyard. I burst out with "What the hell are you guys doing?" They said, "Hey fellows, you watch us be heroes at the end of the month when the boss gives us that we-need-to-break-quota bullshit." I admit that this was an extreme case, but if you can get a group of workers to tell work-banking stories, you will hear some fantastic tales.

Banking work in the sawdust, as was done in the furniture factory, or under benches, in machine shop lockers, under loose floor boards, even in car trunks, or by undercounting, are just a few of the ways I observed workers trying to monitor their own work pace to control the amount that they are asked to produce. I remember a typewriter plant where people would get ahead by taking the extra parts home, then on a day they wanted to take it easy, bring them in to be counted.

If you have not experienced a production line, it is very hard to understand the problem of work pacing. I remember doing things in an emergency, like turning out in seven hours a propeller shaft that normally took twelve or fourteen hours. Obviously I could never do that at a steady pace. It would surely end me up like Charlie Chaplin in *Modern Times*. To expect a production worker to work at his peak for a whole day is like asking a long-distance runner to sprint the whole race the way he does in the last 100 yards. It is simply impossible to do, yet some production-hungry industrial engineers expect that. The foreman at Vass would say, "After all, you produced thirty units this morning. How come you only made ten this afternoon?" I answered, "Because I wore myself out this morning." He did not seem to care about my explanation, just sort of shrugged and said, "If you can do it in the morning, you can do it in the afternoon."

I was learning that I might double or triple my productivity for a short, fixed period of time, but I could not possibly keep up that double or triple pace continuously without serious consequences to my health.

Bennet Kremen, writing in the *New York Times* about the Lordstown, Ohio, General Motors assembly plant told how workers doubled up (buddied) to relieve each other on the line. Some people in the Auto Workers Union were peeved at Kremen for suggesting that one employee on an assembly line could do the work of two; this surely could be seen as evidence that GM might be right when they complain that the workers are not giving a day's work. Workers on a production line may help each other by doing two jobs for a given period of time, but that certainly does not mean one person could do both jobs continuously. I can recall times when I did the work of two or even three men for short time periods. Can this possibly suggest that I could do that continuously and hope to survive? I think not. The problem that employees in manufacturing have is that supervisors continue to harass employees for increased production once the idea takes hold that workers can be more productive. They become extremely aggressive in constantly demanding more. That is how workers learn to pace the amount of work done for a day, a week, or a month. As Max said in the furniture factory, "We give just so much and no more."

A few years ago I visited the Volvo truck plant in Göteborg, Sweden. I spent a day observing work teams assembling trucks. In the afternoon, about three o'clock or three-fifteen, the place seemed to come to a halt as workers began to wipe their hands, wash up, and generally to appear as though the day's work was through. I figured my watch was wrong, because time-zone changes throw off my inner clock. Since quitting time was four o'clock, I asked one of the men what was happening. He looked at me quite surprised saying, "We made our thirty trucks today and that's it. Not even another bolt goes on today."

That example of production pacing is common in many parts of Europe. When I asked the Volvo management about it, they acknowledged the problem, yet they had no idea about what to do. As one manager put it, "What good is participation, team building, and all that stuff if I cannot get one more truck a week?"

Workers in manufacturing try to get some control over the work pace because they are fearful that if they do not, the speedup will kill them. Whether it is true or not is of little consequence because the tradition creates a fear that is real.

At Vass Ice Machine, together with Teddy the Greek I was becoming actively involved in the day-to-day activity of the union. We processed grievances, negotiated contracts, and prided ourselves in holding the company to the letter of the agreement. I was enjoying our union's success and that led to our thinking about how to become more actively involved.

# Union Organizing

One night after the local union meeting, the Young Turks were sitting in a bar sort of complaining among ourselves about how poorly the local was being run. At that time Local 402 of the IAM was made up primarily of old-time skilled craftsmen, mostly Germans. Though they worried somewhat about the Young Turks, they liked our "spirit." As we talked that night, the Greek suggested I take a job in a big plant that we knew was unorganized. If I organized the place from the inside, we would have a large number of new members, which would give us a substantial base of support to run in the next local election. The place I was to get a job, Nathan Manufacturing Company, had about 1,500 employees making various kinds of lubrication equipment.

I had an interview there and was offered a job as a setup man on the turret lathes rather than as a machinist. I had never done setup work on turret lathes. The interviewer said that if I was half as good a machinist as I claimed, I should learn the new job in a few weeks. When I went to the union hall to tell the Greek and my other buddies what happened at Nathan's, they loved it. I would now be working on the production floor. From an organizing viewpoint that was far more important than the toolroom. As the Greek reminded me, it was a natural thing for us depression babies to take jobs we knew little about; we learned on the wing. Your hope was to pick up enough information from the people around, as well as from supervision, to see you through the first couple of weeks. Winging it required social techniques of being able to warm up to a person in the plant who would help you out.

There were about 100 men in the turret lathe department,

primarily Italians. The plant was an old five-floor red brick factory building with wire-gate, pull-cord elevators. The general foreman introduced me to the turret lathe supervisor. There seemed to be an easy good feeling of camaraderie with lots of yelling and name calling, and a pall of smoke hanging in the air from the cutting oil, which I would learn to get used to. Everything was covered with a fine coat of cutting oil, including the men who worked there. The operators wore long oilcloth aprons, which gave some protection from the splashing oil that came off the lathe and made them look like butchers in black aprons. I had to get to learn how Italians love to tease each other about almost everything: sex (especially the size of one's organ), cars, clothes, knowledge of sports, politics; but any derogatory cracks about mothers, sisters, or daughters were taboo. Uncles, brothers, OK—but I once saw Tony Gillotti get an instant fat lip for making a crack about Mike Russo's mother. They turned out to be a good bunch of men, some of whom realized my knowledge of turret lathe setups was limited and were quite willing to help.

As I began to understand how to set up turret lathes, the operators began to bug me for long-run setups. Willie DeAngelo said, "Look, I need to sit on my ass and study the daily scratch sheet, so give me some long runs." All of the twenty-five or thirty men whose machines I was setting up seemed to be avid horse fans. Every morning before the starting bell rang, there was an eager waiting for the arrival of the *Morning Telegraph*, a now defunct daily newspaper devoted almost exclusively to horseracing. When it arrived it was read carefully (mostly in the toilets), and the inevitable "Waddaya gonna get today" argument started and went on for most of the day, or at least until the race results were known. I learned about jockeys, fillies, mudders, saddle weight, parlays, touts, the flats, and trotters.

Next to long runs, the operators wanted a lot of machine change-overs or downtime, the time allowed the operator for machine repairs or tool changeovers. This permitted more leeway to argue the day's lineups as well as to discuss yesterday's results. Fewer work tasks to perform permitted more time to socialize—more schmooze time was a constant objective. As a setup man I was busy figuring out the new setups, what was the best tool progression, how many operations could be combined, how to keep a good cutting edge on the tools, and so forth. Now and then I might catch a little conversation. When I did, I would try to turn it to the union issue. Over time I began to find myself envying the operators, who seemed to worry little about the work tasks and were free to think about horseracing, baseball, boxing, politics, and, as Willie said, "Of course I think about pussy." While there were different interests in the various departments as well as from plant to plant, the one universal was sex. Fantasizing about it was the one sure way workers had for dealing with the boredom and monotony of routine work.

As war production heated, an increasing number of women began to work in factories; until that time their presence had been represented by conversation, fantasies, and pin-ups. Now their arrival in person added a startling new dimension. Girls in tight sweaters and uplift bras typical of the thirties made many a man's daydream suddenly real. What an effect this sudden presence of women had! Wow, some guys went nuts when they saw girls in sweaters, tight pants, and loose blouses in the summer. In the screw machine department Al Pupo would spend much of his day maneuvering to get the new girl inspector to come over to his machine in the hope she might bend over. As he explained it, "Just to see her teat, man, just to see, not all of it like the nipple. No man, just a little teat. That'll make my day, and even the old screw machine will look good."

As the women arrived in the plants, there came to be an increase in factory dates, love affairs, humping in the back of storerooms, a little feeling up, and an awful lot of flirting and teasing. A new schmooze factor was introduced in the form of seduction. The excitement of the hunt and games between the sexes are hardly noticed in white-collar workplaces that have always had both sexes present. But in those days at Nathan Manufacturing women were just on their way to factory life. Their feminine qualities instantly added a more human feeling to the plant, and I sure loved it.

As I worked in the turret lathe department, my doubts about being a skilled worker increased. The operators seemed to be having more fun than me, playing the races, fooling with the girls, and feeling free. It was true that as a setup man I was making more money, but the pay differential between a skilled worker and a machine operator did not seem to be worth the added responsibility. Many of the operators like Al Pupo felt that way. As he put it, "You gotta be nuts to worry about all that shit of blueprints, gauges, plus and minus. Me, I just worry about pussy. That's all."

In the meantime, we kept moving along with the organizing effort. We had put together a good organizing committee that would meet regularly to review our progress. It was becoming clear that the skilled workers were offering the most resistance to unionization. This was not an uncommon problem. Many times I would hear, "Look, I am a skilled craftsman. I don't need to associate with operators. I know what I am doing and that's what I get paid for. Why should I put myself out for some guy who won't help himself?"

As a machinist and toolmaker I always felt we had the most underpaid job in the whole roster of occupational titles. My years in the labor movement were beginning to teach me some things about workers. Much of the reason for tool and die makers' individualism, for instance, grew out of a sense that skill makes you a superior being, and only inferior humans need the support of each other.

While I was wondering about skilled workers' aloofness and indifference toward their fellow production workers, I received a good opportunity to find out more about it. One day I was handed an unrequested transfer from turret lathes to the toolroom. As I would learn later, the transfer was made in order to get me off the production floors. The company had learned of our unionizing efforts and was getting nervous.

The toolroom was on the top floor. Saying good-bye to my friends in turret lathes, I told them we would be in touch. Those who were union supporters knew what was happening and were anxious to let me know of their support. There were about thirty-five quiet men in the toolroom, a big change from the prattle of the production workers. They were making jigs, fixtures, and production models.

The toolroom work was not at all similar to doing turret lathe setups. We worked in a big spacious area and each of us had our own workbench. I was introduced to the foreman, John Prinze, a quiet, shy man who seemed very at home in his long shop coat. He sort of said something into the air about being glad I was there and was sure I would get along well. It seemed to me at the time that he was aware of my union activity and that I had been sent to the toolroom to be watched. He gave me some blueprints as he said, "OK, Bob, make this gauge. We need it right away." I was tense as I studied the gauge prints. The work was totally new to me. I asked the guy on the bench next to me about the tolerances of plus or minus one ten-thousandth of an inch. I said, "They gotta be kidding." "No," he said, "most of the gauge work around here is like that." I started to get scared, for it began to dawn on me that I was being set up. I had not done this kind of work before and simply did not know how to proceed.

I remembered that when I was in the turret lathe department someone had said there was somebody in the toolroom who was sympathetic to the union. The foreman was already hanging around my bench seeing whether I was asking somebody for advice. He said to me, "When are you going to get on with the job?" I said to him, "I think I left some of my tools in the turret lathe department." I said I wanted to go down and see if I could find them. He said, "OK, but get right back here."

I waited until he walked away, took the blueprints, slipped them into my shirt, went down to the turret lathe department, and asked Al Pupo and some of the other union supporters who was the guy in the toolroom who was sympathetic to the union. They told me it was Henry, but they weren't sure of his last name. They said that he ran a milling machine up in the toolroom.

I ran back up to the toolroom, asked some of the guys who Henry was, and they pointed to a tall fellow with a crew cut, running a milling machine. I went over to him and asked him if he could meet me in the toilet. He was kind of surprised and troubled, but shut off his machine and came with me. We went in and I told him that I had been transferred from the turret lathe, and I thought they were trying to set me up to get rid of me by giving me this gauge to make.

I couldn't tell whether he was going to help me or not. I showed him the blueprint. He kind of whistled and said, "That's a real tough gauge if you've never made that before. Why don't you go over to the stockroom, get the stock cut, start to rough it out; it's going to all have to be ground-finished. And then get somebody you know at the union tonight who is a good toolmaker and let him go over it with you." Henry was my instant friend—I could have kissed him. I was saved!

I went out, took the blueprints, went over to the stock room, told the stock clerk to give me the material to make the gauge, and then began to do what's called the roughing work. I understood this process generally and I could stall for time, even if it went faster than I wanted it to. Then I could go down to the union that night, find a good toolmaker, and have him tell me just how to do this.

I got through that first day, but John Prinze never took his eyes off me. The minute he saw me talking to any of the men, he was over to ask me if I had a problem, or if I needed any help, or why was I talking to men around the floor. It was clear that I was being watched, and that John's instructions were to make sure that I didn't wander around the building. My problem now was just to keep the job.

That night I went to the union hall, found a couple of good old-time toolmakers, showed them the blueprints that I had taken out of the plant. They sat down with me and were only too pleased to give me step-by-step instruction about exactly how to make this particular gauge. One of them gave me his telephone number and said that if I ran into any trouble I should call him up and let him know, and he would help me out.

I came back to work the next morning and began to work on my gauge. Nobody paid any attention to me. The men were very indifferent to how I was making out. If I asked somebody for something, there was a shrug of the shoulders. It was a very cold place to work. Each man went about his own business, nobody paying much attention to anybody else. Once in a while there was a little conversation between a couple of men. But each one of these toolmakers was his own person, and didn't seem to care much about anyone else around the floor. I heat-treated the gauge, hardened it, did all the grinding on it, and a small amount of lapping work as well.

I successfully completed the gauge and it passed inspection. I was then given a drill jig to make for a pump body that had twenty or thirty holes to be drilled, counterbored, reamed, and tapped. The tolerances between holes were considerably less than the gauge had had: only plus or minus two-thousandths of an inch on the finished part, which meant the jig was plus or minus five ten-thousandths of an inch. I had to heat-treat the parts to a specified hardness so that the jig would not wear out from all of the cutting tools.

As a toolmaker I had an awful lot to think about. It consumed all my time and left me little or no opportunity for union talk since I had little or no chance to leave the toolroom. The company had succeeded in boxing me in. The work was very absorbing, but not in a creative way. The attention to very small dimensions and tolerances tended to make toolmakers into loners, sort of withdrawn into the geometry of work that had little romance. The toolroom was low on camaraderie and even lower on schmoozing. Toolmakers seemed less interested in playfulness and sexual fantasy than plumbers or foundrymen.

Most of the toolmakers I worked with tended to be conservative, withdrawn, and kind of distant—not at all like plumbers. I now think the skill requirements made of them are too demanding. A toolmaker who makes jigs and fixtures, which are tools that are used for doing machining operations on parts, must concentrate on each step of the toolmaking because of the close interrelationship of functions.

Toolmakers may carry around a thousand dollars' worth of tools and many times more than that in responsibility, and this responsibility exhausts them almost the way boredom exhausts production workers. In years to come when the plant had been unionized, I would have many opportunities to walk around in it. I would take advantage of that whenever I could to get out of the toolroom for some laughs with my old friends in turret lathes. Playfulness is such an important element in work satisfaction, and yet it is hardly recognized in the literature on workplace problems. The toolmakers and other skilled workers I have met seemed to be a lot less creative than we generally expect. It is possible that we confuse the carefully instructed skilled worker with the more traditional but truly creative craftsman.

We finally organized the plant, won the National Labor Relations Board election, and before long I was working full time for the International Association of Machinists.

# Union Official

With the successful organization of the plant, we went to Ricci's Bar on 116th Street and Second Avenue to celebrate the National Labor Relations Board certification of our victory. The strategy of the Young Turks was working. We now had recruited more new people into the local union than the entire old membership, which meant that in the next local election we could name our slate. We did, and it was elected. I became president of the local, Arthur Ronan, the local's organizer, and Teddy the Greek, secretary. Ronan never knew beans about organizing, and I would spend years teaching him.

Being president and working as an organizer for the local was the second job in which I was not required to make a "thing" or maintain equipment that makes "things." There was a shock at the sudden change of no more clock punching or changing into coveralls or responding to bells for the coffee break, lunch, and quitting. It was as if I had been let out of a cage. Suddenly I had a whole new sense of freedom for myself, and yet I felt a certain guilt about those left behind in the plant. I found I had a sort of subconscious continuing concern that I was no longer productive, for what I was now doing was no longer measurable. How was I to know whether I was productive? I must confess that since I left the shop floor I have never been able to answer that question satisfactorily for myself or my fellow union officials, or for professionals, academics, or consultants.

My entrance into the world of nonmanufacturing jobs was marked with the storage of my beautiful oak toolbox with its dozen little drawers full of all kinds of fine tools. My new work instru-

ments turned out to be talking, dictating, writing, and paper passing. For a long time this proved to be very troublesome for me, as I
would notice was the case with many other union "pie cards," a
derogatory term used by the Wobblies to identify full-time union
bureaucrats. When I met old friends from the plant at union
meetings or gatherings I would explain to them why they were
better off than me. Al Pupo or Mike Provenzano from turret lathes
would greet me with, "Hey Schrank, when you comin' back to the
shop? We miss you, man. Jesus, you were lucky to get the hell outa
there." I would dive instantly into my defensive explanation, "You
guys are better off than me any day. What do you know about the
long hours I put in, the harassment, the troubles we have every
day?" As I talked, I would develop the pained look of the new labor
leader who still has guilt feelings for having managed to get himself
out of the factory while his friends remained behind. Though we no
longer punched clocks, many of us put in far more time than we did
in a plant. But still, I think most of us considered it a better deal
because we controlled our work time, coming and going as we
needed. I was often part of a team of organizers where coordination
and working together were critical.

    I was also initiated into a world that I had known nothing about
in the factory called "the lunch meeting." I would learn in time that
this midday potlatch would turn out to be the most rewarding
activity of the day for many people. No longer having to meet
production quotas and without the worries about piece rates, lunch
became an open-ended celebration of food and company. I was
giddy with joy, arranging to meet different people for lunch without
a worry about time or quotas. The change from a tightly supervised
and controlled activity to an almost total freedom in which I could
allocate my own time made me euphoric.

    Did the euphoria cause me to work hard? Yes, and no,
depending on how "work" is defined. At times we put in twelve- to
fourteen-hour days with sometimes a Saturday and Sunday thrown
in. Yet, as I think about it, it was so hard to separate working from
schmoozing that I often went to the union hall just to see what was
happening. What was happening was a bunch of guys sitting

around schmoozing about jobs, tools, politics, baseball, and women.

I don't want to give the impression that I did no work as a union official. There were many tasks to be performed, such as negotiating the yearly contracts (being an amalgamated local, we had close to one hundred agreements), organizing plants, processing grievances, arranging educational programs for stewards and committeemen, and attending meetings, meetings, and more meetings. The job was great fun. It had a variety of activities, plus the exciting challenge of organizing nonunion plants, which turned out to be like planning a small-scale war: the union against the boss.

As local president, eventually I had to memorize *Robert's Rules of Order,* because when the fights came, I sure had to know what I was doing. My major activity was organizing because we, the new leadership, were determined to have the biggest, most powerful machinist local in the city. Organizing meant going to nonunion plants in the morning at start-up time or in the evening at quitting time. The immediate objective was to spot someone who you might walk with to the subway or car, and to start talking about the plant. "Do you have a union at Cutler Hammer Electrics?"

"Yeah, we got a company union but it don't do shit for ya."

"Well, I am from the Machinists and we would like to organize this place, give you some security, get you higher wages."

"Look, buddy. Good luck, but don't involve me, I cannot afford to lose this job."

The guy hurries to the train. He wants to shake me, but I stick with him, even get on the subway train wherever he may be going. He keeps moving fast, scared he will be seen with me.

"How many people work there?"

Thoroughly annoyed now, he says, "About 800."

"How many women?"

"About 300."

"How many skilled workers?"

Now he has become mad. "Hey, bud, I told you I don't want to get involved. About eighty or ninety. The biggest gripe is the chiseling on the piece rates. And don't send no Jews around here. There ain't none working here. You gotta get the women in the plant. If you don't get the women to sign up, forget it." He's talking. Now I feel good. Maybe I got me a recruit. "The old guys will never sign up, so you gotta get the new guys and the women." With that he gets up and goes into the next car. I get off at the next station, take a train back to the union hall, announce to the hangout crowd, "I know the issues at Cutler Hammer." I sit down and begin to write a leaflet about how Cutler cheats its workers on piece rate.

It's well after five now as the other organizers begin to drift in, and I tell them what I have learned. They too have talked to some Cutler Hammer workers. We compare notes and agree on a strategy that will have women distributing leaflets on the line every morning. We will then go for a women's organizing committee inside the plant. A strong women's committee we figure will shame the men into signing union cards. One of the organizers picks up information that the skilled workers are unhappy because the pay differential between skilled and unskilled employees is too small. While I felt that the status needs of skilled workers tended to make them unreliable partners with production workers, the machinists' union had a tradition of supporting the craftsman. This made me decide to go along with a special effort to bring in the skilled workers.

The next step in our organizing efforts at Cutler Hammer was to learn everything we possibly could about the company. First we got a Dun and Bradstreet report and went over the financial operations and the credit rating of the company. How many plants does it own and where are they located? What does it manufacture in each plant? Are any of its other plants organized? If so, with what unions? Can they shift production from the target plant to other plants? Can they stand a strike, and for how long? Who is on the board? Is there any interlock with other companies or banks?

The organizers would engage in an endless argument on strategy. Much of that grew out of our varied backgrounds, resulting in widely different value systems. Some of us were ideological, while others were pure and simple trade unionists. Among the ideologists were those with a belief that ultimately the only solution for workers was some form of socialism. The various shades of believers included socialists, communists, Trotskyites,

Wobblies, de Leonists, and once in a while even anarchists, who were forever accusing me of "selling out the workers with contracts."

In spite of our ideological differences most of us were activists, and that resulted in some kind of agreement to act, and we did. As soon as we gained a few supporters and learned something about the plant's operations, we decided to hold a quick meeting outside the plant gates in the morning or at quitting time. It was at these plant-gate meetings that ideological differences would become more apparent. With the depression not very far behind, people were haunted by fear of a layoff and there was a compelling interest in job security and higher wages.

Peter Narob, a guy who had joined the union with me at Vass, had lived on skid row and never forgot it. He ended up being frightened of poverty, and so became one of our trade unionists. He would speak about how "the union will get you more money." I would rejoin with the need for dignity and self-respect in the plant, and talk about the basic inequalities between owners and workers in society at that time. Actually this combination of evangelism with everyday needs turned out well. Evangelism is the necessary catalyst that gets people to act on things when ordinarily fear would have them fully paralyzed.

A primary organizing objective was to get a committee of union supporters inside the plant. This meant we had to visit workers in their homes to convince them that supporting and even joining the union was worth the risk. The wife, usually referred to by workers as the "old lady," was often suspicious of outsiders, and early on as an organizer I would learn that if I could persuade her to go along with the union, my chance of signing up her husband improved 80 percent. I would often sit in the kitchen of some worker's home in Brooklyn or Staten Island trying to convince his wife that the union really was going to make their lives better. The women seemed less willing to take the risks of getting involved in a union organizing effort. At home they were isolated from any group feeling developing at the plant in support of the union.

I remember visiting workers' homes in places like New York

City, Elmira, Buffalo, and Butte, Montana. For the most part they were neat, clean, and lacked any signs of culture; a universal drabness seemed to pervade these people's lives. Later when I traveled to Europe, I began to understand that the lack of interest in books, arts, and music was less a class than an American phenomenon. I began to feel lucky for having grown up in a European intellectual, working-class home where Socrates, Plato, the Bible, Michelangelo, Beethoven, Marx, Debs, philosophy, dance, poetry, music, and art were part of our everyday life.

Day in and day out, through rain, snow, and heat, the organizing drive at Cutler Hammer went on. At the beginning it went poorly; the employees were just too scared. We won their confidence a little at a time. The need to appeal to the Italians and the Irish at Cutler made me go and learn about ethnics. In fact, the union was the place to experience almost all kinds of ethnic attitudes, such as husbands' attitudes toward their wives. Michael O'Toole, a long, lanky fellow with a heavy brogue would attend meetings when there was beer served, stay close to the tap and never leave until the barrel was empty. Michael would say, "Well, I'm just a bum but me old lady will take care of it." "Michael," I would say, "how is your wife going to straighten out the mess your drinking makes? You never go home when you're on a bender, you spend all your money on booze. What can she possibly do to salvage you?" Michael would kind of squint down on me and get a silly grin, saying, "I tell you Bob she's a genius, me Molly. She can make somethin' outa nothin', even me."

One time I went to Eli Hill's, a Finnish worker's home in Montana—he had invited a few of us for dinner, after which we were to write some lyrics for a union song. Eli was an old Wobbly married to Heidi, a young Finnish woman who had blonde hair that hung down over a most beautiful pair of breasts. When I arrived, I was delighted with this unexpected treat. As the others came, we men gathered in the tiny nine-by-ten living room, where there was just enough room to move between the big overstuffed sofa and the glass-top coffee table by putting one foot in front of the other. As the honored guest I was given the big blue velvet chair in the corner

with the little lace doilies over the overstuffed arms. Heidi ran in and
out of the kitchen with drinks in little cut glasses that were only
used on occasions such as this. On one of her trips I said, "Heidi,
how long have you been here?" She looked at me sort of
embarrassed and started to say something, when Eli jumped in with,
"Oh, she has been here for fifteen years and comes from a small
town in Northern Finland." Then he lapsed into Finnish, at which
point Heidi just scurried off. We drank, talked union, then
adjourned to the dining room. It was smaller than the living room,
with just enough space for the table and six chairs. As we sat down I
was waiting to see where Heidi would sit, but she never did anything
but run back and forth serving the dinner, picking up the dirty
dishes, and all the time taking her cues from her socialist husband.
Leaving that night after we wrote the lyrics to "Miners Local Union
Number 1 Forever," I was kind of sad that there was no way I could
make contact with Heidi. She had really turned me on, but the rule
"don't fool with the members' wives" prevailed.

In the home of a French worker the twenty-four-year-old
daughter was immediately told upon my arrival to go to another
room because there was a young man present. The wife was kept
away almost as much as the daughter. Was it to avoid being seen by
a strange man, or was it just the provincialism of working class life?
The families of American-born workers were considerably different.
In good weather we usually ended up in a big backyard barbecue.

So much of the work of a union representative is done at
meetings. It seems I've been attending meetings ever since the time I
hung onto my father's hand, my head no higher than most of the
other men's pants pockets, and we went to a meeting celebrating
Eugene Victor Debs's release from prison. This form of communication seems so universal, that I have speculated for some time now
on its meaning. Is it simply two or more people sitting around
talking? No, that's no good. They could just as well stand on a street
corner. Maybe a meeting is two or more people getting together for a
specific purpose. But what about a gathering at Duffy's Saloon?
That has a purpose—to drink and maybe talk. Well, I have tried to
differentiate between the time spent at meetings for a purpose, a

goal, a specific outcome, and the time used for conversation, gossip, movie reviews, or sports talk—schmoozing, and I have come up with a most disturbing 80 to 20 ratio at best, 80 for schmooze and 20 for productive time.

The Debs affair was a mass meeting of true believers coming to pay homage to one of its saints. It was a delicious event with the hall vibrating with joyous energy. This kind of meeting, also held by fraternal or business organizations, secures continuity through the idea that "We meet, therefore we exist." At the union, minutes of the meeting were the evidence that we exist, because we met. We had an endless string of committee meetings—executive, planning, auditing, pension, education, negotiating, youth, women's Christmas party, and many more. In these the work was to review, develop, recommend, or suggest. My hunch is that meeting as a form of work is a good job satisfier, since it fulfills our basic need to schmooze.

Working in the labor movement was also to experience an endless series of meetings beyond the local level. There were district, regional, state, negotiating, and central labor councils, and on and on. The life of a union organizer was also helping me to learn that the ultimate schmooze meeting was a lunch or dinner in a good restaurant with five to seven gemütlich people, and one or two sexy women to divert us from the weighty business questions we came to consider. This type of meeting, a sort of potlatch palaver in the name of work, gives a sense that the Protestant ethic is still with us while we enjoy a terrific dinner. More and more we keep the Protestant ethic myth alive by the confusing of schmoozing and work.

During the years I was in the labor movement the issues of power and control were still in a state of flux. I was a radical young man who was heard to say as I stepped before the microphone, "I am speaking for the brothers and sisters who work in our plants." I was considered by at least some people in the higher bureaucracy as the representative of the rank and file at many conventions, council meetings, and as the opposition to the International Union. It was a fun role that made most meetings and conventions a lot more interesting and exciting. As the opposition, we were constantly on the lookout for a weak spot or soft underbelly as the fertile attack zones. It was cowboys and Indians all the way, and we loved every minute of it. After each of these encounters the "good guys" would gather in a saloon, cafeteria, or delicatessen for another meeting to review our performance in order to do better next time.

Local 402 was growing rapidly. The members and staff represented a wide spectrum of politics, from the simple reformers who just wanted more money and shorter hours to those who really wanted to overthrow the whole capitalist mess and install a workers' government in its place. The right wing was far more unified than the left, who ended up fighting more with themselves than with their enemies. We could never agree on how the revolutionary "workers' paradise" should be run. For those proposing a new society like my father's IWW model of One Big Brotherhood, there was more room for optimism than if you favored the dictatorship of the proletariat as exemplified in Russia. The first was a lovely dream that had never happened and probably never would. The second was a very different problem. While it did demonstrate that a "workers' revolution" could occur, it turned out to be a terrible drag on the propagators of a workers' government. I found myself caught in the awful dilemma of being anti-Soviet and thereby admitting that the workers' paradise had turned out to be a huge torture chamber, or trying to identify with some other workers' liberation movement. The trouble with the other liberation movements was an obsessive anti-Sovietism that led to compulsive Redbaiting. The negativism of that obsession always left me cold, though I knew that much of what they were saying might be true. Another option was to become a business trade unionist and try to duck the ideological issues for a time, hoping that somehow things might get better. The ideological differences did not yet affect our devotion to organizing the unorganized and building the union, but in time they would have old friends at each other's throats.

Though our political tendencies varied, we were still a band of true believers with the religious fervor of a movement, which made the job a most exciting experience. In some small ways we were convinced we were changing the world, a band of true believers who never tired of work. We were as religious as any Calvinist reformers; transforming work into a religious activity is a most forceful motivator. The Russians and the Chinese know this, and have made their revolutions into religions to spur people on to work.

The fraternity of the International Association of Machinists made each of us feel like a member of a larger tribal group. It gave me a sense of a greater identity, but it also created a territorial imperative, or as it is known in the labor movement, "our jurisdiction." As I have changed careers and worked in different worlds, I have been impressed with our strong need to be part of a clearly identifiable tribal group. I have a sense that with the decline of craftsman guilds and the new nationalism since WW I trade and professional tribalism have been increasing, as witnessed by the proliferation of voluntary associations and societies.

The many union conventions, conferences, seminars, and special national bargaining meetings that members and officers of locals attended were all opportunities for re-energizing by bringing the faithful together to convince each other of our superiority over the Comanche tribe (the employers) or the Crow tribe (the Teamsters). There were many differences within the IAM until it came to territoriality-jurisdiction disputes with other unions. For instance, we fought with the boilermakers for years over the issue of who scrapes the joints in high-pressure steam lines. The machinists were instantly united with the war cry, "Steam joints our jurisdiction. We will never yield." The whole convention was on its feet, thumping and stumping. "The boilermakers shall never pass into our territory." Convention after convention would preoccupy itself with this kind of territoriality. Who puts up a metal wall stud: an iron worker, a sheet metal worker, or a carpenter? Whatever might have divided us, our jurisdictional disputes with other unions were an instant unifier.

As a union pie card, the more conventions, conferences, meetings, lunches, dinners I attended, the less chance there was of my ever going back to work in the shop. Though there was a growing guilt about being corrupted by a life of long lunches, endless coffee breaks, and marathon meetings, it was dawning on me that my desire to go back to the plant was shrinking in direct proportion to the length of time I stayed out of there. And like most pie cards before me, I would soon reach the point of no return. The Wobblies understood this and considered the pie card phenomenon the major corrupter of union officials. They had a rule that a pie card could hold a full-time union job for no longer than two years, and then back to the plant he went to reacquaint himself with reality.

Being a pie card no doubt was corrupting, but it also gave me an opportunity to learn about jobs in which one did not have to put up with a time clock, quotas, and supervisors. I was learning a new definition of a job as a place where, rather than being incarcerated for eight hours producing some quantifiable thing, I had almost total freedom to schedule my own work and move around at will. Working in the factory, I felt an underlying desire among the workers (particularly the young) to get out, to escape; and yet after a period of time, most of them gave up hope and resigned themselves to their fate.

In the toolroom at Nathan's, when five of us sat around a workbench at lunch time, Fat Rudy would say, "I would have been an engineer except my father died, so I had to go to work." He was a big man whose shop apron was draped over his huge beer belly. "My kid is not gonna have to work in a dump like this. If it's the last thing I do, I will see to it that he gets an education so he don't have to spend his life in some dumb factory."

Rudy hardly finished when Mike Bihik cut in saying, "My kid's in college already. He's goin' to be an accountant, a CPA. Accountants don't work in dumps. He's goin' to wear a white shirt and a tie. Be a real gentleman, not like us." One by one each man would make his declamation against factory life for his children, his ultimate projection of himself. In the beginning I would sometimes ask, "Well, why do you think you're here?" "Because we are stupid and this is all we can do," was often the reply. Some skilled workers, like Ted Peckechek, felt differently. "You have to know what you're doing to make jigs and fixtures. Most people who go to college wouldn't know beans about this stuff." He was right, yet I felt as if Peckechek was a dying breed. Hardly anyone in America cares about skilled workers, so why be one.

The fact that society does not care much about manual work means that for the people who do it there is little sense of being valued. "My kid will make it" may just be another myth for many, since the kid may have no more idea of how to make it than his father did. Many sons of blue-collar workers end up where their fathers left off, yet there are increasing numbers who make it out.

Being an elected union official was one of the most exciting jobs I ever held. It was full of challenges, not from "things" or tolerances or hardness, but from a concern for people, their needs, wishes, and dreams. Imagine working to fulfill dreams. It's both gratifying and disappointing, but the stuff that dreams are made of is what makes living fun. It is too bad that social scientists have not been able to sense this. Rather, they try to quantify the dreams. A quantified wish may become a science, as in scientific socialism, but the dream quality is destroyed and maybe that's why it never works.

In those burgeoning union days, we sang of our solidarity—our commonwealth of toil that is to be. For many believers the "Hieronymus Bosch of Soviet socialism" turned our dreams to nightmares. The people who worked in the labor movement in its early days and when I was there in the rebirth of the thirties were the dreamers of change. Irrational and unscientific as many of those dreams were, we were the somnambulists who thought of how to change things for the better.

Some of my first lessons regarding worker satisfaction and dissatisfaction I learned in those early union organizing times. Now there is a body of literature and research about worker satisfaction that generally suggests that 85 percent of workers are satisfied with their jobs. The data inside me make me somewhat uncomfortable with that 85 percent figure, as I recall how reluctant workers were to deal with that whole issue. It is just too devastating a question.

When we approached a plant to organize it, assuming no work had been done inside, the individual workers at first contact almost always tended to be hostile. Mostly out of fear, they would proclaim to us, "Everything is OK here. You guys are just outside agitators and troublemakers. Why the hell don't you go somewheres else?" In a small town the outside agitator troublemaker charge was reinforced or sometimes introduced by the local press. Workers would say, "We like the company" or "We get along OK here and you guys are disrupters." I guess we were the Wobblies "fanning the flames of discontent." Union organizers were often accused of being outside agitators, and many of us were rabble-rousers who had learned our craft arguing in New York street corner debates whether the path to world revolution was via Leon Trotsky's permanent revolution or the New Economic Policy of Vladimir Lenin. That took up many evenings on Tremont Avenue in the Bronx, but it was great fun, since it also included lots of early liberated women with whom I started out arguing the five conditions for revolution and continued the argument in bed. In a crusade based on dreams there is an unusual kind of passion that seems to spill over into personal relations. Some of the greatest love I have felt in my life was for the people I crusaded with in those organizing days. I don't recall how organizational theory deals with that, yet it made us far more effective than our numbers would suggest.

I would now define what we were doing in those organizing days as helping workers enlarge what Geoffrey Vickers calls their "appreciative system." An appreciative system goes beyond values; it goes to the ability to see not only what is but *what is possible*. Fixed values tend to make people, particularly blue-collar workers, feel that the condition they find themselves in is determined by some kind of predestination and that they should accept their fate. Many workers accept the most oppressive factory conditions as a kind of fact of life because their appreciative system is limited to that condition. I first became aware of people's potential for change by watching what happened when workers substituted a collective concern for the every-man-for-himself approach (which leads to the alienation of "the lonely crowd"). In the organizing days I never felt alone or alienated because the crusade welded us into a solid group. An organizing group might start out with maybe three or four people. It grew as workers—often with great potential danger to their own jobs—would join the small band of dreamers. Once part of that band, if one needed friends, camaraderie, money, or love, they were all there. Time and time again in those movement days I would see workers who said, "I am satisfied with my job" call us outside agitators and troublemakers, and suddenly, as if in a religious conversion, become part of the union group with a central concern for the people around them. It was scary sometimes to see individuals join the union and see this most fascinating change occur.

Bliss Manufacturing was a plant of a couple thousand "satisfied, happy workers" who for many years had been represented by a company union. In spite of a most vigorous long-time organizing campaign that consisted of regular daily leaflet distributions, house visits, and continuous careful committee work inside the various departments, on the day of the voting we were very unsure of the outcome. Most of the employees in the plant were fearful, had never really warmed up to any of us, and always kept their distance.

The election was a squeaker, for the union won by only twenty-seven votes. A bunch of us were celebrating our victory in a typical old neighborhood bar with the formica table tops, tired mahogany woodwork, and the smell of old beer. As we were reviewing the months of effort it required to finally organize this place, we wondered if this bunch of frightened workers would ever win a contract from the company. Sam was the oldest among the organizers. He had been a hobo, a Wobbly, and he took showers immediately upon arriving anywhere, a hangover from his hobo days when it was important to shower upon arrival since one never knew when the next opportunity to wash would be. Sam was a short, fat fellow, who was so eternally optimistic that defeat was incomprehensible to him. He would respond to my cynicism by insisting that "what we need to do is immediately start an intensive educational campaign to raise the class consciousness of these workers. Don't worry, Bob," he would say, "once they understand the nature of their exploitation, they'll respond. Don't worry." Peter Narob, always annoyed with Sam's optimism and radicalism, would cut in, "Sam, you're full of bullshit. We will never make union men outa that bunch of finks." With each round of drinks the argument became more heated. Finally we agreed to take a series of special measures to help these Bliss workers learn what a union was about.

After each one of the twenty or thirty departments had elected a steward, we set up classes to explain the meaning of a union contract in terms of pay and working conditions. At a general shop committee meeting it was agreed to hold meetings in each department and ask each member to go over the nature of a union contract, writing out clauses that they wanted in the agreement. It was a slow process, but without any of us realizing it, some interesting changes began to happen.

I remember it climaxing at a general plant meeting with a couple of hundred people present, when old John McDermott, a Scotsman in his sixties with a huge head of white hair, quietly stood up unannounced in the wrong order of business (we were also teaching *Robert's Rules of Order*) and began to speak softly but forcefully in his burr, "I've been workin' here for well on to thirty-two years now. I don't have much time left before I am forced by age to retire with a pittance that I could not even comfortably starve on. So, I am glad that all of you will now have a chance to repay those bastards who made us crawl like beggars in Calcutta, seeking a farthing. In your presence I want to thank God that I have had a chance to become a man again before I die."

He sat down. There was a long silence as the organizing staff just looked at each other in stunned disbelief. I was chairing the meeting and I remembered the difficulties we had had in getting McDermott to sign a union card. He was the most pious and respected old man in the place. Now he had let loose all his pent-up anger. Suddenly, like a wave breaking, the hall of people stood up in a spontaneous demonstration of approval with people shouting, "That's how it was," "He's right," "Now let's get even." I began to rap the gavel for order, but no one heard. People turned to each other, telling how awful it was to be treated as children, to be constantly humiliated. I stopped my gavel rapping, totally disbelieving what was happening. The organizing staff from the union finally gathered together in front of the podium. We just laughed at each other as a great glow of joy ran through us. We had witnessed the birth of a people's collective concern. There was nothing to do after McDermott but let people take the floor to tell their own stories of indignities committed against them by foremen, supervisors, the personnel department—the company.

What gradually emerged as a central issue of concern for these workers was a terrible resentment of years of servility to the supervisors on the plant floor. The more those workers expanded their appreciative system, the more militant the most recent company supporters became. In a short period of time this plant that we never thought we could unionize was the base of militancy in our local union. Many of these workers became friends of long years' standing, and I was only to lose the support of some of them in the worst years of the McCarthy witch hunts. The labor movement prepared workers for struggle against the company. Being only narrowly political, as in its favorite slogan, "Support your friends and punish your enemies," it in no way prepared the workers for any political attacks.

André Gorz, the French radical economist, commenting on the workers' dissatisfaction issue, points out that the outcomes will be qualitatively different, depending on whether workers are dealt with as individuals or collectively. Most attitudinal surveys about work satisfaction lose much of their usefulness because they tell nothing about the people in a plant as a collective group. Yet for the most part that is how they work, as an integrated system. Since in workplaces the formal and informal work group is a critical element in how workers feel about their jobs, dissatisfaction beyond griping can be interpreted as disloyalty to the group, and expressing it is therefore not encouraged, particularly to outsiders. The union gives legitimization to the group feeling, extending it beyond the immediate work area, where it tends to form, to the whole plant. The change that occurs when an informal group of people becomes legitimized is one in which they experience a sense of elation, the excitement of new-found allies. This legitimization of feeling unleashes an entirely new source of energy.

Many behavioral scientists studying workplace problems tend to overlook this collective energy when they deal with the issue of participation in decision making. It may be that behavioral scientists and industrial engineers generally have had little experience with the phenomenon of a bunch of individuals coming to sense themselves as a collective. Yet this was the pivotal force that allowed us to organize Bliss.

Thinking back on it, before Bliss was organized, the working conditions, wages, and other benefits were not all that bad. Pay was only slightly under union scale, benefits were not too different from most union shops. What was very different was a subtle system of paternalism and subservience that had gradually emerged. It demanded that employees ingratiate themselves for small favors, almost the way children seduce their parents to gain little rewards. Subservience in adults creates a resentment that may grow quite imperceptibly over time and can burst forth in what appears as an unwarranted, extreme militancy. The source of the action is a resentment against a system of conduct that deprives people of their adulthood. This paternalism is not a case of evil supervision, though on occasion that is possible. It grows out of the institutional arrangements of power and authority. First-line supervision is pressed by managers above them to increase productivity. Supervisors do this by pressuring their subordinates, the workers. In unorganized plants many workers find that one way of dealing with these pressures is through the seduction game of wooing superiors in order to secure favors and obtain recognition. As we all have experienced, being seductive, aside from being degrading, is one helluva lot of work. When workers in Bliss became a collective, they discovered an alternative to the bowing and scraping. The effect was electric when the energy formerly used to control their resentment was suddenly released in the interests of the group. It was an inspirational peak experience as the group gained an awareness of its collective position of strength, which dramatically changed the participants' appreciative system. There was a new insight into the impact of subservience on their behavior. It was a most dramatic example of experiential learning.

When I was in the labor movement, the issue of how much control the workers would gain through their union was probably more significant than it is now. I think it is an issue, though there is a reluctance to recognize it. The issue of who participates in decision making or in general management skirts the problem of who controls what. Within the confines of a rather conservative ideological stance, the AFL-CIO has carried worker participation in management as far as it could. This conservative position grew as a reaction to the early socialist influence in the labor movement. Many of the ideological issues in the early years of the unions revolved around questions of control of the means of production. In the early 1900s the IWW was propagating worker control or the brotherhood of the working man via the One Big Union. Daniel de Leon, Debs, Haywood, and Hillquit, all either in unions or close to them, were advocating the workers' ownership of the means of production as the only real solution to workers' problems.

The employer groups were scared to death of the ideologists and fought them bitterly. (See, for instance, Pinkerton's *Strikers, Communists, and Tramps.*) The employers' efforts against the socialist ideology resulted in the pure and simple trade unionism of Gompers who, unlike the socialists, assured the owners that the AF of L had no interest whatsoever in depriving them of their property rights or their right to manage. I believe much of the present hostility in the American labor movement toward worker participation in management stems from this earlier controversy, even though it may no longer be valid because of the much more public nature of ownership of major corporations. (In *The New Industrial State* Galbraith sees the corporation as a public institution.)

The issue of participation in management as a measure of control becomes even more critical when applied to the public sector, where there are thirty-five million employees ostensibly working for the taxpayer. Who has the right to control this work force? The elected officials? But they are, after all, politically beholden to the civil servants for their election. The way the public employee unions are moving, I am not sure they do not already have control of some institutions, even though they have not assumed its management functions. That may be the next step.

The old AF of L leaders, in their belief that decision making was purely a management function, may prove to have been influential to the extent that we have learned so little about *how* workers can participate in decision making. Since the experience with work reorganization in the socialist countries has been so disappointing, as S. M. Miller notes in his writings on neosocialist thought, the idea of socialism, if it is ever to get off the ground again, will require a lot of work to be done on some new models. The model of worker participation in Europe outside the so-called socialist countries, which gives workers representation on the boards of the corporation and in work councils, is implemented within traditional hierarchical organizational arrangements. Without some real changes in these traditional structures, the arrangement becomes a cooptation, placing the worker representatives in the position of approving the existing drama by making them actors in the play. The issue of worker participation in management might better be framed in terms of some new organizational structures for achieving the work of society. Unfortunately, since the Wobblies and the Socialists, very few people in the labor movement give this issue any serious consideration.

Another observation based on my union experience of the thirties is about work motivation. My work experience has always given me real doubts about man's intrinsic desire to work. In movements like the organizing drives of the thirties, we just worked like hell. How many times in the wee hours of the morning in some godforsaken flea-bag hotel did I gaze at the yellowed, peeling wallpaper and wonder what the hell I was doing here. I was a true believer addressing my coworkers as Sister and Brother in a crusade for the brotherhood of man. Such belief needs to be mythological, so that it cannot be easily reified.

I saw that kind of belief and commitment again in the civil rights movement of the sixties, which motivated people to work with no regard to pay, hours, or working conditions. It seems reasonable to conclude that when people believe, they become highly motivated. Luther and Calvin must have known that when they assured all us poor humans that we would find salvation in work. Now, as long as the workers believed that, there was plenty of motivation to work.

What are we in for as religion fades and there are fewer true believers? Will the motivation to work decrease correspondingly? If it turns out that the drive to work is strongly correlated with believing, then I would have some doubts about Herzberg's notion of increasing work motivation by making the work itself more challenging. If believing in work is an important factor in motivation, then it probably cannot be created by some task arrangement. Witness the need to keep people believing in a continuing revolution in China and now in Cuba, in order that the rice continues to be planted and the cane crop maintained. With the advent of the welfare state and the explosion of nonwork-type jobs, the growing problem will be who will do the dirty work. We need to understand this as we try to figure out who does what job, and how compensations, benefits, and amenities are distributed.

# Politics

As president of a local union that was doubling its membership every six months, I was becoming quite well known around the union. I would find myself almost every night around the bar of the German Labor Temple in the Yorkville neighborhood of New York with Sam, Pete, and some of the old Germans who were still active in the local.

The country at one time was full of labor temples, mostly built by unions like the Machinists that were descended from the craft guilds. When I joined the IAM, I had to learn secret signs and salutes, somewhat like the Masons, who always confused me with their finger-fiddling handshake. (For a long time I thought that these handshakes had something to do with sex.) Now they are no longer called temples but union halls, and many of the unions that gathered there have given up the secret signs and rituals. Back in 1943, unions were becoming more respectable, as the FBI and special police groups kept them under surveillance, often with the cooperation and encouragement of the national leadership.

The Yorkville Labor Temple in those days was still a hangout for nostalgic pre-Nazi German radicals. It was built of heavily carved mahogany paneling, was furnished with bentwood chairs, and always stank of mustard and sauerkraut and old stale beer. It was a man's place and few women ever showed up there.

It was in one of these labor temple sessions that we began to talk about expanding "our," meaning the local union's, influence around the Machinists and the AF of L generally. As Johnny Hienze, an old-time brewery machinist who looked like a turkey hawk, put it, "We are the fastest growing local around; we got a terrific president who knows the rules, meaning *Robert's*, and speaks beautifully. What the hell. Let's start shakin' this sleepy union up." John wasn't radical or anything; he was just being bitten by the success of the Young Turks. He was sharing the feeling and was getting an appetite for more. Before that evening of beer and scheming was over, it was agreed that we would reactivate a dormant part of the union called the New York State Council of Machinists, and I would run for its president.

While these state councils were devoted primarily to political and legislative activity, they also played the important function of giving local unions and districts an opportunity to come together independent of the International Union. The council soon held a convention of local unions in Rochester, New York, and I was elected state president. I was to hold that job, along with the presidency of my local, for about nine years, in which time I would be introduced into a new work world—that of politicians and legislators.

The very first job the State Council of Machinists decided to undertake was getting F.D.R. the Democratic nomination by main-taining and promoting his support in the labor movement as he prepared to run for his last term. The CIO was pretty solid in sup-port of a fourth term, but the AF of L Executive Council seemed anxious not to support him, probably due to what they felt was his overcoziness with the Russians. It did not seem at all clear early in 1943 that F.D.R. would get the nomination. There was much dis-content with Roosevelt in the AF of L building-trades unions, which seemed to grow out of the anti-Left feeling that dominated so many of the policies of these unions.

The machinists' union was out of the AF of L at that time, hav-ing refused to pay its per capita tax in an argument over jurisdiction with the boilermakers. It was strongly pro-F.D.R., and within a few months of the convention that elected me, the state council's executive board, meeting in Rochester, instructed me to get a fat suitcase, hit the road, and get every state and local AF of L organiza-tion on record to support F.D.R. I was to organize committees, put some money-raising machinery in place, and build a rank-and-file organization.

I wrote a pamphlet for the State Council of Machinists, "Why AF of L Members Are Supporting F.D.R." It was enormously successful among unions and became a rallying point in winning labor support for F.D.R. Among other things, the pamphlet implied that the AF of L leadership was selling out "labor's greatest friend, F.D.R." The anger this aroused toward me in some AF of L circles was destined to bring about a major showdown later in my union career.

I traveled first through New England, making friends with Joe Nimrod, who would become the president of the New England Council of Machinists and was a powerful Roosevelt supporter. Together we lined up most of the most influential unions. As I traveled, I began to meet candidates running for every conceivable office, from coroner to president. I could not believe how many elective jobs there were; I kept handshaking candidates everywhere I went.

The work of a political campaign presents another one of those situations in which the work itself is extremely hard to identify. It is a hobby and a skill that involves politicians running for office, though they are almost inconsequential compared to all the hangers-on, pollsters, advisers, analysts, speech writers, and camp followers, and often pretty girls who lend glamor, sex, and machismo to the candidate.

With a few exceptions, most of the politicians I met were very cynical people. One whom I remember so well was Senator Robert Taft of Ohio. I had written what was probably my most agitational piece of work—a pamphlet on the Taft-Hartley Act called, "This Is Aimed at You." As I look at the illustrations and read it now, it was not just "fanning the flames of discontent"—it was lighting them. Senator Taft invited me to meet with him in order to "point out the various errors, misstatements of facts, and propaganda that you have written." He was a tall, thin, business-faced man who looked me straight in the eye and talked to me off notes on small file cards. I knew he was supposed to be our archenemy, but damn it, I really liked him. I liked the trouble he took to talk to me. Mostly he had an enormous amount of integrity.

Senator Lehman was a nice man, but then again, he was wealthy, and politics can be sort of a fun hobby for the rich. There was an underlying assumption that if people were in politics, they had some selfish motive for power or something they were after for themselves. Yet they kept talking all the clichés about some greater cause. My first encounter with the question "What do you want?" was with a powerful state committeeman who asked me why I was so busy organizing all those plant committees in support of F.D.R. When I replied, "To elect him," he said, "Oh, for Christ's sake, stop the bullshit. What do *you*—you, Schrank—want?" I became confused and troubled, for I still believed that all the Democrats were the good guys who just wanted to elect their candidates. But I was to discover that many were strictly interested in the local organizations that needed to elect people in order to control the patronage. Some, like the Bronx Democratic organization under Ed Flynn, also controlled their Republican rivals and so assured a mastery of the patronage no matter who won.

I think it was this political juggling activity that made almost all the people in this business so very cynical and susceptible to corruption.

"What do you want? What do you want?" would ring in my ears, especially after Joe Ryan, famed head of the International Longshoremen's Union and notorious for his underworld connections, put that question to me as an ultimatum in a Syracuse hotel room. That made me very nervous, and I figured I had better come up with something or this guy was going to have me outfitted with cement shoes. He continued, "What's the matter, Bob? Don't you like your job? Listen, how about a new Cadillac, some luggage? Listen, go get yourself a new wardrobe at Brooks Brothers and charge it to me." All this because I was secretary of the Labor Committee to Reelect Bob Wagner to his last term. I was at the state AF of L convention, promoting Wagner against the building trades candidate, Curran.

I told Ryan, "Look, Joe, none of these things interest me. I really thought that we, the labor movement, owed something to the father of the National Labor Relations Act, which made organization of the mass production industries possible." I could feel myself making a speech. I was addressing Joe Ryan in his hotel room at 2 A.M. "There is no way that the unions will ever get away with it if we fail to support Bob Wagner. We owe him so much, no matter if he is a very old man. He deserves our best effort."

"Oh, bullshit! Why don't you quit speechmaking." Now he was irritated. Jumping out of his chair, he pointed his finger. "Listen, we got a lotta nice pussy around here. Why don't I get you one. Go up to your room, get a good fuck. You'll feel a lot better. Maybe you'll even quit making speeches, and I'll talk to you in the morning. What do you say?"

I tried to cut in with another speech about how I was not about to be bought out with a piece of ass. Besides, the issues here were of utmost political significance, and so on, but he just kept going, never looking at me, "Listen, people tell me you're a Communist. Now I don't believe that, but for Christ's sake, use your fucking head. You do business with us and you don't have to worry." Still ignoring me, he was on the phone, and the next thing I knew I was being ushered out of the room into the hall. I was introduced to Lily, and Ryan said as he slammed the door, "Have a good time. See you for breakfast."

When I was first elected to the presidency of the state council, some newspaper reporters told me about the whore trap, yet it was one of those things I never quite believed until it happened. Some old Wobbly friends had warned me to look out for booze and women as the number one corrupters of labor leaders. I saw that happen with poor Joe Doorman, a left-winger who had managed to become the international vice president of the Culinary Workers Union. I knew he liked booze, having seen him bombed on many occasions, but what I didn't know was when he got himself gassed, his fancy for women rose correspondingly. They forced him to resign his office in disgrace when he was confronted with some glossy six-by-nines of himself in bed with another union official's wife. Using your wife to set a guy up. Now, that's an example of extreme tactics. In the struggle for power and control it was just expedient. As a friend commented, "Well, he's lucky he didn't end up dead in a lime pit."

So here I was at 3 A.M. in the lobby of the Hotel Syracuse with Lily, who was kind of cute with her teats half out. I was lonesome, tired, half-bagged, and I thought, "Oh hell, why not. She might just be nice company." Anyway, 3 A.M. is another world.

But when she addressed me as, "Oh Bob," I sobered. Whores have a way of saying your name like they have known you for six years. "Let's go to my room. It is so much more comfortable."

"What do you mean? All hotel rooms are the same."

"Oh no," Lily said, "not mine."

The lady was telling me something, or my paranoid center was now in full control of me. Her message seemed clear. Her room was rigged for sound, or for pictures, or with a Mickey Finn. I saw myself on the glossy six-by-nines in high porno. No way was I going to get caught in whatever was going on here. I said, "Listen, honey, how about a cup of coffee?"

"You don't like me, do you?" she said.

"Of course I do, but I am not sure about the people who pay you. By the way, who does?"

"I don't know, I work for this guy."

"What guy?"

"Oh none of your goddamned business. You're just a pain in my ass."

We finished our coffee and I told Lily good night. Her parting shot was, "You are one cold lousy bastard. You're gonna get me in trouble."

"File a grievance," I said, and I went to bed.

The next morning I decided I had better call a meeting of the executive board of the State Council of Machinists to tell them what happened the night before. The twelve or fifteen men listened hard to what I had to say. "These are dangerous people you are fooling with, Schrank," said Steve Gallagher from Oswego. "Hope you know what the hell you're doing." Then came the wisecracks.

"When you gonna get the Cadillac?" "Come on, Schrank, was she a good fuck?" When we have even a little corruption on our minds we detest resisters, and in this union work there were endless temptations, from little bribes of a bottle of booze to a mink coat or a Cadillac. The temptation may be imperceptible, little gifts or small favors that may just grow over time as the receiver finds that it isn't so bad after all. While I found this to be a general condition in some unions of the AF of L, it was not nearly as prevalent in the Machinists. I like to think that the reason for this was the strong socialist tradition, especially around the old railroad lodges, many of whose members used to tell stories about Eugene Victor Debs and the American Railroad Union.

The state council was doing a bang-up job for Roosevelt. Probably because of that, in 1944 I was asked by the international president of the Machinists, Harvey Brown, if I would consider working full time on the Democratic National Labor Committee with Dan Tobin, president of the Teamsters Union. I talked with the local union executives, and told them about Brown's suggestion. They were delighted with the recognition. I called Tobin and made an appointment.

It was early April, a beautiful spring morning, when I arrived at the Biltmore Hotel (headquarters of the Democratic National Committee). It was one of those old, well-maintained hotels with grand woodwork, large rooms, beautiful bathrooms—the kind of place I thought the rich stayed in. The secretary went into the adjoining room and announced to Tobin's secretary who I was. All I heard was a raspy, loud, barking bullhorn voice yelling, "Come on in here, Bub. We've got a campaign on."

I went in. Tobin was a heavy-set older man with a huge head of white hair. He stood up, came around the big executive desk, shook my hand with a wrestler's grip. "Hello, Bub, you're from the Machinists, right? Now there's a bunch of fuddy-duddy pansies. In this business, boy, you gotta be tough. You gotta go in there and kick 'em in the ass hard like you mean it. Christ, now you take poor Harvey Brown. He don't know whether to shit or go blind in the AF of L. One day he's withdrawin' cause he ain't getting his jurisdiction, and next day he's payin' his back per capita. Now, if he'd just stay and fight together with me we could whip 'em all. But he's scared of the Teamsters. He will never stand up to no one. I hear you're a scrapper and a good campaigner, so I'm gonna give you Pennsylvania. I want to whip old John Lewis's ass so he'll never forget how he betrayed F.D.R., labor's greatest friend. Now, how you gonna do it?"

"Well," I began. I had no idea what I would say, as I was in no way prepared for this hurricane of an old man. He interrupted, "Look, son, these guys in labor already forgot what the Great White Father [that's how Tobin referred to Roosevelt] done for 'em. Why, half those stupid bastards, including your Mr. Brown, would be selling apples if it weren't for him. Look boy. Come up with a plan on how to get those coal miners to vote for Roosevelt and get it here real quick. And yeah, how much will it cost?" As I left, rushing out to my new-found mission, I heard him yelling to his secretary, "Find Bub an office, and a secretary. Give him whatever he wants."

That night I dug up every friend I had who knew anything about elections to tell them about my charge from Tobin and ask for suggestions. Before the night was over, we had drawn a plan. The key was to use the railroad unions, who solidly supported Roosevelt. Their network of members would be organized through the locals to carry Roosevelt literature, buttons, and posters to every pithead in the coal fields, and arrange "Vote Roosevelt" rallies at every important train station in the state. Not a coal car was to move in Pennsylvania without leaflets, posters, pamphlets, and buttons. Every caboose was to become a moving field campaign office for Roosevelt.

The next morning at 8:30, woozy-eyed from being up most of the night and excited to cloud nine, I was explaining the plan to Tobin. He listened attentively, kept nodding his head in approval. Finally he said, "Damn good plan, Bub. Will we have to pay the railroaders something? Can't expect people to work for nuthin'."

"No, I don't think so; most of these railroad union guys love F.D.R. You don't have to pay them. Now, it might be good to put a few of their men on the payroll between now and election day to act as coordinators to make sure we cover every town in the state."

"Good, how much do you need?" Our budget was about $125,000. He said, "Double it, boy. You're thinking too cheap. At least $200,000. Son, you're gonna have to pay some of those dumbbells to distribute that stuff. Let me know how it goes."

I had a map in my office covering a whole wall, with pins stuck in every mine, railroad yard, and major plant. Using the railroads as our conduit, we went ahead. We started by holding a series of conferences in Pennsylvania with the rail unions, who enthusiastically supported the plan of action. It worked so well that we carried the coal fields for F.D.R., beating Lewis in the process. The night of the election found many of the labor committee people at the Biltmore awaiting returns. As they began to come in, we became delirious with joy watching "our" assigned areas go for Roosevelt. To my utter amazement, the reward for our success in electing F.D.R. would be an offer of a big federal job—a payoff for my contribution to the campaign. This is the nature of political work. If the candidate is successful, he is expected to pay off his supporters with various appointments, based on their importance to the campaign. I was still just a true believer who hardly comprehended the payoff talk and was naive enough to have thought we were in it because our candidate was the best.

In those Biltmore days, I came to know many leading Democrats. On more than one occasion in the early morning hours, I would help to get the Democratic national chairman off the hall couch where he had bedded down for the night, unable to make it to his room. Those who had helped him out the night before were sometimes invited to breakfast for a staff review of the campaign. The chairman, between coffee and rolls, would lift himself off the high-backed judge's chair. At first I thought his underwear was twisted, or he was rearranging his balls. Then I realized that he was lifting his weight off his ass in order to fart.

I hardly cared about anyone else at the Biltmore besides Tobin, for outside of him there was little or no concern about electing

F.D.R., and that tended to affect everyone's morale. At the beginning of the campaign, the hotshots like me did our own work, ignoring most people around us. Besides, we had a certain optimism that made us feel that something might yet happen if we were patient. The chairman responded to our complaints about the inaction of many committee staffers by saying that his major problem was the goddamned New York oysters that kept giving him all this gas. Well, yes, I thought, that about sums up his major interest—his gas.

Tobin had an almost religious devotion to F.D.R. and felt that few of the Democratic party regulars, including the chairman and the secretary, really gave a damn about that 1944 Roosevelt campaign. The work Tobin did to elect F.D.R. is a classic example of building a parallel institution, when the parent institution has begun to sit on its hands. In this case it was the Democratic National Labor Committee, as a way of overcoming the inertia and even outright sabotage of the old-line crowd on the Democratic National Committee, who had lost their interest in Roosevelt and his New Deal programs. Tobin did not trust the traditional money sources to support his efforts. He was concerned that they might not deliver, so while at the same time pressing the organization, he went out and raised his own funds. The labor committee ended up with its own fund-raising drives, a speakers' bureau, and public relations shop, as well as its own radio and newspaper campaigns.

Tobin was a master at creating a sense of great urgency, which he sustained by endlessly barking orders, calling people to brief him immediately when they returned from the field, in order that he could say, "OK, that was a good job, Bub. Now get on a train or plane and get out to Pedunkit. We got a problem there." He ceaselessly demanded action.

I remember one morning when he was dispatching a group of us to Buffalo. "We got trouble in places like Buffalo because the Catholics are being scared away from Roosevelt by the Red issue. Find out what the hell those dumb bohunks are beefing about." It was the usual parting shot. I asked him, "What do you suggest we do with them?" He yelled back, "Give 'em all some free kielbasa and sauerkraut. How the hell do I know what to do? That's why I'm sending you there. Figure it out when you're there. Find out from the local Teamsters how to get to the key people in the church, the fraternal organizations, and the clubhouses. Polacks do as they're told. You just gotta find out who does the telling. Don't waste your time with a lotta literature. Most of them can't read and those that can will read it and still do as they're told. Our Teamster man there knows that whole bunch. Find out from him the bishop, cardinal, or priest who's gotta be coaxed or pressed, and do it. We just better carry Buffalo or you guys will be helpers on a coal truck." Well, we ate it up, ran down to Grand Central Station, and grabbed the Empire State Express to Buffalo.

Next to Tobin, there was one other person who generated some campaign enthusiasm—Eleanor Roosevelt. She had an electric way about her as she periodically walked through the halls of the Biltmore. Stopping in headquarters or our office, she would smile, saying, "I am Eleanor Roosevelt." I was embarrassed that she should think that I did not know who she was. She just went on, "What is your name? How are things going?" Instantly I believed in her and began telling her in rapid fire how things were not going well at all, how the headquarters were filled with drunks and hangers-on who did not seem to care if we won or not. She seemed a little startled, yet she listened. In the most measured way she said, "Well, of course, you're young and new to this game. Don't be disappointed too soon. You have a long way ahead of you if you want to see change. But now tell me specifically what you need."

I was being told to calm down, cool it, take it easy, things are not as simple as you would like them to be. I told her we needed more money for our work in Pennsylvania and then showed her our plan for winning in the coal fields. She asked, "How much do you have, and what do you need?"

"We have about $125,000 and we need double that so we can put a Roosevelt campaign manager in every railroad caboose in Pennsylvania. We want to turn every one of those cabooses into a rolling campaign headquarters, but we need more full-time organizers, more specialized target literature, more signs, buttons, everything."

"How much more?" she asked.

Really unsure now I said, "Double what we have." I was really embarrassed.

But she smiled that little smile and said, "I'll see what I can do, Bob." I was ecstatic that she remembered my name. She did that with the young staff people throughout the headquarters.

Within hours of Eleanor's visit Tobin called me into his office. "What the hell did you tell Eleanor?" I was scared by his tone and told him what had transpired. Slowly that Irish pixie smile came on him. "Listen son. We gotta work with these damn fools around here, so you be careful what you tell about 'em and don't go saying we ain't got enough money from them. You know that every cent we've spent, we have had to raise ourselves. Now, don't do that again. But I'm glad you did it, and since we are electing him it's about time we got some dough outa this outfit."

I started to apologize. "I hope I didn't embarrass . . . ." He cut me off, "Now don't go apologizing for what you done or you'll become a namby-pamby like those leaders in your union. How would you like to come to work for the Teamsters? You're not gonna survive where you are anyhow. You know that, don't you? They're convinced you're a dangerous Red radical or something. Well, don't worry. We'll get you a good job when this thing is over. By the way. What the hell do they pay you in that cheap outfit anyway?"

"One hundred a week, but I have turned down increases since . . . ." I was about to say I did not believe that union officials ought to get paid more than the highest-paid worker in the shop. Tobin did not want to hear any of that "bleeding liberal talk." He cut me off, "Now look here, Bub. It is OK to be devoted. Christ, look at me. Nobody works harder. In this campaign I don't know what is going on in my union while I'm here. But you gotta look out for yourself too, or you're gonna find yourself out on your ass freezing in a cold winter night, and if you ask your friends for a handout when they see your ass out there, they'll go right by as if they never knew you. Bub, you're young, on top, and smart, so make it do something for you, or you'll be sorry."

My conversation with Eleanor paid off. Within a week the labor committee received a pledge of more money, and with it we stepped up the campaign in the final weeks.

Many of my Machinist friends would visit the Biltmore for breakfast, lunch, dinner, midnight snack, drinks, or just to hang out. Sometimes I felt as though it was a little like Jackson's White House when the squirrel hunters came to sup. Thousands of workers had become part of a new labor movement during the war. Many of those who came to visit the Biltmore, which in 1944 was still a classy hotel, had never been in New York or had never seen the inside of this kind of hotel. They would come to my suite with its adjoining office. I would call up room service and order lunch. In a few minutes a waiter arrived pushing a table. Freddy Lupo from the old automatic screw machine gang flipped. "This is it, Schrank? You mean all you do is call up and they send it?" "Yep, that's all there is to it."

Other machinists would just wander in and out of the bathrooms, the suites, the restaurants. One guy said, "Can I take a shower in there?" "Of course, go right ahead." They just could not believe this kind of living and kept saying, "Schrank, how the hell will you ever go back to a machine shop after this?" Or the railroad machinists, who were the staunchest F.D.R. supporters, would taunt me with, "You'll never bust nuts again after this, Schrank" (a term which refers to the nuts used as fastening devices, not the male anatomy).

At the Biltmore I was beginning to learn something that has been continually reinforced ever since: how society maintains class separation. When I first arrived there, I was not that much different from the machinists who came to visit—overwhelmed with the infinite amount of luxury in the lives of the wealthy businessmen associated with the Democratic National Committee. I was even more surprised at the banality and the incompetence of some of the elites, the people who had power to run things. Late one night after a series of difficult campaign meetings that seemed particularly dumb, I was struck with the reason for this class separation. If the average blue-collar worker learned that the tycoons of business and industry were not much more competent than he was, it might cause things to change much faster. Hence the separation. The public relations image of industrial leaders, like Hollywood stars, has little or no relation to the real thing, but it keeps the public thinking that our naked emperors are draped in gorgeous gowns.

As everybody knows, we won the election, handsomely carrying Pennsylvania. Tobin announced to me the next morning as I was cleaning out my desk, a little sad to leave the Biltmore, that I was to come to Washington to attend the inauguration. "Now, Bub, you'll get a chance to meet the Great White Father. Make sure you are ready to tell him what you want, in case he asks."

Together with a mob of inauguration invitees, I caught the 6 A.M. train out of Penn Station. In short order people were showing their status by announcing whether they had an invitation to the stands, the halls, or the White House. Tobin had seen to it that I had a White House card, though originally I had just made the stands. I felt alone on the train; most of the people seemed to belong to some political club. The Washington station was mobbed when our train pulled in. I walked to the Capitol with thousands of people just streaming toward the inauguration ceremony. I felt a sense of being on the in as I flashed the various passes I had been supplied with.

The inauguration was a letdown; Roosevelt looked just plain tired. I walked to the White House, wondering how many times I would do this. At the White House, after endlessly showing passes again, I found myself on a long presidential reception line. When I made it to him, Roosevelt looked so drawn and worn I thought the poor man should just go to bed. Tobin seemed to ignore his condition as he introduced me to F.D.R. in his wheelchair. Close up, I was again shocked by his debilitated physical appearance, to the point that I almost could not look at him. I was suddenly sad, feeling he would not live long.

"Mr. President," Tobin said, "this young man, Bub Schrank, won Pennsylvania for us, and we owe him a lot. Now that crowd, with Bill Green [then president of the AF of L], are going to do him in, so let's find something for him to do where he will be safe."

I wanted to say that I was not worried and that besides I was not interested in a job. The president looked at me sort of quizzically. "Thank you for your help. You're a very young man to be tangling with those old gray-headed buzzards. Be careful they don't get you."

The line of people pushed us along. Tobin said he would call me to Washington in a few weeks, and we separated.

When I met Tobin in Washington in a few weeks, as agreed, he seemed harried. His face had none of the campaign joy left. He had received promises of judgeships for the prosecutors in charge of the case against the Dunne brothers in Minneapolis.

"But Dan, the Dunne brothers aren't guilty."

"Those Trotskyite bastards ought to be shot at daybreak."

My ears seemed to deceive me. This couldn't be the man I had learned to respect and love during the campaign. It was not the same Dan Tobin of the Biltmore. He was now the cynical union leader without a cause. As he was telling about his judgeship problems, he suddenly looked at me. "The best I can do for you," he said very apologetically, "is the administrator of Yellowstone National Park. Now that's a great opportunity, boy. You'll have security and it will get you away from that bunch of pansy Machinists, who will chop you up as feed for buzzards before they are done with you. They are just too damn respectable for your radical ways. When the police Red squad comes, they'll just crumble. Lovestone and his crowd were complainin' to me about you. You know what I told them? Mind your own goddamned business, and what the hell is the AF of L doing with its own intelligence agency anyhow?" Dan was mad because of his judge troubles and the idea of union police bugged him. "Jesus, I would like to be left alone. Now, about this Yellowstone thing."

I began to laugh, thinking he was kidding. He became annoyed that I thought so lightly of his fine offer. "Dan, this is just a plot on the part of the AF of L to get rid of me." I relished that notion because I strongly believed in plots and this one seemed so flattering. "Dan, this is just one more scheme carried on by fools to get rid of me and send me off to Yellowstone Siberia. No way is that going to work. I love what I am doing. I intend to continue that." Years later I had an occasion to visit Yellowstone. It was one of those moments when I wished I could turn my life around or give myself a good swift kick in the ass.

I turned the offer down. Tobin was sad. "OK, Bub, if you ever need a favor, remember I owe you one. You're a good campaigner." So this is what politics was about. You help me, and if I get elected then I help you. I hung around Washington for a few days, meeting with various political types, and the cynicism just kept growing in me like a weed. I was beginning to feel as though politics was nothing more than a trinket-trading Casbah. My problem was that I wanted to believe that the welfare of the working people was more important than some silly payoff. Of course I was full of high-flown ideas about noble deeds, good works, and so on, but I was learning on the job what was expected behavior.

I found politics a pretty seedy business, particularly as it related to legislative bodies. The hangers-on, the camp followers, the pretty girls seemed to outnumber the real people around the office. The hangers-on cooed sweet things in the ears of the politicians, who sometimes began to believe what they heard and entered a kind of celebrity fairyland of television cameras and goggling audiences.

Tobin's predictions about my limited life in the machinists' union eventually turned out to be true. Roosevelt died, the war was won, a long period of transition to peacetime began, all of which created enormous problems of shifting allegiances. Harvey Brown called me to say he wanted to see me in New York. We met at the Hotel Pennsylvania.

Harvey Brown was a sort of simple man, sincere, but not very bright. "Bob, I have information from the FBI that you are a Communist. I want you to leave the union because you are an embarrassment to me. Now, I know you have to make a living, so I am arranging a job at Schlitz Brewery. You will be a vice president at $25,000 a year."

I was upset, and I could not believe that Brown would do all this on the FBI say-so, like so many other union leaders during the McCarthy days. "Harvey, I signed the non-Communist affidavits under the Taft-Hartley Act. I am not now a Communist, OK? But what you need to know is that I am not going to recant, cooperate with the witch hunters, or be intimidated about who I talk to."

He didn't care what I was saying. "Look, if you fancy us to get you, we will, so why not save yourself all that grief?" He looked at me for a moment. His large jowls gave him a hound dog look. He became speculative. "You know, Bob, we are in for bad times. The political pendulum is going to swing to the right. Harry Truman can't stem the wave of reaction. We got bad days ahead." It was a dirge all right; I felt like the undertaker was here to measure me up.

"Harvey, I think we might just as well have a fight because it's better to deal with right-wing reaction by resisting it than by walking to the executioner's block. That's not my style."

"Bob, we will beat you, believe me. Everything is on our side, the government, business—and the members will desert you on the political stuff. You'll see."

We shook hands as I left. I asked if the fight was on. "No, think it over, talk with your wife. Don't be hasty. You have a lot at stake here."

We never met again privately, though we became protagonists in a bitter struggle that would go on for years. I had to run for election every year as state president. Brown started after me by bringing dozens of international representatives into the state to campaign against Schrank for a few weeks before the convention. Year after year I would beat them in the voting. It was an exhausting time, with FBI agents waiting for me at my home, alternating between mornings and evenings, tapped telephones, intercepted mail, threatening telephone calls, coworkers pleading with me to be more cooperative. One evening I drove up to my garage. Sure enough there were the two shoe salesmen from the FBI. I got out of the car as though this was all brand-new. One said, "Hey, Mr. Schrank, can we talk to you?"

"What do you want? You know everything about me. What more do you want?"

"We would like you to help your country by telling us what you know about Communists in the unions. You could be so helpful."

"Hey, fellas, you know more about that than I do, now don't

you? The party is shot full of agents. Why don't you just let me be?"
I started to walk away with the two of them right behind.

"Can we talk again sometime? We really appreciate this."

"No, I don't think we will have any more talks. I just want to be
left alone." And I went in the house quickly, closing the door for
fear they might come in.

Congress passed the Taft-Hartley Act. I saw it as part of the
reactionary darkness settling over the land. I wrote the pamphlet
"This Is Aimed at You—An Exposé of the Taft-Hartley Slave Labor
Law." On the cover was a scared worker with a gun pointed at his
head. It was an instant best seller. The state council had okayed it,
but Harvey Brown was furious. Not only was I not retreating as he
had advised, but I had the "audacity" to write and publish "this
attack" on the officers of the union that strongly suggested that the
Taft-Hartley Act would have been inoperative if all the unions had
refused to participate in the signing of non-Communist affidavits.

What a ludicrous thought that seems today—a whole labor
movement rushing to swear that they were not Reds. The international executive council of the union expelled me from the union
for not having their approval to publish.

Events now followed one another in very rapid fire. As soon as I
received the telegram advising me of the council's action, I went to
the union hall, removed the records, withdrew all our money (considerably over $250,000) and put it in safe-deposit boxes. When the
Internationals arrived to take over, there was nothing there. They
were furious. Our local's lawyers went to court on my rights under
the First Amendment. After a long, drawn-out case known as
Schrank vs. Brown, we won, establishing in law the preservation of
constitutional rights within organizations as well as the right to seek
redress in the courts without exhausting one's remedies in the
union. It was a great victory for the rank-and-file members, but it
was my death knell in the labor movement. They would never
forgive me for this "audacious" act of seeking redress under our
Constitution.

Brown retired. His successor was smarter. He just bought out all
the people around me, including some very close friends, who

because of "their families" could not take the McCarthy pressures. I was expelled from the IAM. After I lost the vote in my local union, I no longer cared. I had run out of steam. The Left was getting more and more difficult, and the pressures just wore me down.

I went back to work in the old Nathan Bliss plant that I had helped organize. The workers were glad to see me, yet they felt bad about what had happened. One of my old friends, Henri Bonnheimer, said, "Why the hell did you have to open your big mouth so much? You had to be there on everything, letting niggers into the union, fighting the per capita tax, supporting all those radical bills in Congress. Christ, man, if you just minded your own business, you would have made V.P. easy." There was a lot of that feeling in the plant. But anyway, the work there now just bored me. I simply could not get interested again. The Mine, Mill and Smelter Workers offered me a job as an international representative. I took it, glad to get out of the plant.

My job in Mine and Mill was not that different from the work in the IAM, except that I found the left wing that controlled much of the union as difficult as the right wing in the Machinists and, in many ways, just as corrupt. My disillusionment was complete. I reached the point of believing in nothing. I was laid off from Mine and Mill, went on unemployment insurance, hung around for six months, and ran out of money. I had a family to support, so I began to look for work.

Because of years of militant union activity, I found myself terribly blacklisted and unable to find employment in production. I applied for a job as a die setter at the Ford Motor Company plant in Mahwah. The personnel interviewer acted as though he had struck gold. He was ecstatic. "We are really hunting for die setters. You can start right away. Come back tomorrow, bring your tools, and be ready to go." I was very excited; finally I had connected.

I came back the next day ready to go, checked in at the personnel department to pick up my badge. The interviewer looked at me. "Who you kidding, bud?"

Trying hard to be shy and speaking in my most innocent tone, I said, "Gee whiz, what's the matter?"

"What's the matter? Who you bullshitting? Your name lit up the whole fucking machine. It not only came on tilt, but the bell rang. Get it? The *Red* bell. Stop wasting your time around here. Go get a job in a sausage factory or something. Forget the auto industry. They will never hire you."

I felt so frustrated. All the old depression unemployment fear rose inside me. "Where is the 'machine' that knows so much?" I asked him.

He was sort of candid with me. "It's in Detroit, has a record of everyone who is or ever was a union agitator, a troublemaker, an organizer, a Red, or any shade of pink."

Driving home at night, I stopped at a bar, had a few drinks, and figured I had to forget going back into a plant. I had to do something different. I had to make a living. I did not care much about the labor movement anymore, and I was thoroughly blacklisted. I wondered what would happen if I applied for a job in management, outside the bargaining unit, on the "other side." Would I have to be a bastard? Well, I was going to find out.

# Management

I went to a fancy Madison Avenue employment agency, and within a few days I was on a new job as a foreman in the machine-building and maintenance division of a small retail data-processing company. After spending so many years fighting the bosses and their managers, becoming part of management proved to be more traumatic than I had expected.

I began to relax into being the foreman by spending a lot of time talking to the employees, listening to their beefs and suggestions. In the main, their suggestions were strictly work-related—the grinders are inaccurate, the spindle on the Number 4 miller is off, the light over the jig borer is insufficient, and so on. Then I spent sleepless nights asking myself, What will I do if the company tells me to do something to the employees that I find I cannot do? I said to myself, You're part of management now. You have to learn to play the role. But what if that role turns out to be a bastard? I will just tell them they can shove the job they know where. On and on the paranoia grew until things proved not to be as bad as I had feared. Once again, the anticipation was far worse than the fact.

I began to remember the things workers beefed about when I was a union officer. Now I was determined to pay attention to the conditions of work. After all, I rationalized, even the socialist brotherhood in any form had to have some kind of supervision. I kept asking myself: Could I supervise others without myself becoming a mechanical robot?

There were about forty-five men, almost all skilled workers, in the department. There was no union. My first efforts were to become familiar with the work as well as to straighten out job order systems and establish cost centers and parts inventory. The plant manager was pleased with what I was doing. "You're doing a great job, Bob, keep it up." Now, I thought, I can start paying attention to working conditions.

I started by improving the ventilation, cleaning up the toilets, building an eating area, getting the windows washed; generally making the physical surroundings more pleasant. The employees loved it; and with no urging on my part, production began to increase. I had become an instant success, yet I did not have to do anything as a foreman that I considered antithetical to the interests of the workers, whom I now called employees. My paranoia was decreasing. I was beginning to enjoy being in management. I would learn in time that as a supervisor I used McGregor's model Y, the humane, participative, open management style. What I had fought so hard as a union organizer was what McGregor called management X, the traditional, authoritarian style.

Most behavioral scientists concerned with workplace issues have so little understanding of the part that unions play in alleviating working conditions that it is no wonder union leaders become frustrated: They find practically no recognition in the behavioral science workplace literature of the role of the labor movement in humanizing work. Without the work of the unions, it is hard for me to see how American business and industry could even consider the next steps toward autonomy, participation, and codetermination.

My relations with the men in the department were easy-going. I would walk around checking on the work, doing quality control and at the same time kidding about the difficult jobs, sports, politics, and sex in about that order. Thinking back, second only to being competent as a toolmaker machinist, the most important management quality I would say I had was a good sense of humor. The work itself I sort of knew by rote, and I could get answers, too, by consulting others. That was never of any earth-shaking importance to me, so I would joke about what had to be done. The men would sort of laugh, yet they rushed to meet schedules. That turned out to make me look good.

I told each man when we finished a job how he had done in

terms of both quality and time. We joked a lot about how long it takes to get things right. Humans seem to have an almost limitless ability to solve mechanical problems and at the same time show an enormous inability to understand how to live with themselves and each other. I began to see the function of humor as a way of acknowledging the absurdity of the human condition in the face of this apparent contradiction.

I began to attend engineering expositions and conventions, meeting many men whose lives revolve around the design and development of machines. I remember a dullness about them, as though the gray of the steel had entered their souls. Compared to plumbers or my old union friends, they seemed like a drab lot. An old saying suggests that "dull people find dumb work." Well, I don't think so, because I too felt a certain lifelessness growing in me. The machines themselves seemed to be making ceaseless demands for the improvement of their efficiency, and their demands were draining my life energy. I had started to carry a small pocket notebook with me to jot down little ideas for improving or redesigning machines. It was a constant challenge to keep them from wearing out and at the same time make them do more for less.

There was something new in that engineering experience that I only recently have come to understand. It involves the nature of conflict in work. Working with machines has conflicts and tasks that involve objects and materials, all of which are inanimate. People are used as the instruments of the objects or machines. Engineers deal in the main with these inanimate things, whose only resistance is in the limits of their physical nature. They lose the human, living, dynamic element in work. Over time I found engineering work comfortable and absorbing, but my only challenges were excessive friction, unstable raw materials, tighter machine tolerances. I was becoming a very neutral person whom I was gradually getting to dislike. For someone who had tasted the excitement of human conflict in the unions and national politics, there was not much romance in developing a better rack and pinion mechanism for a high-speed press.

In contrast, the issues in the labor movement almost never were concerned with objects. They were the problems of people, of their working conditions, pay, and benefits. Union work also required me to take a stand, one that might be unpopular with management, and at times with the members. In the very neutral, alienated world of engineers there is a sense of being above or beyond the conflict issues, a sort of technological person. I found engineers reserved, expressing little or no curiosity outside of their engineering specialty. Compared with the openness of the average shop worker, their interest in sex, for instance, was a hidden, secretive business.

I was attending an engineering convention in Chicago, and because my company did considerable business with a major electrical manufacturer, I was assigned a lovely female friend to keep me company, if not warm, in the windy city. Helene, who had been "Helen" back in Des Moines, was a model-type—tall, skinny, and shining from an endless round of soaps and lotions. She had been trained in charm. We went to dinner, and for most of the evening I plied her with questions about her job. "I am hired as a bridge to customers like you, in order to further expose the potential buyer to our product line." I fantasized: Helene and I go to my room. We get into bed. We are about to go to it when out comes the newest high-speed gear box sample. "You were saying . . . ."

"We are hired to give understanding to the customer."

"Do you go to bed with all the customers?"

"The decision is up to us. Now you must understand we don't *have* to. After all, we're not just call girls, but if we desire to, we can."

"Is your pay scaled to going to bed with a customer?"

"No, we get a flat rate a day during the convention, but if you want to be called back, you have to build a reputation for being friendly."

"How many conventions do you do a year, and what kinds?"

"Oh, maybe fifteen or twenty of all kinds: pharmaceutical companies are great, with doctors; then there are engineers, dentists, printing companies, truckers, political meetings." Helene was really enjoying the interview. She laughed. "I draw the line on morticians.

Darned if I am going to have some undertaker work me over. No siree. Every job has to have its limits."

"How do you like this engineering crowd?"

"They're OK. Most of them are not like you. They don't talk much, and they're very secretive, so you have to meet them in their rooms, and they don't want you to know their names. They seem to be scared. I don't know of what. Now you take truckers. They're tough, they could care less, and they are great spenders."

Helene was a little like the engineering convention. We seemed to be friendly enough, but when we got down to it, I would not even call it a wham, bam, thank you ma'am. There wasn't much wham in the whole business. Helene said, "Most engineers like it that way, and I have to keep passion out of this business or I might offend someone." This was one of my first encounters with sex as a cool medium.

My efforts on behalf of the company were rewarded by promotions, first to chief plant engineer and then to division engineer responsible for three plants. As the demands of the job increased, I found myself increasingly committing more of my life to the company. To the envy of other managing engineers, I began to be consulted by the vice president in charge of production at the head office of the corporation. I was now mixing with the corporate executives, traveling first class, eating at 21 Club with three corporate vice presidents to discuss the Swedish operation. Good food, fine wine, the best cigars—I felt big, contented, and sure I had made it. After all, the labor movement didn't want me, so why should I feel guilty about sitting here in the 21 Club making it? I thought Bertolt Brecht was stupid. Am I supporting corporate oppression if I share in the power, or can I use my position to humanize existing institutions? An irresolvable contradiction, or a paradox. Why be a man when I can be a success? Listen, Bertolt, class status is so damned insidious. You think that a little socialist shit can affect the intoxication of being accepted into the higher reaches of the corporate world. You're nuts. I was moving up, and, by God, I liked it.

Though sometimes deeply buried in our unconscious, the drive upward is everlastingly present. Being summoned to an audience with king, pope, president, secretary general, or prime minister gives us a heightened sense of importance, power, status, no matter how cynical we feel toward an institution. Even if I did not actually hold the power, just being in its presence was heady stuff. Anti-establishment people (we used to call them "radicals") suffer a heavy ambivalence.

I was now working for corporate headquarters. I found myself becoming more involved, absorbed, single-minded, with an excitement for equipment deadlines and new ideas that created in me a general sense of euphoria. Yet there was a difference between this kind of work and the labor movement. What was it? Slowly I was missing the old companionship, the wonderful conversation of all my friends in screw machines, turret lathes, and the machine shops. The management world was a circumspect one full of innuendo, nuance, correct dress, and carefully choreographed behavior. The result was little or no spontaneity, no feelings, no physical contact. All this meant zero sensuality. I was beginning to miss walking with my arm on another guy's shoulder at a union meeting. Doubts began to take root about whether I could make it as a corporate executive.

One winter night in a fine old Boston restaurant, the corporate boys from Yale and Groton, having belted down a few too many martinis, kept asking about life on the outside, the plant, the union, sex. I had a growing feeling that I was being spied on by a bunch of Harvard Business School voyeurs who seemed to sense something missing from their lives but were not sure what. I was missing something too. A short time later the vice president in charge of production, having learned that I was "getting antsy," said to me, "Schrank, you are too smart to lose; if it is the last thing I do, I am going to shoehorn you into this corporation."

I was going to college at night, having been urged to do so by the company, when they learned that I had no school beyond the eighth grade. "You're corporate material, but you will have to get a degree." College was a real growth experience, and it was reinforcing my distaste of corporate managing. I was on my way out.

Some doubts have grown in me about engineers and managers. The first has to do with management's ability to manage, and the second has to do with behavioral science notions about work, motivation, and job satisfaction. In my days as a union official, there was a fantasy that corporations were homogeneous, single-headed, efficient monsters systematically exploiting workers. Talk about being convinced by one's own propaganda! Institutions and professions now appear to me as tribal groups defending their turf—territoriality: their secrets, sacred bundles, and their leaders and tribal councils. When I moved from the union tribe to the corporate tribe, I learned some of their secrets. They were fumbling around pretty much like the rest of us, yet they were better able to conceal it through public relations, with its handouts, image building, color slide and sound shows. Then there is always the secrecy that is called up to "protect us from our competition" or from other tribes, but this is usually baloney since it is more often used to hide mistakes from the world at large.

The loss of perspective on their lives, the lack of joy in their work, seemed so natural for the engineers. Yet I became very involved in what I was doing, even though it made no social sense. It was so absorbing that it caused me to lose interest in a world of feelings and sensuality. Was it sublimation? I would doubt it. Maybe it happens because the work is with metals or plastics, usually to close tolerances in measurement or composition or both. The thing— the object, the task, the gear, cam, housing, nuts, bolts, timer— engulfs and dominates one's life until an obsession like building a better zipper takes over all thought and no one thinks to ask what was wrong with the button. The pressure of corporate life to come up with new products makes managers and engineers fearful if they do not constantly create and innovate. This makes for individual competition resulting in a lonely crowd. Productivity for engineers does not indicate the quantity of work produced but rather what new ideas or improvements they have generated. The pressure to come up with solutions to problems sends at least some competent engineers off into dealing or specializing.

I think that engineers and managers would rate considerably

higher on the alienation scale than most unionized workers. The competition of managers vying for recognition and position creates little trust, and that means little human contact or concern. The corporation I worked for was liberal and easy-going, but even there the higher up the totem pole you climbed, the faster they went for your jugular. Life in the corporation tended to be isolated and cold, with some fucking, no love, and little sharing of sexual fantasies. It all reminded me of Wilhelm Reich's *Listen Little Man*: "Security is more important to you, even if it costs you your spine of life."

The gentility and civility of engineers and managers seemed to make them less sensuous, robust, and less aware of the organic qualities of life. They often struck me as being without affect because of their preoccupation with a large inanimate object or some minute, trivial part of it. It is the syndrome of overspecialization that Mumford talks about in *The Pentagon of Power*, when one becomes so highly specialized in the head of the pin that in time one no longer knows what the rest of the pin looks like, or worse, what it is used for. And there I was, totally involved in the feed mechanisms of continuous-web letterpresses.

Was this group of managers and engineers more satisfied with their jobs than plumbers or machinists? In general I would say yes, but I would add that most of these men were so completely and exclusively focused on the "head of the pin" that they had given very little thought to what they were doing, why they were doing it, and at what cost to themselves. In the recent NASA layoffs, some aerospace engineers had been forced into new careers. In an interview with one of them who opened a hot dog stand, he said he had suddenly discovered—guess what—that there was more to life than Wernher Von Braun's "bigger and better rockets." "I love owning my own business, but more important, I am my own boss."

Managers and engineers tend to lose their concern about people because of their total preoccupation with "the product." In my case, feed mechanisms, the product, took over most of my psychic energy. Such narrow frames of reference have an impact on how managers and engineers view other people. Preoccupied and obsessed with the product line, they can begin to view people, or the workers, as obstacles to reaching their objectives.

In the whole production matrix, people are probably the most frustrating for managers since they constitute the most difficult variable to control and predict. No matter how predictable society tries to make its members through its various socializing mechanisms, people continue to give managers the most trouble. Managers are always complaining about "those workers." "If only they would do what we tell them or learn to follow instructions, we would surpass all our quotas." It is this obsession with the product and the consequent neglect of human needs that could fill case-history books with stories of management's insensitivity to workers. This insensitivity is often turned around and explained as a "lack of worker motivation." Workers become strangers to many managers and are seen only as an extension of a piece of machinery in which a capital investment has been made. This leads to the engineering dream of eliminating the "human element" in production.

A good illustration of this phenomenon came up in a union negotiation. Sitting around the huge conference table in the mahogany paneled conference room during an intensive collective bargaining session with the Republic Steel Corporation, the company was reciting a litany of how much production time is lost as a result of lateness, extended coffee breaks, lunch time beyond the bell, and early quitting. The whole discussion seemed kind of absurd, so I kept encouraging the industrial engineers to give us the data on what the lost-time factor added up to. Out came the slide rules as the figures multiplied upward. "The company has 5,000 employees in this division. Estimated loss on starting time, seven minutes; on two coffee breaks, twelve minutes; and quitting ten minutes early. That makes a total of 2,400 hours a day." The company was very impressed with these figures. After all, they were clear evidence of the cost of malingering.

I said, "I would like to have a recess." It was agreed. The company representatives left the room, and the union committee remained. I asked the committee members how many times the average worker went to the toilet during the workday to pee or shit, and how long did each function take. After some bickering back and forth, we agreed on three times: two short and one long, the short about seven minutes, including travel and smoke, and the long about fourteen minutes. We calculated an average of twenty-eight or thirty minutes per employee lost a day in the toilet. I asked the committee if they would permit me to bargain away at least some of that time, or in other words, if we could reduce the toilet time in exchange, let's say, for a couple more holidays. Everyone appreciated the absurdity of this, but they were happy to join the dramatic fantasy that would reveal the production engineers' thought processes.

When the company representatives returned to the bargaining table, I put forth our propositions, in the course of which the absurdity of it all seemed to carry me away. "We are not only willing to reduce defecation time, but we have recently become aware of a pill that, taken each morning, would assure the employer of no defecation on company time." Noticing on the other side of the table the industrial engineers all playing with their slide rules, the committee members almost blew it with their giggling.

Charles Hunsteter, chief of production engineering, a pudgy fellow with thin strands of hair plastered to his sweaty forehead announced, "You think it's funny. Well 1,166 hours a day at $5.00 per hour labor and overhead cost, $5830 a day times 250 workdays a year: $1.500 million a year." The figures so excited him that he said, "Schrank, I don't know if you're kidding or serious, or what. But the fact is this could change our entire competitive position, and I would hope you would give our company first crack at it." Well, the poor committee members thought they would bust. The company attorney, a little more reality-oriented, was embarrassed by the joke and changed the subject. On the way out the door at the end of the session, Charlie said, "Schrank, you may be kidding, but this could be an extremely useful tool in production scheduling."

That incident epitomizes a particular kind of industrial engineering management viewpoint that I am amazed to find still prevails in some manufacturing companies. How to perfect a completely programmed person in order to eliminate the human element from technology continues to influence the thinking of at least some behavioral scientists and industrial engineers concerned with productivity and worker motivation.

How fulfilling is engineering and managing in terms of Maslow's higher-order needs of autonomy, creativity, and self-actualization? Blue-collar malaise is explained by some social scientists as caused by an absence of opportunities for autonomy, decision making, creativity, and self-actualization. I have often wondered to what extent these elements were present in the work life of engineers and managers. And though it may be true in some cases that persons of this rank in organizations have more opportunity to be creative and make the decisions related to their work, nowhere in the literature is an even more important question raised, that of the *purpose* of their creativity. What is it used for? In its most extreme form, the question of how one's creative energies are used is what confronted the atomic physicists when asked to perfect the bomb. What tends to get lost from Maslow's schema and its application to the workplace is the moral issue that asks: What does my creativity create? What is the impact of my self-actualization beyond me?

When I was busy increasing the speed and feed accuracy of high-speed web presses, it caused an isolation from living things that tended to negate the human concerns at the workplace. Relationships were important to me in terms of how they complemented my machine. I became caught in the treadmill of making better widgets, forgetting what I had learned many times as a union official when workers would say, "Listen, Schrank, I don't give a fuck for the junk we make here. I am here to make money so I can get my kicks outside of this dump." That often repeated basic philosophy of work stirred my subconscious as I wondered, How much do I really care about increasing the speed and efficiency of high-speed dumbwaiters?

Compared to managers and engineers, blue-collar workers seem more able to shed their work concerns at the end of the day. Workers are more concerned with security and pay than the product. Managers and engineers are concerned with upmanship. To get there, they must efficiently deliver a product. Different jobs create very different kinds of anxieties. Workers' concerns have most to do with security, wages, hours, and working conditions, but these tend to be group concerns that create a common bond. Manager-engineers tend to be primarily preoccupied with their own performance as a way of getting ahead—getting ahead of someone else—and thus produce a highly competitive, individualistic, non-group life.

I believe blue-collar workers are able to shed their workplace anxieties more easily than managers because of less responsibility as well as a deeper resignation to their situation. Since Karl Marx, much of the literature on work alienation has had to do with blue-collar workers, but I experienced them as far less alienated than managers or engineers. Workers at least had each other. I have a hunch that some of the literature on blue-collar alienation written by behavioral scientists is more often an expression of their own malaise and alienation than that of the workers. The longer I was in the world of managers, the more I missed my union buddies, their ribald spirit, our singing together, their sensuousness, their sexuality. By comparison, managers were a deadhead lot who had traded humor and sensuality for the role-playing Kabuki world of the corporate headquarters. I have met more people having fun as clowns on one plant floor than in all the very many corporate headquarters I have gone in and out of.

Engineers, managers, or behavioral scientists, with their compulsive, competitive preoccupation with "making it," tend to see this as a paradigm for all workers. But many workers are not interested in "making it" in a career of power and responsibility, or even in increasing their autonomy and creativity. Some blue-collar workers prefer to make bowling the center of their lives. That may be a greater demonstration of autonomy and creativity than building a better high-speed gear box.

# Human Services

With all my years of working I never realized how little contact I had had with social workers, psychologists, and counselors until my job at Mobilization for Youth (MFY). It was in 1963 that I was to experience a new world of work—another tribal work group called the human-helping professions. Mobilization for Youth was conceived of as a first in large-scale social science experiments. The experiment was to test the hypothesis that an opportunity structure would act as an alternative to delinquent behavior. The theoretical base for this effort was set forth in a book by Richard Cloward and Lloyd Ohlin called *Delinquency and Opportunity: A Theory of Delinquent Groups.* Their argument is that juvenile delinquency is a reflection of the inability of society to supply the necessary means by which people can achieve the middle class status by which society measures success. Cloward and Ohlin's work draws heavily on the work of the French sociologist Emile Durkheim and the American sociologist Robert Merton. Cloward studied under Merton at Columbia University, where both are now professors. MFY was to be a concerted, multidimensional effort at creating opportunities and thus overcoming the handicaps of being born poor. The multiple approach was to confront the problems of delinquent youth by dealing with the whole family, providing skill training, promoting employment readiness, handling drug, housing, and legal problems and those of unwed mothers.

I came to MFY through a sociology professor at Brooklyn College who one day asked me, "Why are you wasting time running some plant when you could be making a real contribution to solving some of our country's problems? Our new president, John Kennedy,

wants to do something about youth unemployment and delinquency. There is this new project on juvenile delinquency. They
need somebody who knows something about work. Stop wasting
your time. Go talk with them." The professor's comments had a
marching ring to it. Could this be the old union organizing days?
Anyway, I was getting bored with gear ratios and quotas.

I went to Avenue B and 2nd Street for the MFY job interview, in
the heart of New York's lower East Side ghetto. As I parked the car I
began to remember the place from my childhood, but it now smelled
from the grease and garlic of the latest immigrant Puerto Ricans.
When I was a kid, my father had taken me here on a Sunday to go
shopping. It had smelled from the kosher pickle barrels that stood
on the street. The Italians I had lived with in the northeast Bronx
would refer to it as Jewtown, or Kiketown, a place to shop for a
bargain if you were smart enough to outwit the Jews. For the most
part, the Jews had gone by now, except for some old people left
behind by their kids, who had made it out to Glen Cove, and the garment workers who lived in the Amalgamated Clothing Workers
Housing Project. Many of the older stores were still Jewish-owned,
though the neighborhood had made bodegas, Puerto Rican grocery
stores, out of them.

I walked up Second Street, passing great mounds of garbage
breaking out of old shopping bags, broken furniture tossed in the
street, and from each open doorway that pungent, dark smell of
peeling paint, piss, and rotting wood. The whole scene intensified
my sense that I was about to enter a crusade. Here I might have
another chance to fight for the poor and the downtrodden.

I was interviewed by a variety of people at MFY, many of them
social workers. I could not understand why, but my experience as a
machinist, union official, and plant engineer seemed to fascinate
everyone. I was led out into a long hall in which there were dozens
of little cubicles, each big enough for a small desk and chair. The
counselors assembled in the hallway, and I was introduced as
someone from the "real world of work." I was to hear this phrase,
"the world of work," many times, and I thank those social workers

for helping me formulate my first thoughts about work, makework, and nonwork.

There was an extended negotiation concerning salary, since MFY was offering a figure considerably less than what I was making at the corporation. It was agreed that I would take a few days to think it over. The more I thought about it, the less important the money became. I was about to enter a new campaign, to create opportunities for ghetto youth in order that they might begin to behave like the rest of us.

I was hired by MFY and assigned to set up the first on-the-job training program (OJT) for MFY youth. Later I would become director of the work programs. In the main the kids who came to MFY were problem teenagers who had difficulties with the law, the schools, or narcotics, and who, in the normal course of events, would not be considered for employment. I spent a lot of time meeting with individual employers, associations of employers, and personnel directors of large companies, trying to convince them of the benefits of the OJT program. As an incentive to hiring our enrollees, the immediate benefit was a reimbursement from MFY of up to one-half the enrollee's salary, in exchange for which the employer agreed to train him or her in some skill. The carrot of salary reimbursement was quite attractive to some employers. I explained to them how MFY would make the kids "employment-ready," by teaching them some elementary things about jobs, like coming on time, and that all the employer had to do was teach them a skill.

We were able to place enrollees in welding shops, kitchen cabinet factories, furniture repair shops, department stores, and gas stations. Gas stations seemed like a good work situation because the demands were intermittent and, like most adolescents, MFY enrollees seemed to have trouble with highly repetitive work. I learned quickly at MFY that poor minority youth have about the same emotional needs as most other adolescents, except that their poverty does not permit them the luxury of trying to discover who they are.

Since there is no fixed flow of activities, gas stations afford the employee a lot of schmooze time. There is time to sit around and talk to each other, customers, passersby, or friends who stop in. A neighborhood gas station is probably the closest thing to the old country store, where schmoozing was so much a part of the shopping.

One of my first OJT contracts was a gas station on Second Street and Avenue C near the MFY headquarters. It was owned by Barney Hochhauer, an old Jewish man left over from way back when. He had a compassion for our MFY kids. "I vant more than anything for you should succeed in vot you're doing so dat this neighborhood could be like it vonce vas vit nice kids coming in for some air for their bicycle tires. You know, I don't mind dat, but don't you think they should hang da hose back up after they use it? Is dis too much to ask? They gotta learn manners so they could be nice people."

He was a big man with sad eyes and a whispery voice. He would look you straight in the face, "I vill do anything to help make this place fit for humans vonce again. But vot can I do if da kids have no fathers and no mothers to teach them wrong from right? You know vot?" He would pause and, in visible pain, say, "Ve are making animals here, not people. I am not prejudice against anyone: Puerto Ricans, niggers, Chinese, nobody. But ve gotta let each other live; instead ve are killing each other in this jungle."

Over a period of a few months, I placed a half dozen MFY enrollees in Barney's Mobil station. I would stop by almost daily to see how things were going. He would make little complaints and suggestions, like, "Can't you talk to José Ramon about cleaning himself up a little bit, just a little bit? Now dis is not a hospital or a hotel, but how does it look ven a customer comes in and he is covered vit grease? Dat's not nice." He would apologize, "Look, I am not saying he's not nice. Don't get me wrong; he's fine. He just needs to understand dis is a business, not a playground. Understand? OK?" A car would drive in and ring the bell and he would walk off.

While the schmoozing part of gas station work went over great with our enrollees, the selling part did not. They were too reticent and scared to talk to customers who they felt were "strangers." Their lack of any social experience outside the ghetto makes these youths extremely fearful of people they don't know.

Barney tried hard with the kids, but he was torn between his heart and his pocketbook. When push came to shove, his pocketbook always won out, but he trained lots of kids to pump gas, change tires, and lubricate cars. In a short time we would open our own MFY gas station two blocks away.

The job center at MFY was on the street floor of an old catering hall. There must have been about fifteen vocational counselors who sat in the little cubicle offices, holding entrance interviews, making the job placements, and then following up on them. The counselors were supposed to help the enrollees develop work or career plans and then help them overcome whatever obstacles might stand in the way of achieving their goals. Most of the enrollees who came to MFY were extremely limited in the kinds of jobs they were able to do. They lacked the most elementary reading or measurement skills, such as using a ruler. Many could not read the instructions for installing a part or doing a simple subassembly. The most successful job preparation for these ghetto teenagers was a one-to-one apprentice-type relationship in which there was trust between the teacher, the journeyman, and the student apprentice. Such a relationship can help to dissipate the pressure from the peer group not to make it, a pressure that in turn reinforces an underlying group assumption that "we *can't* make it" in this hostile world.

The MFY enrollees were rejects, for they had failed society's first socializing hurdle, the schools. By the time they came to MFY, they had been thoroughly conditioned to the notion that they were losers, and because of their limitations the only jobs we could get for them were doing menial factory work, which tended to reinforce their negative self-image. This proved to be a most difficult contradiction. Some of the counselors reflected a prevalent attitude toward the poor: "After all, they should be thankful that we got them any job, considering who they are." As in most employment programs, the staff is evaluated on how many placements it makes. The name of the game, then, is placements. The problem was the kids understood this, and more than once Ramon or Maria would say to me, "You get lousy jobs for dumb kids. No?"

Since my work was to develop OJTs, I tried very hard to develop jobs that had some trade or career potential. As I developed OJT openings, there was an immediate pressure on the counselors to fill them. The supervisor of counseling behaved as though it were an auction, yelling, "Come on, let's fill these plumbing slots. This is a great opportunity. Come on now, counselors, we gotta fill these slots. These are good jobs. Let's go!" Like the rest of us, the counselors knew the stories about how much money plumbers or welders make, but had no idea what plumbers or welders do. It was a reflection of how society generally values white-collar jobs and sees manual work as somehow denigrating. But after all, many of them had struggled very hard to avoid the blue collar in order to become white-collar professionals.

Most of the counselors were women and the enrollees evoked a lot of maternalism that the kids loved, most of them having never experienced much mothering. Besides, for many of our Puerto Rican and black young men, it might have been their first chance to sit close to sweet-smelling, good-looking white ladies. The relationship could easily become its own cul-de-sac.

I began to notice that the counselors and social workers would refer to the enrollees as "clients." I could not understand this at first—it was all very new—but later on figured that this was done to objectify the person, as in a doctor-patient relationship. Labeling a kid "client" or "patient" implied that he or she was sick with the problem. This absolved the social situation that produced the pathology. I am not sure why, but it seemed important to the counselors and social workers to have patients and clients.

The resistance to sending enrollees to manual jobs was an ongoing problem. When placement figures dragged, some of the OJT job developers who had come to work with me became angry, and we therefore began to do our own placements. This caused endless staff meetings, in which we wrangled over who was responsible for what. What was becoming clear (and I was to learn this many times over in this kind of program) was that the Department of Labor and the president's Committee on Juvenile Delinquency, the funding sources, wanted numbers—quantifiable results.

The training I had had filling quotas in industry was extremely useful here, for I figured if this is what we have to do to keep our "crusade" alive, we will do it. We were able to get pretty good jobs, from plumbing to keypunch operators, waitresses, weeders, and machine operators. The OJT program was considered a success, and I was about to be promoted.

During the OJT phase of my work at MFY we used to hold open house every Tuesday and Wednesday evenings from 6 to 10 P.M. for enrollees who had been placed on jobs. Because the first ninety days were the most critical, they could come in and talk about any problems they might be having at the job. The meetings were well attended; usually twelve to fifteen people would show for the session. These sessions grew out of a notion that the transition to work was a difficult adjustment time for adolescents. My own experience in the furniture factory was a reminder that we were asking these young people to give up a childhood they hardly knew for the adult discipline and responsibility of a job. For middle class kids, the age when one gives up childhood is constantly being moved up. It used to be twenty-one and is now getting closer to twenty-five. Ghetto youth, who may have to start working at sixteen, feel it is just another punishment for failing, for being poor, black, or Puerto Rican.

At the open house sessions, my role was to act as a referee or chairman while the enrollees went at each other, expressing their many doubts and insecurities about the job. Rinaldo, a very fair-skinned Puerto Rican young man who was well known to the group, started to tell us about his job problems. He had a head of blondish hair that made him look as if he did not belong, and probably accounted for the instant hostility of the group. Rinaldo was saying, "I'm going to quit, because the boss bugs me all day. Man, I can't even shit and he's after me. Man, I mean, 'do this, do that, get this, get that.' "

He had barely finished when the group started to go after him.

"You don't wanna work, Rinaldo, man, you just wanna hang out and sit around the park smoking and shooting up, 'cause you is a fuck-up, man, you is a fuck-up. Whaddya mean he follows you in the shit house? What you doin' in there, man? How many time you go in there, man? Nobody shits all day."

I would try to step in, "Now wait a minute, fellows. Let him answer. You're beating him up with questions. OK, Rinaldo, tell us what's the matter."

Now Rinaldo is totally intimidated, but the group is important to him, so he is going to try to worm his way out. "Well, fellas, you know I got trouble with my mudder, 'cause I don't have no father." The place is roaring with laughter. They taunt him. "Your mudder? Rinaldo, come on, tell us. What kinda trouble you got with your mudder?"

I come down hard. "Lay off him and let him talk!!" Rinaldo goes on, "I don't know shit about my mudder, but my social worker at Henry Street says it's my mudder's fault 'cause she's dominoing me."

By now I am laughing with the rest, and I go over and sit next to Rinaldo, put my arm around him and say, "What's the matter with the *job*, not your mother." Rinaldo, born and raised on welfare in the ghetto, is hep in lots of ways, and he knows he was putting us on and so did we. He says, "OK, Mr. Schrank. You want the truth. The job stinks. All day long I stand by this little press, pushin' in little pieces of metal, the press bangs 'em and that is it all day long, man. Man, I will go nuts doing that. That's a job for a monkey man. I wanna nice job."

I remember the furniture factory days. "I know exactly what you mean." Now, what am I going to tell him? The enrollees are all eyes on me now. How am I going to come out? I am unsure, because a part of me is saying Rinaldo is right about the lousy job. Another part of me is saying that's how it is in a factory and where else can he get a job? Is it just a temporary thing until he can get something better? What is he equipped to do that's better?

"Listen, Rinaldo, I agree the job is lousy, but you get paid, and you might get a chance to move on to another machine and become an operator. Keep moving yourself up so that in time, maybe on your next job, you will be doing better."

There is a sort of quiet in the group. They accept it, but I feel they don't like it. They are wishing I had a magical solution and I am failing them. Now I am getting resentful. After all, I made it out of the furniture factory, so why can't they? When I think "they" or "them" I am in trouble; worse, I am ashamed to find myself pulling the same old psychological trick of holding the victims responsible for the condition. I did not grow up in a ghetto, nor did I suffer the outrages of being black or Puerto Rican in a hostile world.

For ghetto youth, working in menial factory jobs is a continuation of the punishment they may have grown to accept but do not understand. What they need is positive nonpunishing experience. That is why our Bloomingdale's department store OJT project was so successful. It was demonstrably different because our enrollees felt they had made it into the uptown world of "clean people doing nice work." For Rinaldo and Maria, it was an air-conditioned sea of beautiful things, their childhood dreams of heaven come true.

The open house employment meetings were a lot of fun. The enrollees had learned some psychological jargon through their visits with counselors and social workers. I found that although the psychological notions were not wrong or bad, for this population they were mostly irrelevant. Most of the kids who came to MFY had had terrible childhood experiences, but more significant was the fact that they were continuing to live these experiences in the here and now. Their appreciative system was limited to the life of the ghetto. I began to feel that what these young people lacked most was an ability to navigate the system. They had experienced mostly punishment in their growing up. Therefore what for me was a "grin-and-bear-it—things-will-get-better" situation was for them just more of the same old bitterness.

So I decided to do an experiment. All our work program discipline was based on sets of rules, the violation of which evoked various punishments. It was the same old thing over again under the new guise of a youth employment program. I thought it would be a good thing to eliminate the punitive disciplinary rules from the work programs and substitute rewards in their place. When I suggested this to the staff, I had a rebellion on my hands. "What! Give up the power to punish?! Schrank has gone crazy." It took many staff meetings before people were convinced that it might be worth trying some positive reinforcement.

The full impact of trying to eliminate the punitive nature of the program controls was never fully resolved at MFY. I only realize now that when I tried that experiment I had scarcely comprehended the punishing nature of our whole learning system. Our very devoted teachers and work supervisors, as in most of our school systems, simply did not know how to function without being able to punish. The scars from the school punishment were so deeply embedded in these ghetto youths that almost any learning situation created a panic of anxiety that gave rise to excessive noise, tin can banging, and general cacophony as a way of drowning out the terror of more punishment. Rinaldo and Maria's reactions reminded me of Thorndike's experiments, in which he tried to uncondition the learning of cats with electric shock. Substitute a classroom for Thorndike's electric grid that sent the cats into a frenzy and made them unable to learn, and you get a sense of how a learning situation feels to some ghetto children.

MFY was one of the first of the great social experiments of the early sixties, and it attracted many people who were peddling wares to help save the poor. We were quite innovative in some of the things we did, such as acquiring a local neighborhood Shell gas station through the president of Shell Oil and then using it as a training site. That experience was to help me formulate Schrank's first law: If it doesn't work, expand it. And its corollary: The greater the magnitude, the less notice will be taken that it does not work.

People phoned and wrote, asking about how to acquire a gas station for training delinquents or hard-core unemployed. I would try to say, "Look, let me tell you about some of the problems with this sort of training site," and inevitably a voice in Kansas City would say, "Look, we saw the article in *Business Week*, and we think it's a helluva idea. Just tell us how to get the station."

Because of the role of the media in our society, public relations is often far more important than evidence. At MFY I observed that individuals and institutions interested in replicating our programs were not concerned with the outcomes as much as with promoting the idea. I began to perceive that promoting an idea, a program, or a product through public relations can make it become real. Some people begin to deal with difficult and often insoluble social problems through the media, as if the promotion were the solution—as in the case of our gas station, which really did not work as a job training vehicle.

Getting back to the parade of peddlers through MFY, one of the most memorable was Charlie Slack, Ph.D., Harvard. Charlie had developed a hypothesis regarding a therapeutic approach to poor people and their problems. I am paraphrasing, but Charlie's theory went something like this: The poor cannot afford therapy, but, like all of us, they desperately need it. In order to help them reveal their inner selves, instead of their paying the therapist, the therapist pays them. The immediate reward of money reinforces the revelatory behavior leading to self-understanding and should result in new behavior.

Slack proposed to test his positive reinforcement theory at MFY. The chief of counseling at MFY was somewhat skeptical, but a curious fellow, and said, "Look, why don't we get some kids together for Slack, and let's see what happens. What have we got to lose?" We agreed to give Slack a chance to demonstrate his skills.

It was a warm New York summer night when we gathered about a dozen Puerto Ricans and blacks, males and females, in a little room of an old East Side catering building. A few social workers came. As we sat crowded and hot, waiting for Charlie Slack, we ate doughnuts and drank Coke. He arrived late, hurriedly bursting in, making us immediately aware of how busy and important he really was.

Slack was a tall, slim, balding man, and his assistant, whose name I remember as Dr. Werneger, was four feet tall and spoke with a German accent. Slack announced, "I will run the session, and Dr. Werneger will record it." We all nodded. Slack sat his long frame up on a table, which made him appear even larger than he was. He looked around the crowded, hot little room with its institutional, cream-colored, peeling walls. "OK, look, I'm here to pay you for telling us about your feelings. How do you feel about the work programs here, about MFY, or anything you want to talk about? Two dollars for how you feel."

The recorder was busily writing Slack's questions as though they were totally new to him. I wondered where Charlie had found Werneger. There were no Germans on Avenue A and Third Street. Sure enough, Charlie advised us that Werneger was a clinical psychologist from Vienna.

Well, nothing happened when Charlie offered "Two dollars for your feelings." There was a long deadly silence. Slack tried again, "Two dollars for your feelings." Finally Henry, a usually quiet black youth, said, somewhat annoyed, "Listen, man, I wanna job, you know. That's why I am here, and if I could get one, I wouldn't be here."

Unsatisfied, Slack started again. "Two dollars for your real feelings. What are you really feeling? Who will buy two dollars for their real feelings?"

The embarrassed silence just seemed to keep growing until it echoed in my ears. After a time, Ramon said, "Hey, man, what makes you think my feelings is worth only two bucks? That's what's the matter with white folks. They don't even think a black man's feelings is worth anything. Just get me a job, and don't worry about my feelings." It was becoming painfully clear that buying feelings as a therapeutic technique was not working, at least in this setting. The meeting was self-consciously adjourned.

Acknowledging that his experiment hadn't worked because, as he explained, the setting was not right, Charlie Slack moved on. Next time I read about him, he was on the West Side of Manhattan taking kids for a ride in a Cadillac limousine as a reward for "good behavior." I learned later that Slack had been a student at Harvard of Skinner, who was doing some amazing things, such as training pigeons to add and subtract. Slack's notion was to apply operant conditioning to change delinquent behavior. For good positive behavior, the kids were given an instant reinforcement with a ride in the Cadillac. Slack was surprised to learn that there was no behavioral change, only the same round of unemployment, poverty, and rip-offs that characterize the ghetto. The kids just went for the ride in the Cadillac, that was it.

Of the many visitors to MFY by far the most colorful was Bobby Kennedy. He was then attorney general, and many of the original grants to MFY came out of the President's Committee on Juvenile Delinquency, housed in the Justice Department.

Bobby would often come to the city unannounced. His Washington office would call New York for a police car to pick him up at LaGuardia field and drive him to Second Street and Avenue B. It was opera buffa when word ran through MFY headquarters, that "Bobby Kennedy will be here in twenty minutes." Directors of the various activities—multiservice center, coffee shop, homework helper, remedial education, and work programs—were instantly vying with each other to have Kennedy visit their site.

The visit I remember best was on a warm, lovely spring day when even the slums didn't seem so bad. A police car pulled up at MFY headquarters, followed by three black limousines. It turned out that when Kennedy's secretary had called for a police car to meet him, someone at police headquarters advised the borough presidents, the D.A.'s and some other city brass that the "attorney general was coming." Uninvited, they all came to meet him in the Second Street slums. Kennedy, in shirtsleeves, jumped out of the police car, ready for action. Everyone began to catch his rapid-fire style as the doors of the limousines flew open and people bounded out, gathering around him. Nobody seemed to know why or what they were supposed to do. People were now hanging out the windows, wondering what was going on as police cars began to gather. Everyone was jockeying to get next to Kennedy, and Percy Sutton had just made it in the nick of time.

"I want to see the workshops. Have you got a car?" Completely oblivious to the growing scene around him, Kennedy announced what he wanted. That was it. One of our work supervisors owned a VW van and was designated to take the attorney general on a tour. About six of us jumped in the van. Kennedy, sitting up front with the driver, said, "Let's go," and we were off. Behind us were the borough presidents, the D.A.'s, and the police brass, all scrambling into their limousines. The Cadillacs following the van screeched their tires trying to catch up.

Our first stop was an old abandoned five-story school building on Fifth Street that MFY had acquired from the city for workshops, classrooms, and offices. On the top floor in what was once a sliding-wall auditorium, we had our sewing shop. When the place had been used as a school, the sliding walls could be rolled back and eight classrooms became the auditorium. These were now sort of haphazardly rolled open.

Kennedy bounded out of the van and into the school with Anton, the driver, and two steps at a time, dashed up one of the many cagelike staircases. I was in pretty good shape, yet it was hard to keep up with his "vigah." He was in the sewing shop as I came through one of the open sliding walls.

His hand shot out to me. "I'm Bobby Kennedy. What do you do here?"

"I'm Bob Schrank. I direct this program."

"Is this a good program?"

"Excellent. I want you to meet Josephine Falzone. She runs it."

He shakes hands with Josephine. "Keep up the good work."

He starts to move on. I go through one of the wall openings. I meet him on the other side. Out comes his hand, "I'm Bobby Kennedy." "Yes, I know. I'm Bob Schrank," and we go through the same routine.

He is moving all the time; the sliding walls have created a labyrinth. He goes through another opening and we meet again. "Hello, I'm Bobby Kennedy." Now I am laughing, as are the sewing shop enrollees, whose awe of all these important people begins to dissolve as the scene turns Chaplinesque. Kennedy doesn't laugh. He is oblivious.

Just as we are ready to leave, the limousine entourage arrives on the fifth floor, huffing and puffing. Kennedy is about to exit at the other end of the floor. Someone yells, "He's going down." They rush across the auditorium and through the labyrinth of open walls, with people bumping into each other and finally making it through the openings to the down staircase.

Someone tells Kennedy that "they" are trying to catch up with him. He turns around and bounds up the stairs, only to see through the wire fence that separates the up and down staircases the borough presidents, the D.A.'s, the deputy chief inspector, and their party running down the up staircase. There are yells of recognition "Mr. Attorney General!" The group in the down staircase turns to run up with Kennedy, when, at Anton's suggestion, we turn and go down "now that they have caught up to us." It is now a Mack Sennett comedy sequence as the entourage again turns to run down.

Finally, with an utterly breathless group of officials around him, we reach the street, where a local crowd of curious people have gathered. Kennedy says, "Can you expand that program?" referring to the sewing shop. "Yes, if we had more equipment and materials." "Tell me what you need and I'll get it for you." He is off in the van to the next worksite with the lurching limousines after him. Kennedy was supportive of what we were trying to do even if he was a little detached.

At MFY I again found myself wondering about jobs and work, and how the pay, benefits, and amenities are distributed. Though I attempted to make the work projects as real as possible, there was no quantifiable product at MFY. Reporting to the Washington funding sources primarily required computing the number of people who came in and went out of the various centers and the kinds of services received. Human service is such an intangible item; sometimes it just involved a referral from a counselor or social worker.

Having recently emerged from a world of manufacturing quanti-fiable things, I found it difficult to adjust to a marshmallow world of talk that "hopefully, somehow, perhaps," would affect a person's behavior. The tough part is that nobody ever knows for sure what, if anything, is the effect. My own German work ethic tends to leave me uncomfortable about not being able to measure tangibly the results of my work. Counselors, for instance, sat and talked with young blacks and Puerto Ricans about jobs, school, family, the police, and life. The content of the counseling conversation depended on what school of counseling the person had graduated from.

There were constant arguments at MFY regarding who could do what with a "client." You might be barred from conversing with any of them if you were not "professionally" trained. This professionalizing of a particular skill made it arcane to the rest of the world, barring outsiders from knowing what was "really" happening. The counselors would periodically tape-record a session with a client. Then a group would gather in a room to listen to the tape. This was called a case review. This case review business was adapted from medicine to psychiatry to psychology to counseling, making all the participants feel very doctorish.

When I requested to sit in on a case review, there were objections by some professionals on the grounds that I was not properly trained. Well, I managed to sit in on a few, and what I learned was that some staff people were playing Doctor Freud while a lot of enrollees were playing hustle the counselor or social worker. Hustle was played by seeing how much could be gotten in terms of little awards, favors, and appointments. It was obvious that some of the younger female counselors were getting turned on by the high sexual energy of the male enrollees. These enrollees knew it and were having a good time playing "make the counselor wet her pants." Yet many of the enrollees, both boys and girls, enjoyed the sudden interest taken in them. It did not matter what the counseling technique was, the attention satisfied a deep hunger for someone to take an interest.

At the case conferences there would be attempts to identify the pathologies of the enrollees that had led to their deviant or aberrant behavior. The discussion would reflect the participant's exposure to psychological theory. There was an underneath sort of assumption that if people did not behave according to social norms, then there must be some trauma lurking in their psyches that was the cause of such unacceptable behavior.

Though the enrollees had problems, the bigger issues for me were the social and economic conditions of their life experience. The

MFY staff was increasingly divided on this issue. Is it the individual or the situation that is the problem, and if it is the objective condition, then what do we do about the individual? At that time I strongly believed that the situation or objective condition was the major determinant of a person's behavior. This was reflected in how I ran the work programs.

My concept of what work projects for the MFY enrollees ought to be was quite different from that of most of the social workers and psychologists. Their work experience was limited by the very nature of their professional life. Advanced degrees had been the tickets out of menial or manual work; most of them had had no experience aside from maybe some part-time work in unskilled jobs. Many of them had worked hard at becoming professionals in order to make it out of the working class. Now that they had made it, they tended to believe that those who were unable to do the same suffered some sort of deficiency. Some of the staff had come out of sheltered workshops for the physically disabled, where work activity is looked on as therapy. The focus of the work itself is then not central to the person but only important to the extent that it can help overcome a physical handicap.

The influence on my own values regarding work came more from traditional proletarianism, which holds that the working class is the most potent force for change; if we could help these young people become part of the stable working class, they would not only have made it for themselves but would represent a new force for change in the black and Puerto Rican communities.

This is still the view of people associated with the A. Philip Randolph Educational Fund, such as Bayard Rustin and Ernie Green, and is reflected in their efforts to create opportunities for blacks to become part of the construction industry. While I continue to support the rights of minorities to enter these skilled jobs, I have far less hope that this will satisfy the blacks' desire for equal status. I began to understand the resistance of many black youths to doing manual work as I analyzed how the benefits from work are distributed. Since they do not perceive the manual blue-collar worker as having made it, the idea of belonging to the proletariat does not have the attraction for young blacks and Puerto Ricans that it had for someone who believed that the working class was the vanguard of a coming revolution. The questions asked of me by the young blacks and Puerto Ricans at MFY about why they should take "lousy jobs that don't go nowheres" started me on a long journey of reevaluating how the benefits of jobs and work are distributed in society.

The projects that I was involved in developing at MFY were based on the concept that to be meaningful, work should be socially useful. This meant that our work projects needed to be based on what the community wanted done. Reflecting this policy, we built new bleachers in the baseball diamonds of the East River Drive Park, reworked the sitting and recreation areas at public housing projects, rebuilt the inside of a number of community centers, completely rehabilitated old slum tenements.

Social utility as the cornerstone of our projects was best exemplified by an MFY sewing shop project. We put the sewing shop together with equipment hustled from the International Ladies Garment Workers Union, which they gave us on the condition that we sew rags for the "wiping trade." The ILGWU was concerned that MFY not become competitive with their employers. Of course we did not, and I doubt that anyone believed we intended to. We did sew some of the nicest children's clothes that the lower East Side folks had ever seen. We made clothes for people who could not afford to buy them. To demonstrate to the enrollees the socially useful character of their work, we would sew hundreds of children's garments, and twice a year they would carefully pack them in cartons for distribution to children living in migrant labor camps in Long Island and New Jersey.

The whole sewing shop gang of about thirty eighteen- and nineteen-year-old Puerto Rican and black kids would become increasingly anxious as we talked about "the trip." By the time "the day" arrived they would be scared stiff as they piled their cartons of clothes into the bus at 6 A.M. for the ninety-mile ride to Glassboro, New Jersey, or Riverhead, Long Island. For most, this was the farthest from the lower East Side they had ever been. But I did not know how fearful they were until early one spring morning.

We had a trip set for late in April. It turned out to be one of those warm and lovely mornings when just to be alive is a great joy. Even the drive down along the East River was a pleasure. When I turned onto Houston Street to meet the bus, I spotted a group of our sewing shop trainees gathered together in a little park, passing the booze bottle camouflaged in the brown paper bag. I was driving my Ford convertible with the top down. I screeched it to a stop and without opening the door, I jumped out and stood in the street, screaming at them, "I am not about to take a bunch of drunks to New Jersey so the world can see what a bunch of punks we really are. Why don't you all just go home and drink your wine because that's what I am about to tell the bus driver to do."

I was starting back to the car when Beverly, a beautiful Puerto Rican girl and a natural group leader, took the bottle in the brown paper bag and smashed it on the sidewalk. "See? It was almost full. Honestly, we didn't hardly drink any. Can we go?" she pleaded. "We really want to. Please, we are gonna be so good you won't know us."

I was feeling real lousy about my outburst as I listened to her. "Look, we'll all have a cup of coffee to make sure we're sober." They realized that I was already won over. Beverly and a few other girls walked over to me at the curb as I was collecting my lost temper. "Hey, Mr. Schrank, you really care about us. Man, you sure got mad. Nobody ever gets mad for us, just against us. We're gonna be OK, don't worry, Mr. Schrank."

"All right, get your coffee, and I'll meet you at the bus. But this trip better go smooth or there won't be another." They went for coffee and we met at the bus.

The ride on the New Jersey Turnpike through the farmland went without a hitch as we all relaxed after the early morning flare-up. We were met by a young man from the migrant ministry, who took us to a nearby church meeting room where he briefed us on the migrant camps, labor contracts, pay, and housing. Then the bus went off on the dirt road to a group of chicken-coop-like shacks sur-rounded with the usual assortment of old rotting cars, washing machines, tires, sinks, and so forth. The bus, now looking twice its size next to the little shacks, stopped under a big shady tree.

The MFY trainees took armfuls of the children's clothes they had made. I stood watching Beverly as she stopped each little kid she met and asked them, "Would you like some new clothes?" The shy, frightened black migrant kids, staring, inarticulate and unbelieving, would give a small nod as an acknowledgment. Beverly would step back, eye the kid for size, reach into the carton she was carrying, come out with a pair of cute overalls, and right there in the cucumber field slip the little boy into them. She would step back again, this time to inspect the fit. If it wasn't just right she quickly pulled out a needle and thread and made some quick alterations on the shoulder straps, the length, or the side buttons.

When I looked up from watching Beverly, I suddenly became aware that thirty black and Puerto Rican teenagers from the lower East Side were finding the children of migrant workers in the fields and around the shacks. They would reach into their cartons of clothes, find the right garment, proceed to make it fit, and stand back to admire it. For a long time I had to leave the group to hide my tears of pride and sadness in what I was experiencing.

When all the garments had been distributed, we gathered under the big tree to talk about what had happened. Maria started. "My God, these people are worse off than us. How can the government permit people to live this way?" Others chimed in, "This is unbelievable. Are there more places like this? We gotta make clothes for all these kids. Maybe we should work more hours. Can we get more materials from the mills?" I was so filled with pride that I had difficulty speaking for the joy that swept through me.

In many ways this was the essence of unalienated labor. The enrollees helped design the clothes, made them, and distributed them to the user. The notion of socially useful work had succeeded. Those who did the work had direct contact with the beneficial effects of what they had done.

The migrant camp gave the Beverlys and Ramons of MFY a

chance to see themselves in another frame of reference—that of helper instead of the helped. They experienced a situation worse than their own and felt determined to try to do something about it. That was the important step for them—what can we do about it? They simply had not thought about confronting problems as a "we," as a group, as a collective. Could the experience of seeing the socioeconomic problems of a group of poor people help them to better understand their own situation? That was my fervent wish.

As I thought about these MFY enrollees, I remembered the radical socialist-communist youth clubs in the Bronx during the depression of the thirties and what a powerful force they were in helping us to cope. We did not blame ourselves for the condition we found the world in. Instead we took off after the system that created hunger, unemployment, exploitation, and insecurity. We studied, read, argued, and fought with each other about Stalin, Trotsky, de Leon, Kautsky, Rosa Luxemburg, and Lenin's last will and testament. From this endless Sturm und Drang we learned a lot about how society functions, who benefits, and who loses. Probably more important, we cared about each other, calling ourselves comrades or brothers and sisters.

At the migrant labor camp in Glassboro, recalling those radical youth days, I thought what a difference a movement like that might have made for these kids. Nevertheless, I was becoming convinced that the things we were doing in our work programs were beginning to demonstrate that ghetto people, given an opportunity to understand their problems, might begin to deal with them. I didn't know then that the little body of programs we had developed at MFY to deal with some pressing social issues was about to be picked apart. Even these small efforts would put us on the front page of the *Daily News* as a "commie plot."

The attack on MFY came on a Sunday. I was swimming in a pond in Westchester with some friends when someone called from the house to say that I had better get a look at the *Daily News*. The headline read, "Youth Agency Red Controlled." There followed an incoherent tale of how MFY had printed posters accusing a cop named Gilligan of an unprovoked shooting of a black kid. Furthermore, the article went on, MFY was fomenting a confrontation with the landlords on the lower East Side by organizing tenants into protest and rent strikes.

As I drove back to the city, I marveled at how I had believed I was through with red herring attacks accusing me of subversion, of being a commie agent, of inciting revolutions, when I gave up being part of the organized Left and the labor movement. Here it was again, with the *Daily News* uncovering yet another great plot to overthrow America. As I drove down the West Side Highway, people looked at me from other cars as if I was nuts, driving along laughing. It all struck me very funny. It was one thing to see unions in the basic manufacturing industries as sources of potential revolution. But a bunch of psychologists and social workers fiddling around the lower East Side of Manhattan? Really now! Was capitalism that paranoid?

That Sunday night nervousness and anxiety were already at a high pitch as various staff members called to ask what was happening, what should be done, how to do it, and so forth. I wondered how much my own radical past was going to be an issue again. I was somewhat intrigued and annoyed with the thought that I would have to go through the McCarthy Red wringer again. Yet there was some excitement in being named a witch, or at least it made routine everyday living seem pretty dull in comparison.

When an institution, a union, or an agency like MFY comes under charges of being Red influenced, it becomes extremely difficult to continue normal day-to-day activities. It is hard to know whether to continue doing the organization's work or stop what you're doing in order to defend against the attacks. The McCarthy-type political attack that was launched against MFY was almost impossible to counter. If I am accused of being a Red or having been a Red or cavorting with known Reds, how can I defend myself other than to say, "It's none of your damn business!" Because if, in order to prove my desire to be purged, I acknowledge having cavorted with witches and devils, I then need to name other witches and devils. The problem is always compounded by the revelations from time to time of real subversive spy activity, giving a certain credence to the existence of witches and devils.

As I drove to the city, I was beginning to separate out who were the good guys and who were the informers. Who was manufacturing the "big plot" and why? Damn, this was getting exciting! As ——— had indicated, I had been fingered on various occasions. As a result I have always had an interest in the nature of informers. More information about what happened to America's witch hunt informers of the last three decades might help discourage Red-baiting attacks in the future. After a few days on the front page of the morning papers such attacks are usually deposited in the trash can of history, despised and rejected by both the informed on and the informed for.

When I arrived in the city, I called Margaret, a young radical social worker. "Of course, come on over. A bunch of us are gathering for a strategy session." We spent that Sunday night figuring out what to do at MFY come Monday morning, as well as devising a plan to get us through what the group assumed would be a long and difficult time at MFY. My adrenalin was running now that the fight was on. Margaret and I made love fiercely all night in preparation for the Monday morning battle.

Driving to MFY early Monday I thought about my tendency to indulge in heavy lovemaking whenever I was engaged in a difficult conflict situation. It seems to act as a reminder of what life is all about. I used to do that on a natural urge; then I learned from an old Maine trapper friend, Eagle Eye Smith, that before a storm animals will copulate like crazy. Eagle Eye said, "The most important act for life is copulation, and folks who don't know that just ain't livin'. If you live in the woods with nature, you'll see how natural it is; if animals get scared, that is what they do to reassure themselves. They huddle, stay close to each other, and assure life by fornicatin'." To my mind that's the most useful philosophy of action in the face of anxiety-creating conflict.

At our Sunday night meeting we had agreed on an overall strategy: Regardless of what the top leadership and the board of directors were to do, we didn't want to give way to the attack. We would organize the staff to resist the attacks on basic constitutional rights. We would start to raise money for the defense of anyone victimized by the accusations. And finally, we would resist the dismantling of our programs, particularly those that were empowering the poor!

When I showed up at MFY headquarters on Monday, there were a lot of people milling around one of the social workers. Tom Cattrell met me, pushing a piece of paper in front of me as I entered the building. "We are all signing resignations to protest the attack. Most of the professional staff have already signed as a protest against the *Daily News* charges."

I was flabbergasted. "What the hell do you think that will accomplish? That is absolutely the wrong strategy. Suppose the board accepts the resignations? Then where are we? Out on our collective asses."

Cattrell was unsure now. "It will force the MFY Board to toughen its position and not collapse under the *News'* pressure."

"Baloney. Not to collapse means to defend the programs and the people who are under attack, particularly community and tenant organizations. That resignation strategy is ridiculous; not only will I not sign it, but I will actively oppose it." It was my trade union background that led me to such an unconditional response. I remembered that when the bastards have you under attack, the nature and strength of the resistance not only determines if you win or lose but what will follow when the conflict is over.

The attack on MFY turned out to be nothing but the same old frightened conservative business reaction to some people demanding a small equity. When challenged in the most minimal way even on the far edges of the status quo, property owners need to smack down hard. A small group from MFY was challenging some slumlords to provide services contracted for by the payment of rent. If the services were not forthcoming, the tenants would withhold the rent in escrow until the contract was complied with. Wow, how mild it sounds now, yet it was considered inciting revolution. I have often wondered why people in power, that is, property owners, are so paranoid, so easily threatened. Is their power so tenuous?

There were conflicts at MFY that helped clarify for me the many changes that have occurred in society's attitude toward work. One such conflict was over whether enrollees, when confronted with a problem at work, should be permitted to leave the worksite to see a counselor at the headquarters building. I argued for a reality-oriented school of work, maintaining that the job should be treated as an eight to five responsibility—period. The craftsmen who supervised the work program staff supported my position, partially out of loyalty but also from a conviction that manual work requires a certain toughness that the enrollees had better get used to. I also felt that when people are treated as sheltered clients or patients, their behavior will become dependent. The MFY professionals perceived the carpenters, auto mechanics, and cabinet makers as a rough crowd, insensitive to the human needs of the "client." They were seen as aggressive, difficult to deal with, disrespectful, and even contemptuous of the activity of social workers, psychologists, and counselors.

Some of that contempt, I suspect, grew out of a real jealousy of the status position of white-collar professionals. In terms of status, the pros clearly had it over the craftsmen. They received higher pay, were not governed by the clock, worked in a relatively comfortable air-conditioned office, and could coffee-break and schmooze almost at will. The resentment this inequity created was expressed constantly by the blue-collar work supervisors. I began to see this phenomenon at MFY as a microcosm of what was happening in our whole society.

During one of the regular discussion meetings, I asked some enrollees why they went to the counselor so often. What emerged was this: Talking with a friendly lady in a nice little air-conditioned office was a lot better than building concrete bleachers in a hot summer sun or in rain, or putting up heavy sheetrock walls, or greasing cars in the gas station. Louis, a really tough Puerto Rican, looked at me as if trying to decide whether to say it or not. "Why you trainin' us for dis shit job when you people got all the good jobs sittin' on your ass all day in a nice air-conditioned office, just bullshittin', man, just bullshittin' all day? Man, we wanna do that too, so we come down for counselin'." What was I to say? Was I to tell Louis that we had gone to college (I was in my senior year) and received degrees that gave us this right to sit around and talk while they worked? My God, I thought, the enrollees perceived this place as a plantation, and they just wanted to sit around the mansion with the rest of us.

All that the black and Puerto Rican enrollees heard from the work program staff was work, work, work, while what they perceived in the office was a group of predominantly white people sitting around all day in conversations—and that was also called work. The assumption about socially useful work programs was proving to be only partially true. But I remembered how I felt working in a factory, and I could empathize with the kids. It seemed to be an almost irresolvable contradiction for the MFY youth, as it may be for most manual workers.

The work genie that lives inside me will sometimes poke me in the ribs, as he did once when I was at the Aspen, Colorado, conference center, discussing workplace problems. The genie said, "Hey, you guys in the Bingham open pit copper mine, do you think what we are doing here is work? Is this work? Funny what passes for work."

The conflict between manual workers and intellectual, or white-collar, workers was present in the staff and may have affected the enrollees. The carpenters, auto mechanics, and cooks were in a constant state of unease. "Why do you give us production quotas when all the time those professional people sit around talking, drinking coffee all day, and getting more money?" I was insistent that the only way a work experience can be related to the world of production is through a sense of urgency. We therefore tried to keep to a production schedule for each job. The work program staff felt it was terribly unfair, and that created a real cleavage between the blue- and white-collar workers at MFY.

MFY was unique in the way it brought together manual and

intellectual workers. Most of the social workers, psychologists, counselors, had little experience, and that resulted in less understanding of manual, physical kinds of work. When they referred to "the world of work," it struck me funny, an implication that *we* were in some other world. I often wonder, now that I have my Ph.D., do I dwell in the "world of nonwork, the Big Rock Candy Mountain"? I have observed that people who work primarily with their brains, the mind professionals, have a vague fearfulness of people involved with tools of violence such as hammers, wrenches, and powersaws. Their sexuality was both attractive and scary to some of the female counselors and social workers.

Because MFY was an important social experiment, many hours were spent in discussion with counselors, social workers, and psychologists. I gradually sensed a certain defensiveness, an uncertainty they had about their work, and since I was moving into this world I was interested in learning how their uncertainty was dealt with.

Most Indian tribes have a precious bundle of artifacts like eagle feathers, bear claws, a scalp from an enemy tribe, all representing the wisdom of the tribe. The tribal council looks after the bundle and adds or detracts artifacts as new wisdom is acquired. Think of professions as tribes who create institutions, like the American sociological or psychological associations. The precious bundle of the professional societies may consist of theories, traditions, jargon, and most important, territoriality. Territoriality came to light at MFY as case workers would insist that they alone, not group workers or psychologists, could see "really disturbed people," or they alone could make referrals to the psychiatrist. Counselors would then huddle and announce that "we are trained to do case work" and the tribe would call up its sacred bundles, the literature that would establish territoriality. When it came to unemployed youth, economists would enter the fray by announcing, "It is an economic problem that would best be treated by pumping up the economy in order to have a tight labor market."

Another thing that has struck me about the activity of various professional tribal groups is that people on the outside do not seem to care much about another tribe's internal struggles. Professional tribal organizations perform the function of reinforcing the raison d'être for the profession, thus protecting it from doubters, detractors, or outsiders.

In some ways MFY was a microcosm of the blue-collar, white-collar, and professional labor forces and the work differences between them. All the jobs at MFY shared the overall objective of helping youth to gain full employment. What I found so startlingly different in responsibility was the accountability of the specific work tasks. The blue-collar crew had to come up with quantifiable production. As it turned out that was the toughest job. Even though they had considerably more freedom at MFY than is usually permitted in most private-sector jobs, they still had to quantify each day's accomplishments. What may have aggravated a sense of inequality between blue collars and professionals at MFY was the close proximity of these two kinds of employees. Yet I think awareness of that inequality is now more prevalent in almost all workplaces, if not directly, then through communication within families or through the television. The ability of an employer to quantify an employee's work output is the source of much anxiety and concern to the person being measured. The quantified employee is always aware that production is being measured, so they lose some freedom of choice regarding how to go about their tasks. In my new job as an intellectual worker, the lack of any productivity measure was something I had to get used to. As with most of the professionals, I spent considerably more time on the job than my required 35 hours, considerably more time than the blue-collar workers. Central to my hypothesis about the inequalities at work is the notion that time spent on most white-collar service jobs has no correlation to the work performed. This may be one of the reasons for the declining interest in blue-collar work.

The day-to-day, on-the-job life at MFY was unusual, interesting, and satisfying. What I found to be most satisfying was not just challenging work, but the high level of schmoozing. Schmoozing at places like MFY is difficult to separate from the daily activities of "meetings." Meetings were a central part of our activities in which we considered how much an enrollee should be paid, how many enrollees a counselor or case worker should see in a day, what new work projects should be undertaken, rules for the work programs, reports to the funding agencies, preparing for review committees—meetings, meetings, meetings.

The professionals have another benefit denied blue-collar workers—attending conventions, conferences, seminars, and retreats. While at MFY I attended my first behavioral science convention. It was very much the same as a Navaho tribal gathering. The elders of the council presided up front at the potlatch dinner, passing traditions to the initiates and making awards for daring, bravery, or contributions to the welfare of the tribe. In contrast, the blue-collar workers were left out. They did not belong to a tribal group or travel to its ceremonial gatherings.

I dwell on amenities of the job—the freedom to work at one's own pace, to break when you wish, to come in late, go home early or late, shop in the middle of the day, take a long lunch hour, get paid by the week or month—because I believe this may be the stuff of which high levels of job satisfaction are made. It is the unequal distribution of job amenities that I believe to be the cause of much of the growing blue-collar resentment.

As MFY was grinding down, many of the work crew supervisors did not go back to their old production jobs. Some became vocational teachers; others went to school to get degrees, and still others went on to projects similar to MFY. They had experienced the freedom to schmooze, and had a taste of the nonproductive world of service. It reminded me of the old ditty, "How you gonna get 'em back on the farm now that they've seen Paree?" only now it should go, "How you gonna get 'em back in production after they've had the freedom to schmooze?"

# City Commissioner

One day while I was still at MFY I received a call from Donald Elliott, head of the New York City Planning Commission and close advisor and friend to Mayor John Lindsay. Elliott said, "Hi, Bob. You have been recommended to head the Neighborhood Youth Corps for the city of New York." Very much surprised, I asked who had recommended me. He said Judge Kohler, who had once been a judge in the California Family Court and was now head of the Youth Corps. I had met Mary Kohler at the city-wide meetings of Youth Corps program directors. I was surprised at the recommendation since I had no intimation that she was going to suggest me for the job. (Is this the way most people get jobs, by becoming part of a network of people who then support each other? This was my first experience with a political job appointment.) I advised my superiors at MFY of the call from City Hall, and most of them felt good that we were receiving this kind of recognition. Since Judge Kohler was anxious to leave the job, I thought my appointment would be imminent. Months dragged on and I finally asked her about it. She said, "I think they are investigating you, but that ought to be completed soon."

I continued working at MFY, periodically checking with Judge Kohler about what, if anything, was happening. A few months later I was in her office one morning on some Youth Corps business when she asked whether I had heard anything about my appointment. I told her that I had not, at which point she became quite annoyed, saying, "I just don't know what all this stalling is about." She picked up the phone and made a number of inquiries to Elliott and others around City Hall on my appointment, but with each call she became more indignant. "Honestly, Bob, this smells like a runaround—a 'continuing investigation of Schrank's character!' " Having been told that the FBI was investigating me, she turned to me, holding her bosom and sucking in a lot of air, and said, "Well, I think there is something funny going on here and I will get to the bottom of it." She picked up the phone, and to my amazement the next thing I heard was, "I want to talk with J. Edgar." The judge told him she wanted to know "what is holding up the FBI report on Schrank." I don't know what Hoover said, but the judge seemed pleased. Just so sweetly she said, "Oh now, thank you, J. Edgar, that is so kind of you."

She hung up. Within minutes a Mr. Maloney of the New York FBI office called the judge to say that they had no request from the city to investigate Schrank. "Well," she fumed. Slamming out Elliott's number on the dial she said, "Now, Donald, what is going on here about this Schrank thing?" She told him about her conversation with Hoover and the call back from Maloney. Elliott claimed he was unfamiliar with the whole business. He thought the New York Police Department was investigating Schrank.

In the meantime I was told to go see Mitchell Sviridoff, who was head of the New Haven, Connecticut, antipoverty agency and was about to be named head of a new superagency in New York City, to be called the Human Resources Administration. The superagency idea had grown out of a notion that the integration of human services under one umbrella organization would make their delivery more efficient. I traveled to New Haven for my interview with Sviridoff and that seemed to go well. Sviridoff and I, it turned out, had a common bond; both of us had come out of the labor movement. A godsend in any job interview is the discovery of some common interest between yourself and the interviewer. If the interest is as esoteric as having come out of the leadership of the labor movement, it can be a strong bond, as it was and remains for Sviridoff and me. He asked me to outline my ideas for the Neighborhood Youth Corps. I told him that my experience at MFY had taught me the need for work assignments that had enough real substance to challenge the enrollees. Having worked as a sheet metal worker, he said he knew what I meant by "challenge." Mike, as Sviridoff is called by people who know him, has a rapid-fire mind that can quickly grasp the essence of a problem. In years to come we would often commiserate about our work experiences as we tried to make sense out of the behavioral science jargon about workplaces that seemed so strange to both of us. What has bothered us most is the overemphasis on pathology and a lack of understanding of all the benefit, pay, and security problems. We had a good visit. He said good-bye. "Mayor Lindsay will call to confirm the appointment." He came to New York some months later to be my boss, and what I consider very unusual is that in time he became a real friend.

When I met John Lindsay, he struck me as an extremely handsome man. Unlike most politicians I had met, he seemed far too polished, looking more like a male model than a politician. His St. Paul's School training keeps him at a distance. It was probably this coldness that turned off most blue-collar people. It is one thing to have gone to St. Paul's, it is another to wear it like a concrete picket sign. I respected his civil rights commitment, particularly his record in Congress, but like most people around him, I never really knew him.

In my conversation with the mayor I told him that he needed to know about my youthful left-wing activities. He was immediately uncomfortable and began to shift around in his seat, almost visibly annoyed at my bringing up tales of old diseases. He swept his hand across his Louis XIV desk, saying that he didn't care about that. "But, Mr. Mayor, if somehow or other it comes up, I do not want to hear you saying, 'Gee whiz, Bob, this is a surprise. If only you had told me.'" He seemed amused by it all and laughed, sort of dismissing the notion with a "well, we don't really want to think of those dirty things" sort of attitude. It would not be too long before he would be surprised by a speech in Congress about how "dangerous radicals" were running the antipoverty programs in New York City.

I was hired by the city of New York as a civil service appointee. I was now a crusader on the public payroll who thought I was going to show them how to run an effective training program for the poor, the blacks, and the Puerto Ricans. In going from Mobilization for Youth to the city job, it literally was a move from a shack in the ghetto to a mansion on the hill. My daily trip into the slums of the lower East Side was over. My new office was in a modern steel and glass tower. I had moved up to the twenty-first floor from a job on the streets to a bird's eye view of lower Manhattan, a block from City Hall.

In contrast to the fifteen staff people that I inherited, who sat at desks in a large open space, my office was completely closed up to the ceiling. A few staff employees had partial partitions, signifying higher civil service titles. I learned that the higher up the civil service job hierarchy a person moved, the more privacy one was entitled to. Clerks Grade One to Four, a desk; administrative assistants, a five-foot partition; and so on up until you arrived in your own private office. Then you have earned your privacy.

I liked my new office. It was about ten by twelve feet and had a glass wall with a movable drape that separated it from the rest of the staff. It was light, faced the street, and had a telephone with four lines and an intercom to my secretary. I soon learned from some of the old civil service hands around that I had been "done in." Henry Roberts, who had worked in the city's finance office for over a quarter of a century, stood in my office doorway and looked around, shaking his head as though things were bad indeed. "At your level you should have an office twice the size with a rug, two phones, and a credenza. Call up Jonas at real estate, tell him you're a director at a Grade Twelve level and you are entitled to a bigger office, another phone, a rug—and don't forget the credenza."

"Henry, what the hell is a credenza?"

"That's the thing behind your desk where you keep your keys, your ashtray, some liquor, and an extra telephone so if you have people in the office and you don't want them to hear you, you can talk facing the wall." I was laughing, but he cut in, "Schrank, you don't know the city like I do. If you want respect, you gotta have the office right."

During my stay as a city employee my workplace would be

moved a couple of times. I never bothered much about offices and their decor. Neither did I intend to make a career out of being a civil servant.

When I came to work for the city, most of my staff of a dozen people was already there. Like most employees, they were all nervous about the new director and overanxious to prove how good they were. Helen Mannyford, a rich girl who had defied her family, married a Jew, been thrown out of the social register, and come to work in the poverty program, became my assistant. Quite a few of the Youth Corps staff were civil servants, while others were temporary appointments. The regular civil servants were annoyed with our new sense of urgency, the crusading to get the job done, but we had to meet large new payrolls and fill our training and placement quotas, as well as plan and develop new programs. In the process of proselytizing, prodding, cajoling, and threatening the regular civil servants, trying to win their efforts on behalf of what we were up to, it began to dawn on me that there simply was no reason for them to put out. There was no incentive, therefore no motivation. In the civil service system there is little or no reward for performance. The result is generally a "why bother" attitude.

Helen, other staff members, and I would hang around the city's manpower office "after the close of business," as it was called by the federal civil servants of the Department of Labor, from which we received funds and to which we were responsible for program activities. If we had known the enormity of the problems we were to encounter, we might easily have sat around crying.

During my employment by the city I held two jobs, first as director of Neighborhood Youth Corps and then as assistant commissioner for manpower programs, responsible for operation of the city's job-training programs. The Neighborhood Youth Corps was a federal antipoverty youth effort that was directed both toward in-school youth, who worked twelve hours a week, and out-of-school youth, who worked thirty-two hours a week. The money for the Youth Corps came directly from the U.S. Department of Labor. The city had to contribute 10 percent matching funds in order to be eligible for grants.

What does a director of the New York City Neighborhood Youth Corps do? Before leaving, Judge Kohler spent considerable time briefing me on the city's Youth Corps contracts with the federal government. When I first came into the job, the city was receiving about $15 million from the feds and it all had to be contracted for. The judge was adamant about the need for accuracy in drawing these contracts or, as she warned, "the city could be most seriously penalized." With the average contract running 150 to 200 pages and with a half dozen or more to do a year, I could easily have spent full time doing contracts. However, Helen and the rest of the small staff were bright young people, some of whom had been associated with the civil rights movement. They had a real commitment to the program and were therefore willing to come in on weekends to do contract proposals for the Department of Labor and the Office of Economic Opportunity (OEO). My immediate staff had the same crusader's feeling about this antipoverty effort as I did, and unlike the average civil servant we were a small band of true believers who worked all kinds of unlimited hours.

For a time I would worry about the judge's admonitions ("Bob, be extremely careful in developing a contract"), but little by little as the pressure mounted to get the contracts out, care and concern were sacrificed for speed. Eventually, in the pressure cooker of street riots, contracts tended to become sheer fiction as we tailor-made the proposals and the reports to fit the federal guidelines.

Jane Norman from Ohio was as tall and skinny as Helen was short. She had a ridiculous puckish sense of humor that included making rooster noises in meetings and submitting endless excuses for being late and absent (including two I had never heard before—in the first one she had fallen off a doctor's examining table and broken her wrist, and in the second, she called one morning to say that she had slipped in dog shit and could not make it to work). Because I was in the position of authority, I was faced daily with decisions as far-ranging as whether Jane's excuses were acceptable, to how much money the Hasidic Jews of Brooklyn should get for Neighborhood Youth Corps slots. In the case of the Janes of the world, managers are constantly faced with decisions about what to do with them. The decisions are usually influenced by three elements: balance—are they worth the problems they create; personality—how much are they liked by fellow workers; and connections—are they related to, or a friend of, someone higher up in the company or hierarchy. When it comes to keeping a job, it is better to be liked, as Jane was. She was a good worker, productive and sometimes imaginative. She was invaluable in our weekend contract development sessions, always able to come up with the city's 10 percent contribution to the program. While the federal guidelines said the city had to contribute 10 percent to the program cost, it also stipulated that this contribution could be "in kind," which meant a service or free space or, as Jane said, "We have to show them that we can give that which we didn't know we had." She would laugh and laugh; the absurdity of the world that some of us would experience periodically registered on her all the time.

To be eligible for the Youth Corps, the enrollee's family had to earn less than the minimum standard of income as established by the Department of Labor. The eligibility of each enrollee had to be approved by the city's central manpower office. The Youth Corps had had up until this time a maximum of six or seven thousand enrollees. The numbers were now constantly climbing as "the crusaders" cried, "Give us more for the poor," and they did. In the summer of 1967 we reached an enrollment of 50,000. The staff would look at income, number of kids in the family, and other relevant information reported on the forms. We had two large rubber stamps, one that read "eligible" and the other "not eligible." When there were a large number of intakes, most of the staff would be doing "eligibilities." As program director and commissioner, I had rapidly learned how to satisfy the federal guidelines. Unbeknownst to me at the time, the kids in the poverty neighborhoods had also learned how to "meet the guidelines." I can hardly remember a single "ineligible," except in the summer youth programs, when now and then some uninformed middle class kid from Forest Hills would apply for summer work. Jane would laugh hysterically as she sat and slammed the "eligible" stamp on the applications. She would giggle in her throat. "Hey, Chief, do you think everyone is just filling out the forms according to the requirements and none of it is true?"

I now believe that all of us kind of play a game of beating the guidelines. Middle class people do it with expenses written off on their income tax. The temporary or laid-off employee does it with unemployment insurance. Welfare recipients give the kind of information that makes them "eligible," as do food stamp recipients. Beating the guidelines, the regulations, the rules may turn out to be the last great challenge left to us humans, now that we have conquered most of the frontier. Fulfilling the guidelines has also made me very suspect of government-collected data. Recently the Department of Labor began to have some doubts about information it was receiving from the cities, counties, and states. A field check by an independent research outfit indicated some inaccurate information reported by local prime sponsors about whom manpower programs were serving in their communities. Such reports are "meeting the guideline requirements."

No longer using the subway, I was now driving to and from work. I was part of a class of people who have finally made it out of the subway and are now liberated to sit in daily traffic. We are a sort of smug group in our own automobiles, with a new status symbol of "the better the car, the greater you are." Most of us have our radios on, and the station you tune to may further identify your status group. Behind the wheel it's sheer aggression, with everyone vying for the one car space ahead or trying to beat the light. Many mornings by the time I made it to the office, I was so full of traffic anger I could have punched somebody in the mouth. The trek home at night was often bumper to bumper like the morning, yet I liked it better than the subway. For while I might be waiting for the traffic to move, at least I was sitting comfortably unsqueezed, listening to the radio and not being shoved around in a packed train.

The work of a director or a commissioner, while in many ways similar to most other administrative jobs in a service industry, is not at all similar to the management responsibility in manufacturing. In a service industry the work can pretty much be what one wants to make of it. In a way you don't have to really do anything, and yet if you wish to be an influence, you can intercept many pieces of paper for approval or introduce new policies or programs into the department. In manufacturing, the administrator or manager is usually held responsible for the productivity of his plant or department, and because there is most often a quantifiable outcome, performance is easily measured. The argument that it is impossible or difficult to measure productivity in the service sector began to strike me, when I worked for the city, as somewhat self-serving: It is much easier to work on a job where there is no productivity measurement.

There were dozens of manpower programs in the city that had to be approved by me, yet I saw few of them because I simply had no time. We solved this dilemma by holding the sponsoring or operating agencies responsible for them. As a manager, this put me in a posture of reacting to complaints. Many of the organizations participating in the city's manpower-training programs were church groups, and separating their religious activities from the training programs required constant effort. But the Hasidics were by far the most difficult. Once I received a complaint saying that the Neighborhood Youth Corps enrollees working in the Hasidic camps up in the Catskill Mountains eighty-five miles from the city were working seventy hours a week instead of thirty-two. I rushed one of our staff people up there to investigate. The Hasidics were wonderful in their "innocent" ignoring of guidelines. Rabbi Lugarsky would storm into my office exclaiming that "we have our own rules that you, even though you are a nice person, cannot possibly understand."

"Rabbi," I started to say, "I really can't be concerned about the rules of the Hasidim."

He was a short man who looked like a barrel in his black frock coat and broad-brimmed hat with his long locks of hair dangling over his ears. At my suggestion of "rules or guidelines" his eyebrows went up. He became taller as he lectured me. "The Hasidim have their own rules that have governed us for hundreds of years. How can *you* think that *you* can make new rules for *us*?"

What we had here was a failure to communicate. "Rabbi, I will write you a letter outlining what is permissible for you to do with the money you receive from the city, and I will give your organization two weeks to comply. If you do not, we will withdraw the money." He nodded his head in agreement and left in a huff for City Hall to complain about "that unsympathetic, maybe anti-Semitic, director you got over there on Church Street."

Manpower training was still a fairly new program area, and because this was a period of rapid growth it required that we start lots of new things. Our small city staff felt our major contribution should be the development of new program ideas, which we would brainstorm at our regular city office staff meetings. With the birth of a new program notion I would assign a staff person to develop the idea on paper. We would then run the new program as a small-scale experimental model, and later try to replicate it on a larger scale. We learned a lot about the difficulties of replication. Programs that work well in one setting may not work at all in another, as happened with our building maintenance training activities. Or a small successful program set up as a model could be a total flop when replicated on a larger scale. We had developed a good building maintenance training program with some of the private hospitals in the city. They were training Youth Corps enrollees as maintenance plumbers, electricians, and glaziers. The enrollees loved the program. They became highly motivated, received good training, and worked hard, and we were able to place them in other jobs.

At a meeting of the city-wide coordinating council I reported how well this maintenance training program was working and suggested we do it at eight of the city's nineteen hospitals. It was agreed our next trial run would be at Bellevue Hospital, the city's largest. It was a total disaster because the skilled help at Bellevue mostly told our black and Puerto Rican helpers to "get lost, come back at quitting time, go to the movies," and so forth. What we were learning about program effectiveness was that success had more to do with the people who were running the program than it did with its design. The design could be rational down to the finest detail, but if, as was often the case, the people running it did not particularly care about the participants (who might be black or Puerto Rican), then nothing of much use would happen in the program.

It was 1967, and Mayor Lindsay was trying his damnedest to be responsive to the black and Puerto Rican communities. One of his instruments for this purpose was the Urban Task Force (UTF), which he established under the direction of a former newspaper man, Bill Monday. The Task Force's mission was to keep its collective ear to the neighborhood ground, alert for what was happening (particularly in ghetto communities), and to head off troubles, especially the kind that can lead to riots. Keep in mind that this was the late sixties, when communities used rioting as a way of expressing their impatience with the promises of the Great Society programs.

I was assistant commissioner now, responsible for the operation of the city's manpower programs. I was appointed to the Task Force to represent the city's manpower agency. As we met early every Monday morning in the Blue Room at City Hall, I began to see us as the true Monday morning quarterbacks, carefully reviewing the events that had occurred during the past week, with particular concern for the weekends. Saturday and Sunday during the warm weather, with its long daylight hours, were considered the most riot-prone time in the ghettoes. The head of the Task Force, Bill Monday, was one of Lindsay's "bright young men." He was a humorless, grim fellow who took himself very seriously, probably because he operated out of a conspiracy ideology, which suggests that everything in the world is run by some plot or another and one's major function is to find it. This was a time of endless demands; for decentralization of neighborhood schools, increases in hospital care, more welfare and Headstart programs, summer jobs for youths, swimming pools, and traffic lights, with all the interest groups using the streets as a forum. They marched, sang, paraded, and demonstrated, all of which created contact with a police force that had little or no sympathy for this new street phenomenon. Members of the Task Force were to act as go-betweens in order to avoid confrontations between the police and the demonstrators. When we learned of a contemplated street action, we would inform the police through the chief inspector and, with luck, a negotiation for agreed action would take place. Ironically, this complemented the Task

Force director's conspiracy notion, since even the "spontaneous demonstrations" had been secretly orchestrated at City Hall, unknown to the participants. Sometimes these scenarios sounded as if they were taken from a movie script.

The Monday morning Task Force sessions were attended by about fifteen or twenty people sitting around the huge table in front of the marble fireplace in the Blue Room of City Hall. (The mayor would sometimes drop in unannounced, which helped to explain the good attendance.) The director, in his deadly monotone, would open the meeting with a discussion of some weekend occurrence, like the Yippie antiwar demonstration in Grand Central Station that had resulted in a series of arrests. He was visibly pained by the breakdown at Grand Central and blamed the police. He suggested that the chief inspector explain "why the police had to move the way they did to arrest so many Yippies." I suspected that the director had already held a series of talks with the Yippie leaders and the police. They had probably worked out a scenario that the chief inspector and his cops had not understood, and so they had screwed the whole thing up. The chief inspector, even more solemn than the director, an archetypal police officer trained in monotones, replied, "I did not issue the order for the police to move in on the demonstrators until the perpetrators climbed up on the main Grand Central information booth and were making speeches from on top of the clock."

I suddenly realized that a person becomes a perpetrator only when he or she breaks the law. But what was the law that the chief inspector thought he was protecting? I leaned over to Commissioner Cyril Tyson, a black man with a good sense of street humor, and said, "Hey, Ty, is he worried about the clock losing time or what?" Ty asked the chief inspector the same question. The inspector thought seriously for a moment. "It was the job of the police to protect property and that's what time is, in this case as represented by the clock." It struck a few of us as funny, but not the director. He was snarling at the chief that the police were to blame because he had worked out an arrangement with Jerry Rubin, the head of the Yippies, and the police had failed to stick to the script. As I listened to the inspector and the director, I had the feeling that a Kabuki script had been agreed to, but that someone in the Police Department had not been able to resist the opportunity to bust some of those long-haired heads for the benefit of the TV cameras. The Task Force experience allowed me to understand how the media had created the phenomenon of the agreed-upon protest script. There was nothing analogous to it in our union-organizing efforts.

Other Monday mornings found us gathered in the Blue Room to discuss the allocation of jobs to various neighborhoods and fights that were going on between Puerto Ricans and Italians, or blacks and Puerto Ricans, or Hasidics and blacks, or Poles and blacks, and so on and so on. The director and some other Lindsay aides tended to become utterly exasperated with people who did not fully appreciate the weightiness of some of their decisions. I was beginning to feel that people like me, appointees working in the public sector, tended to overestimate our importance. Some of the Lindsay aides at City Hall behaved as though the future of the city hung on their every act, while most of the civil servants acted as though they could not have cared less. That tension resulted in the isolation of the "apocalyptic" appointees from the civil servants who, for better or worse, really run the city.

My job at the Task Force was to make youth jobs available to the "hot neighborhoods." The director had a strategy of "buy out the leadership," which I did not respect, and I told him so. I believed that unless the city developed meaningful jobs for blacks and Puerto Ricans, things would get worse in the ghettoes. There were many telephone calls to me from the mayor's office, from councilmen and congressmen, requesting or demanding job slots. While I had to listen patiently, I carried out most of the job distribution through a group that Judge Kohler had organized, called the City-wide Coordinating Committee. It represented the minority organizations in the city, which were my own base of support in the community.

Among the many surprises I received as commissioner was a startling telephone call on September 27, 1967, from the Washington bureau of the *New York Times*. They asked me if I was aware of a speech that a congressman from the Bronx had made that day in the course of introducing an amendment to antipoverty legislation on the floor of the House of Representatives. In his speech the congressman had attacked me as a radical and called on Sargeant Shriver, head of OEO, to withhold any funds for the city of New York until I had been discharged. The congressman's amendment to the OEO legislation required that no one who had ever been or was presently connected to any organizations on the attorney general's subversive list could be an administrator over a certain level of pay in any antipoverty program. With few house members present, the amendment was introduced on the floor of the House of Representatives and was carried on a voice vote. On the morning of the 28th, there were two issues confronting City Hall: First, what to do about Schrank, and second, what to do about the amendment.

Late in the afternoon of September 27, I began to receive telephone calls from a variety of people suggesting different things that I might do. A few callers, some close to the mayor and concerned that I might be an embarrassment, suggested I resign. But the main sentiment seemed to be expressed by Reverend Milton Galamison, who said, "I sure hope you're not going to let any of this scare you, now are you?" I assured him I would not.

Early on I talked with Mike Sviridoff, who had become head of HRA. Knowing how I enjoyed a hot debate, Mike said, "Now, Bob, I suggest that you try keeping your big mouth shut, at least long enough for all of us to sit down and try to figure out what to do about the congressman who's creating these problems. I'll arrange a meeting with the mayor as soon as possible." Reluctantly, I accepted Mike's suggestion to shut up, but told him that if the mayor wavered in the face of the congressman's attacks, I would go it on my own. In the meantime I was being called by newspapers, wire services, and television networks asking me to comment. I would have loved telling the congressman off, but my agreement with Sviridoff made it hard for me to say anything. I did give John Kiffner of the *New York Times* an interview over the telephone, making a few observations on how I came to be hired and what was known of my radical past by the Lindsay administration.

The next morning, one of the mayor's chauffeured cars picked me up at my house at 7:30 and took me down to City Hall. As we drove, I had a feeling of importance; people would look into the chauffeured car, but of course they had no idea who I was or why I was there. When we arrived at City Hall, I was told to go straight to the mayor's office and talk to no one on my way.

As I came into that Louis XIV office, the mayor was there along with Mike Sviridoff and a number of other people, all set to huddle on today's crisis. Most of these huddles are to develop a script for the media—"What are we going to say to those damn television cameras?" Henry Cohen, an HRA administrator who was an old city hand, had taught me the usefulness of being one of the world's slowest talkers. In this kind of crisis situation, his languorous way of talking might make you sleepy, but at the same time it helped remove a lot of the anxiety and tension. In this emergency he was invaluable. His calm manner and firm commitment to civil rights tended to calm down some of the others who seemed quite upset and disturbed, as if I had tarnished their leader. One of them suggested I quit, and another kept making cracks about how my Communist past was burdening the poor mayor. There were many people around Lindsay in those days who were busy with White House fantasies, and anyone who interfered with that ambition was considered a burden.

Sviridoff's working-class, trade union training stood him up firm. He said to the mayor, "Look, we know all about this sort of stuff and we need to pay as little attention to it as possible. If we tend to business and don't get sidetracked into debates with the congressman, in a few days it will all disappear. On the other hand, if we engage in a big debate, the whole thing can balloon into a cause célèbre."

The mayor, who had been sitting quietly listening, said, "There is going to be a press conference at 9:00. It is now 8:45. I really have to be clear what I am going to say to a roomful of reporters and television people whose number one question will obviously be the Schrank thing." Lindsay turned, looked at me straight, and asked,

"Bob, what would you do if you were I at this morning's press conference?" Lindsay was at his best in this kind of crisis and his clarity on civil rights issues was most refreshing. I liked him for that.

"Here's the way that I think you ought to handle the media this morning, Mr. Mayor. Tell the press what you think of me as an administrator, as a manager, and that you knew all about my past when you hired me; that you employed me because of my record of achievements before I came to work for the city—which ought to be the single most important criterion for employment—and not for my politics. Say that you are sorry that this amendment passed the House, and that you will do everything to see to it that it is defeated in the Senate. You will further resist any witch-hunts that will bring us a new wave of McCarthyism."

The mayor looked at me very intently for a time and said, "OK, Bob, I agree with that and I'll do it." He stood up and we walked across the hall to the Blue Room, which was so full of newspaper reporters and cameramen that the mayor and his entourage could just about squeeze in. One or two reporters buttonholed me on the way. "Look," I said, "I have nothing to say. We consider this a city problem and the mayor will speak for the city."

We crowded into the smoke-filled Blue Room. It may be hard to picture how regal John Lindsay could look in this mob. His tall, thin body, his piercing blue eyes, his love of himself in the public eye makes him appear totally at home in this kind of setting. He came upon the stage like an actor and started to speak his lines. There was a sudden quiet. He talked about the congressman's attack on me and repeated almost word for word what I had said to him a few minutes earlier, adding things of his own for emphasis. He was most decisive when he said that the city in no way was going to be badgered and that any threat to cut off antipoverty funds was simply a form of blackmail that he would not respond to. There were some questions from reporters, but Lindsay remained firm, saying he would have nothing more to say on the matter at this time.

Some weeks later Lindsay told me that the day after the congressman's attack, a delegation of ministers, many of them black, led by Milton Galamison together with Father Robert Kennedy of the Brooklyn diocese and Reverend Presley, came to see him on my behalf, telling him that they "would be very disturbed if the city responded in a way to hunt me as a result of the congressman's attacks." Lindsay said he assured them of his support and was pleased to have me in his administration.

In Washington, Shriver was saying that he was not about to cut off New York City's antipoverty funds. He indicated that OEO would carry on a routine investigation of the matter. Bill Haddad, who was the inspector general of OEO and whom I had met at Mobilization for Youth Day, sent Shriver a telegram: "Sarge, this is a time for balls, not for whimpering. Stand up on this one." Jay Rockefeller, who had worked with Shriver early on, also sent a telegram saying that he hoped he wouldn't waiver.

Many people from the academic community responded with telephone calls, telegrams, and letters to the mayor. The support I received was heartening and made me feel good. And Mike Sviridoff turned out to be right. I did keep my mouth shut and within a few days it all faded from the front pages; yet in an underneath sort of way the people in the city's manpower agency were still involved in it. Considering all the other problems he had, I felt bad in a way for being so much trouble to Lindsay. On balance, however, I think he came out of it quite well. Furthermore, Bobby Kennedy and Javits assured us that they would take care of eliminating the Bronx congressman's amendment from the antipoverty legislation.

I have dwelt on this incident with the congressman from the Bronx only to demonstrate how a person's life remains part of his employment record. The incidents, which had nothing to do with my job, had all occurred at least twenty-five years before; yet there they were in broad daylight as though they had happened yesterday. I have managed to come out of this sort of business pretty well, but I know of people whose lives have been destroyed by informers who have whispered the most negative kind of information into employers' ears.

My work as commissioner required my attendance at numerous

meetings of state and regional agencies where my experience as a negotiator was most useful. This was particularly true at the state meetings, where I made certain that the city received all the monies it was entitled to. The amount of manipulation and juggling that goes on in the various government agencies and jurisdictions can use up the full attention of any number of bureaucrats. I found myself increasingly occupied with this sort of operation and with budgets, until that was all I was doing. In many city meetings, particularly of neighborhood groups, I had to give information on how we were distributing resources. The commissioner's job was an endless political balancing act, and I learned that distributing and administering millions of dollars of public money may make you popular, but that such popularity mustn't be confused with anything personal. Even in our most plush years, there was never enough to satisfy all those who wanted and needed more. The result was that I ended up saying "no" more often than "yes," and more people were angry at me for rejection than loved me for saying "yes." If you need and want love, don't be an administrator.

The primary task of a commissioner was to process the paper and be in touch with funding sources and operators of the major program components. I felt as though I was a central telephone switching exchange, receiving enormous amounts of information, then processing it to be sent out to other interested parties. This kind of managing is important in all bureaucracies, but in larger institutions with thousands of employees it is absolutely critical. How sensitive a large system is to paperwork! In a small organization like a plant of two to three hundred people, processing a payroll or making operational changes is relatively easy. In an institution of 250,000 employees like the city of New York, it is horrendous. Once a piece of paper left my desk, to go to personnel, budget, or the federal government, for example, or to the comptroller's office for a salary adjustment, there was no way of knowing what happened to it. Because HRA was one of the first new superagencies, it was mired in a bureaucratic swamp. Some of the swamp, I think, was created by bureaucrats opposing the notion of superagencies. In a bureaucracy if a person is opposed to a decision, he may nullify it by obstacles.

Because of our problems, HRA acquired two expediters to work on payroll questions, budget modifications, renting space for new programs, and even such relatively minor problems as furniture and telephones. Tony and Alfred, as they were known, reminded me of the two blind mandolin players in the Durrenmatt play *The Visit*, who followed the heroine wherever she went to entertain her on demand. At an appropriate moment in our endless chain of meetings they would say in unison, "Now any problems you might be having on space or payroll, we will be glad to handle it for you." Tony, the short one, and Alfred, the tall one, would both smile and bow a little, not a real bow, just a little Japanese bend. Well, we had terrible troubles in HRA, all right, trying to get people on the payroll, acquire office furniture, or make a budget modification.

I stopped in Suerkin's Bar one night, a routine that would end each winter workday, and found my two friends. They saw me and pushed an opening at the bar so I could join them for a drink. They bought me one, I bought a round, then Tony bought, then Alfred, and so on. We are all kind of high now, so I ask them, "Hey fellows, how come some things go through smooth as silk and others just get stuck?" Tony starts to answer, but Alfred, annoyed, interrupts. He is right next to me at the bar. He looks me straight in the eye and spits as he exclaims, "If I don't like it, I don't approve it, and it don't go nowheres. Get it? It goes nowheres!" "Well," I say, "there is a process that we follow—" He interrupts again. "Well, so do my partner here and me. If we don't like what's going on, it just don't go, see?" Now, I would admit that these two fellows were in an unusual position, but what they said was true for so many civil servants. All they have to do is not pass the paper, and the machinery of government or any large bureaucracy just stops.

I began to analyze the paper passing that was eating up my time as commissioner. There was the daily mail to be answered, field reports to be read and responded to, memos on yesterday's horror stories, checking on new program developments. Then came meetings, meetings with individuals, groups, committees, task forces, monitors, evaluators, reporters, and people seeking funds, advice, or help. Together with the staff I prepared proposals to the federal government for the city's manpower programs, made reports on these programs, read and approved evaluations, investigated complaints and forwarded them to higher authorities when indicated. The sheer magnitude of all of this made it almost completely impersonal. What helped me from becoming just another impersonal bureaucrat was my intimate contact with the City-wide Coordinating Committee. I had developed a warm personal friendship with a number of black ministers who had grown up on the streets of the ghettoes but somehow managed not to be overwhelmed with rage. Many of them remain the most authentic people I know, because they never became superficial in their own struggles toward success. One of these ministers would drop in on me saying, "Robert, let me tell you what's happening with the folks out there." As I listened, I soon found myself thinking that lately my speech had become abstract about blacks and Puerto Ricans, referring to "them" as objects of our activities. These were my mother earth connections, the tie to what was real out there in the communities, a constant reminder of why I was there. I am indebted to these men for helping me to understand a little about being black in a white world.

As I have mentioned, in 1967 there was a major concern about riots. We knew that a big summer program that gave kids jobs could make the difference between burn and no-burn in the city. Lindsay was extremely anxious to keep the ghettoes quiet; if he was to have any chance at the White House he could not afford a major riot. I would split up the staff people in program teams, each of which would be responsible for developing different sections of the contract proposal, following the "fed regs," federal regulations. The program teams would have to come up with a total of forty-five thousand work sites. Based on our past experience, we might assign two thousand to the New York City Mission Society, a Protestant religious mission group working in New York ghettoes. Having agreed to give the Mission Society a certain number of slots, as the job openings were called, we were then confronted by the Jews and

Catholics who wanted equal treatment with the Mission Society. So began a gigantic balancing act of dividing the jobs between the city's many religious and ethnic groups, the awards most often having nothing to do with their ability to administer a meaningful employment or job-training program.

Out of L.B.J.'s New Society programs came a number of rituals for claiming antipoverty funds. One of these was for a community organization to prove poverty in the neighborhood, document it, and come up with a "proposal" for alleviating the condition. The poverty indicators that demonstrated the severity of neighborhood conditions were expressed not only by income (as reported in the census) but by crime, infant mortality, school dropout rates, and by lack of educational achievements. The spectacle of the various community groups vying for a piece of the pie before the city's antipoverty council was right out of the theater of the absurd. People would parade before the council to prove, for instance, that their group of Puerto Ricans in East Harlem was poorer than those East Harlem blacks.

"We have more crime than you and 20 percent more illegitimate births, more suicides. Why, we got the highest dropout rate in the country—our kids are the dumbest—they can't read their own names. So who's poorer?" Raymond Garcia yelled at Jessie Brown in an Anti-Poverty Council meeting at 1 A.M. with a hallful of people yawning at the endless speeches. The council did not get very involved in the fights over the distribution of the manpower training funds. This was the power of the commissioner's job, the ability to influence heavily the decision of "who got what," and I had devised our own mechanism for distribution. As a result, there was a steady stream of people coming to see me for more job slots, increased administrative funds, or just more money for a particular program.

While there was a feeling of power in this role, there was also a certain unease about it, stemming from a feeling that if my judgments about who got what did not fit the political scenario written at City Hall, my days would be numbered. I would give another seven hundred slots to the Department of Hospitals, and one thousand each to the twelve community action agencies. Another staff team would figure out in-kind distribution—the city's 10 percent share of the contract. Jane would sit with a calculator, determining the cost of the space the city contributed to the program. We calculated that a person supervising Neighborhood Youth Corps enrollees used a space eight by ten feet at $6.50 a square foot, or $520.00 of the city's contribution.

As I have said, when I first started in my job as Youth Corps director I would heed Judge Kohler's advice to use care in drawing up contracts. Little by little care faded as Bob Waldgreen of the regional office of the Department of Labor would call and ask, "Hey, Bob, how much more summer money can you use?"

"All you can give us" was an automatic response, since at that time I believed that poverty is best relieved with money.

If it was after 5 P.M., Waldgreen would say, "I know it's after the close of business and I hate to bother you, but how soon can you get a new proposal in here for another 1,500 slots?"

"How soon do you need it?"

"Well, Bob, you know it's almost the end of the fiscal year and we have $6 million of committed but unspent monies. We either allocate in the next two weeks or it goes back to budget."

"We'll take it and get the proposal to you in ten days."

And so it went. The staff would be back in on Saturday or maybe Sunday doing another modification or a new contract. We were making contracts now with such rapidity that we simply had no time to consider their content and, interestingly enough, neither did anyone on the other end. Waldgreen, a hard-working civil servant, would sit with us "after the close of business" to review the budgets. If they added up to the bottom line we were OK; if not, we just had to keep "fiddlin" until they did. After submitting a number of "weekend-drawn contracts," we quickly came to realize that nobody in the federal bureaucracy was interested in more than checking the budget numbers to see if they added up. If the numbers did, usually you were in. Another attitude of the feds toward New York City was that since it is not part of the real world anyhow, why bother with it. That resulted in their leaving us alone except when they went after a potential scandal, in which case they behaved like flies around a cow's ass on a hot day.

While the job of Youth Corps director proved to have less and less substance and more and more structure, my job as assistant commissioner of HRA turned out to be all structure, represented by nothing but passing more paper than I ever could have imagined. In the Youth Corps the budget was flexible enough to permit a certain amount of direct access to funds, but the funds I administered as a commissioner were channeled through the regular civil service organization. The result was that every act requiring approval became a challenge at beating the bureaucracy. For instance, the act of hiring someone required approximately seventeen steps. (It was not uncommon in the early HRA days for a person to be working for the city for six months without being paid because of a breakdown of bureaucratic paperwork.) If I made it through fifteen steps but goofed at fifteen, I had to return to "Go" and start over. A "budget modification" that required nothing more than a shift of money from paper clips to paper towels required twenty-seven steps.

The machinery of the New York City bureaucracy is basically a system of checks that has fed on itself for decades like weeds in an abandoned plantation. By now there are checks on checks that no one any longer understands. It is functional to the extent that it creates jobs for commissioners or agency heads, who are really political empire builders. The more people they have working in their departments, the bigger the agency, the more important the chief. No one seemed to be concerned whether the steps in the bureaucratic cycle were necessary at all. The whole operation was reminiscent of Ravel's *Bolero*, where the same theme is repeated over and over with no apparent purpose.

What little success I had running through the bureaucratic obstacle course was achieved by befriending the old hands who really ran the city anyhow. The chief finance officer of the Department of Social Services, Lou Henam, became a friend and adviser. He was part of the city's old fiscal club of Beame, Cavanaugh, and

Crotti, the accountants who actually ran the machinery of the city government. Whenever I found myself stuck in a bureaucratic swamp, I would ask Lou to lunch at Gastener's, another City Hall hangout. Around coffee the conversation would go something like, "Lou, the feds are saying that we overpaid the summer Neighborhood Youth Corps by anywhere from $50,000 to $500,000. You know what? I don't believe any of it. I think it's just another political attempt to embarrass the antipoverty effort."

Lou would chomp his cigar and say, "Sure we can check out duplicate checks. We just have to return the computer tapes, nothing to it."

"Lou, why don't we do it?"

He thinks, chomps and chomps some more. "Bob, they ain't interested in facts, only politics. They don't care whether anyone got two checks or not, they just want to embarrass the program. The agency is too big and it's getting too powerful. Some people just don't like it."

I plead with him to let me rerun the computer tapes. He says no, he has already been given his orders. "Nobody wants this stuff to look too good, y'know." I pay the check and we leave.

Mike Sviridoff had left to become vice president of the Ford Foundation.

The city's planning agency was developing an idea of creating a dozen multiservice skill-training centers that I was strongly opposed to and which would eventually cause me to resign. My own star was on the decline now, as events seemed to be demonstrating. Sometime after the screaming headlines about "millions stolen in antipoverty funds," little of which was ever substantiated, I was relieved of fiscal responsibility for the manpower programs. Actually, the Department of Social Services was the responsible payroll agency, but some city bureaucrats had become annoyed with me after what happened at a meeting in the office of the city investigator. His staff had found that some Youth Corps enrollees had changed their checks from $14.00 to $44.00 by tampering with the "1." It involved a few enrollees in Queens. I had made the mistake of laughing, saying, "I think that was pretty creative." Laughing among the grim can be a fatal mistake that I admit has caused me some grief in my worklife. The city investigator as well as others in the room became angry, demanding to know if I "condoned stealing." "C'mon, fellas, for God's sake, we are trying to keep these kids out of jail, not put them in. I will get the kids responsible to return the dough, OK?" From the lack of response in the room it was clear that I was alone. I did get agreement with the city investigator that if I would get the enrollees to pay back the money, they would not prosecute. But it was clear to me from that time on that there were a number of people with whom I no longer shared the same wavelength. I knew the distance between us was destined to grow.

My three years with the city were more of an experience with management by crisis than they were with managing crises. This was 1966 to 1969, not exactly a slumberous time in New York. The crises had many shapes and forms, as when groups from a black community in Brooklyn organized a sit-in at the regional office of the Department of Labor, demanding more summer jobs. Willard Wirtz was secretary of labor at the time. Upon hearing at his Washington office about the sit-in, he tried to reach the regional director in New York. The black kids from Brooklyn were occupying the regional director's office. When Wirtz called, to his surprise one of the youths from the sit-in answered the phone. Wirtz announced, "I am the secretary of labor, and I instruct you to immediately inform the regional director that I am on the phone!" The young man from Brooklyn replied, "Listen, mother, I don't give a fuck whose secretary you are, we want to talk to the boss," and bang, he hung up the phone. The mayor, who related the story to me, said that Willard had told him he had never been talked to that way in his life. It was also suggested that an apology from the black kid might help the city's relations with the Labor Department. Privately Lindsay and I both thought it quite funny, and we agreed that it was high time for Willard to hear such language. I assured Lindsay there would be no way to find the kid who insulted the secretary. Lindsay felt as I did but thought an apology would be helpful. Because I found it all very funny it was considered poor crisis management on my part, as some felt I was not concerned enough about the secretary of labor's feelings toward the city of New York. They were probably right.

In my role as commissioner, one of my earliest appointments was a black man I made director of the Youth Corps. He had grown up in a poor family of seven kids, the only one who "made it," having graduated from college. We started out being pretty good friends, and with many of our central office staffers we would sit around "after the close of business" and schmooze about what was happening in the programs. I asked him one day, "How come you made it out of the slums?"

He looked at me quizzically, laughed a kind of nervous giggle. "I just got my ass out of there."

"Well, I just don't believe that. What was the difference between you and the rest of your family? What happened to you that sent you on another road?"

He grew more serious, pondered the question. "Well, I learned to read. I was a shy kid and spent a lot of time alone. Started reading comic books and gradually began reading other things. When I went to school there were teachers who, seeing I could read, encouraged me, so that eventually I got in the air force and I was outa the ghetto and on my way."

How some people manage to make it out of the nightmares of abject poverty has always been of interest to me. We know so much more about sickness than we do about health because of the psychological interest in pathology. My research of those who made it out of poverty indicates a presence of at least one person who cared. Caring meant encouragement, like simply saying, "Yes, you can learn to read"—and knowing how to read is the key to all other learning.

Blacks were pressing hard for power through authority, and I knew my stay in the commissioner's job would not be a long one. Sometime later there would be a demonstration at City Hall demanding more jobs. I had specifically instructed Youth Corps personnel not to get involved in that sort of activity, and they had assured me they would not. I found they were not telling the truth. The Youth Corps staff members said they would not participate in the demonstration outside of City Hall, but on the six o'clock television news, there they were, howling like a bunch of banshees from the top of some cars that some poor guys happened to park there. I felt embarrassed by the whole incident because it implied that as a manager I was unable to control my subordinates. I was fearful that the mayor would be annoyed. As it turned out, I saw Lindsay that night at one of the many Youth Corps summer theater performances we both seemed to be attending pretty regularly. I managed to talk with him about the day's events at City Hall. (Lindsay was always surrounded by celebrity-followers, which made conversation in public almost impossible.) We agreed that the Youth Corps demonstration was not helping our efforts to increase congressional support for summer youth jobs. What to do about the demonstrations? I wanted to fire my whole gang, for I felt personally betrayed. The trouble was they were all black and I was white. "No," Lindsay said, "that will just make them martyrs, so we won't oblige." We managed to agree that they were all irresponsible and could not be trusted. We would not respond precipitously, for it would only increase tensions in the black communities. Later, as I talked with some of those who had participated in the City Hall caper, I knew our friendship, or more important, our trust, was over. We now talked past each other, I as a white man to black subordinates instead of to friends.

As the civil rights movement of the sixties was erupting, there were many instant radicals who would make their appearances in demonstrations, protests, neighborhood groups, or in public meetings. A number of blacks were suddenly calling themselves Black Panthers and doing a lot of loud talking. They had been bitten by a kind of sudden radicalism that I found somewhat strange. The radicalism I knew in my youth was usually arrived at after a long, tough ideological journey through the literature, debate, arguments, and discussions. This new radicalism surprised me, for the converts expected to be supported by the institution that they had under attack. They expected their attacks to be forgiven, and even thought they ought to be promoted for being revolutionary. There was a kind of cooptation in all this that I never quite understood. The radicals I knew expected nothing but a hard kick in the ass from the institutions they attacked—and that's just what they got.

I had better not leave the impression that the whole machinery of the city government was involved in crisis managing. Not at all. Most civil servants do whatever little routines they have worked out for themselves, not caring much about the "big crisis issues." So while life in the city's manpower agency was full of emergencies, the civil service clerks continued to do their nine-to-five minimum. What occupied their time? Well, for example, someone disturbed by our inability to find anything in the files came up with the following system.

March 19, 1966
MEMORANDUM

Mr. Schrank's general file is composed of two divisions: Neighborhood Youth Corps and Economic Opportunity Committee. There have (and will be) instances when a file folder (or folders) must be removed for reference, information, calculation, et al., by one or more employees of Central Control, Economic Opportunity Committee, or (in rare instances) officials and individuals not of Central Control.

To overcome this problem, two lists of cards have been prepared—yellow and blue. The yellow cards represent the Neighborhood Youth Corps file, and the blue the Economic Opportunity Committee. Each folder has a card counterpart. Whenever you deem it necessary to remove a folder, please notify the keeper of the files of this action. He will thereupon note on the corresponding card that you have it in your possession and the date you have taken it. When you wish to restore it to the file, please put it on his desk (NOT BACK IN THE FILE). He will remove your name and date from the card and return the folder to its original position. This procedure would act as an infallible tracer for all folders in transit, as well as proving informative to Mr. Schrank and Jane for pinpointing their locations promptly if the keeper of the files is not in the office.

Another fine example of this sort of document was generated when HRA's committee on sit-ins and demonstrations proposed to institutionalize protest by creating rules for protection from it.

KEY TACTIC                                              CONFIDENTIAL
In cases of office area infiltration, once the demonstrators become evident, Task Force members are responsible for stemming further infiltration by implementing the one-entry circulation system described in Section II. Task Force members must also meet the infiltrators where they are, determine who they are and what their grievance is, and encourage them to regroup in the Conference Room container area until discussions can be arranged.

THE BASIC GROUND RULE
The basic ground rule is that groups may occupy the Conference Room and immediately adjacent areas (see Appendix) on the understanding that there will be no interference with office services and operations. An obvious corollary is that only a portion of a massive demonstration group may remain on the premises, that portion being determined by how many can safely occupy the Conference Room container area without creating a fire hazard or violating a Buildings Department regulation.

Consequently, upon an initial refusal to regroup in the Conference Room container area, infiltrators are advised that their office area activities may precipitate a disruption of office operations and services. While infiltrators must be informed that their problems or grievances can be aired by a smaller delegation from the demonstrators, until this smaller delegation is chosen by the demonstrators and a mutually agreeable time can be set for discussions, all demonstrators must understand that they will have to remain together in the Conference Room container area.

ENFORCEMENT OF GROUND RULES
As can be seen, up to this point the enforcement of ground rules rests primarily on a keen sense of timing and patience, on the artful persuasiveness and firm diplomacy of the Task Force members. All this is, of course, freely counterpointed upon the degree of sophistication of the demonstrating group's own leadership and upon the fluid responsiveness or the sharp reactions of the demonstrators to the climate of attitudes which the Task Force members project.

Once when there was a sit-in on the fifth floor, Jessie Green, the black leader of a Harlem group of tenants, let a bunch of chickens loose in a commissioner's office on the tenth floor. The chickens went clucking around, flying over the furniture while the commissioner kept telling Green that "men of goodwill can always find a way to agree." Green just laughed; he was not at all interested in goodwill, only in program money.

This is what an antipoverty workplace of the sixties was like. In the middle of crises and chaos it turns out that we were expected to develop meaningful programs for ghetto youth. There simply never was the time or space enough to think through meaningful programs for ghetto youth. For the young people in the Neighborhood Youth Corps, the need for a challenging work experience is absolutely critical. If we enforce the same kind of nonexperience that has dominated their lives, we confirm their negative self-image. What they desperately need is a work experience that spurs them to some kind of personal growth. If that has not occurred, it is a sign that nothing has happened, and that nothing will change.

Like most workers, the enrollees in the Neighborhood Youth Corps, or in any youth work experience program, need job orientation that helps them understand the product of the work they are assigned to, whether it be repairing street potholes or a job in a hospital, a data-processing operation, or an air traffic control center. Many of the jobs assigned black and Puerto Rican youth involved simple repetitive tasks with no challenge and therefore no learning. A second critical ingredient for a successful youth work program is the supervision. Supervisors need to have a fierce commitment of support to these young people in order for them to gain some confidence in themselves. Support does not mean control; it means challenging them, showing how, and then getting out of the way.

Probably the single most important thing I learned from the training and employment programs of the sixties was that people unable to read at a fifth grade level are not able to take advantage of any skill-training program. Some people have argued that there are jobs that require no reading. That may now only be true for stoop labor, picking vegetables in a migrant camp. Any decent job that offers a challenge as well as an opportunity requires reading of some kind of instruction. Nothing will make a job dead-end and dumb like the inability to read and comprehend directions.

At the end of all work experience programs like the Neighborhood Youth Corps there should be a job placement potential. I say potential because I know of no way, short of the government's guaranteeing everyone a job, that a training program can assure all of its graduates placement. As commissioner I was able to arrange deals with a few large employers to guarantee a certain number of jobs for our graduates and to develop training programs for them. We had such a program in training butchers for a supermarket chain; upon the completion of training, the enrollee joined the union and went to work at union scale. Clearly that is the best of all worlds. But what about those that we could not place? It was becoming clear again that in a free, open labor market we could not guarantee placement at the end of training. Trying to understand who gets hired and who is unemployed in New York City taught me much about the irrationality of the labor market. It is ludicrous to try to run a college, a vocational school, or an employment training program on the basis of what the job market will be buying in six months, a year, or four years from the start of learning.

In my conversations with major employers in New York, I found that each employment projection was couched in "ifs"—if our business continues to grow, if the market holds, if the unions don't hit us too hard, if our competition does not beat us—if, if, if. Employers are reluctant to make commitments because they want to operate in the open market. In addition, many employers are aware that the majority of the people who participate in the employment training programs are minorities. In spite of some progress, many companies, particularly in the financial district, have done very little to date to increase minority representation in their work force.

What to do about job training that could not guarantee employment? I tried to run the city's job-experience and skill-training programs on the assumption that learning a skill or successfully completing a work task that resulted in a felt sense of "I can do it" might be significant in itself for the person, even if at the end there was not a job waiting. Is it possible to structure the learning itself as a useful experience?

The small, sort of private butcher program success that I have mentioned occurred when we were able to find in one of the institutions where we were training our people a person in authority who had some real interest in the development of good skill development programs. An outstanding example of this was a program Helen developed at Harlem Hospital. She managed to locate a doctor who was the chief of obstetrics at the hospital and who was anxious to develop a program to train young black women as obstetrical aides. Careful planning of recruitment, intake, orientation, training, curriculum, and placement made the program a real success story for the dozens of young black women who graduated. In contrast to our doctor of obstetrics at Harlem Hospital, most city supervisory employees just did not want to be "bothered" with our enrollees, saying, "It's not our responsibility, and anyhow who is going to pay us for the extra work?" These supervisors, like so many people who do routine jobs, had spent years developing a way of doing the least amount of work necessary. Now here were some "bleeding hearts" crying over some poor black and Puerto Rican kids. "Imagine expecting us just to help 'these people.' They must be kidding!" This is a generalization, of course, yet it reflects many of our job development experiences in city agencies.

Because the learning element of a training program has to do with content and not structure, the emphasis on the program numbers tends to negate the most critical element. Moving from Mobilization for Youth to the commissioner's job taught me an important lesson about the impact of magnitudes on program content. In both of these jobs I was dealing with very similar problems. It was a personal experience of not just "small is beautiful," but "small may work where large does not." MFY had about six hundred enrollees and a staff of sixty. At HRA we had anywhere from fifteen thousand to fifty thousand enrollees and a staff of about two thousand. At MFY I knew many staff and enrollees personally. I felt I could have some influence on what went on within the program and was also able to receive rapid feedback on how the program was functioning—its strengths, its weaknesses—so that we could easily take corrective action. It was not at all like that in the commissioner's job. There the magnitudes were so great as to drown out most programmatic concerns. Interest in program content may be directly correlated to a program's magnitude, that is, the larger the program mass, the less the interest in or concern with its content.

This sort of thing probably happens when the technical problems involved in running a large-scale institution become all-consuming and demanding. The result is a complete absorption in the structural problems of outreach, recruitment, hiring, personnel practice, salary scales, discipline, work conditions, reporting to higher-ups, organizational charts, and so on and on. Problems relevant to the content—what is really happening with the work-experience, skill-training, job-training, or remedial classes—tend to get lost because there is no simple numerical way of reporting the experience itself. At HRA we were preoccupied with issues of program leadership, which was primarily a division of the political pie based on *how many* people were recruited, dropped out, trained, completed, and placed. There was little or no concern for the content of any of the activities. Only in a few minor instances, sort of show-case efforts, did we manage to develop a primary concern with the program content.

I think I was generally considered to be a successful commissioner. It was, unfortunately, for the wrong reasons. It was not for running a program of any great content but rather because I made the numbers look good by recruiting enough people to fill all the training slots allocated to the city. With the OK of my superiors and the mayor, we made ourselves appear even better by overspending the allocated monies. That was passed off as both evidence of need and a demonstration of our capability to administer a large program effort. We were the General Motors of employment training.

The lack of concern or interest in program content that I have been discussing was also reinforced by the bureaucratic Washington funding sources, the Department of Labor and OEO. They visited the city fairly often to ask about the same structural problems: How many people had been recruited? How long did they stay? How many were placed? We had a good staff that had learned how to answer all those questions. As time went on, the answers seemed to be less and less related to anything real. I now have a hunch that much government data that are generated by participating local agencies are not at all reliable. The operating institutions simply learn how to make the data fit the guidelines, and that is what the Washington agencies are getting.

In my years as commissioner, hardly anyone that I can remember in an official capacity from the federal, state, or the other city agencies ever inquired much, if at all, about what went on inside our programs. There was simply little or no interest or concern for the nature or content of our outreach or orientation, our remedial classes, our training, how they were run, and, most important, what the enrollees had learned. The interest in numbers was reinforced almost daily, for example when I would casually meet the mayor or other city officials. "I hear you are doing a great job filling all those training slots; that's wonderful." It was clear to me that quantification was firmly in the saddle, riding roughshod over most things substantive. The longer I remained as commissioner, the more I myself experienced a loss of interest in program content. Meaningful work sites, good training programs were becoming a sort of private agenda that Susan, Jane, and I would talk about in our schmooze time, but with a declining conviction that anyone else really cared.

I have explained about my experiences with nonwork as a way of life on the job in my early employment. This notion was substantially reinforced during my employment with the city. At first I was surprised at how skillful people were in using up the time of day and yet producing so little. I have now become intrigued with the notion that most of us want a job with security, as in the military; we want good pay and maximum benefits, tenure and seniority, but there seems to be a powerful inclination to do as little work as possible. If we have job security and basic needs are being met, do we lose our motivation to work? My experience has given rise to serious doubts regarding humans' intrinsic desire to work at all.

Civil service in some ways may epitomize this human desire to have a job as security, and yet do the minimum amount of work permissible. With the exception of a few creative people who have managed to find or develop some interest in the work they do, I believe the desire to have a job and do as little work as necessary may be far more universal than is generally acknowledged. Warren Bennis, in discussing productivity and work motivation in a March '77 *Wall Street Journal* article, said,

There are a host of institutions that have been ignored by most of the economic game plans we have seen in the last several years, institutions that are incapable of having any significant rise in productivity. I would include such organizations as universities, hospitals, welfare agencies, local and state government, some service areas, and all cultural activities—museums, symphony orchestras, ballet companies, and so on. These public sector institutions are for the most part very badly managed. I am making no excuse for them except that I don't think it has been sufficiently recognized that they are not productive and cannot be run exactly like large and efficient productive industries.

I suspect that Bennis's view might be expanded to include a large segment of the work force's service sector, or all those whose productivity is not, or cannot be, measured. While I tend to agree with Bennis, he loses sight of the tools of retribution in the hands of manufacturing managers, tools that are nonexistent in the service sector. There workers have little or nothing to fear, since, if New York is any example, a civil servant is simply never fired. What I have said about the punitive nature of schooling and work preparation in our society is relevant to this problem. Experience makes me wonder whether humans will in fact work at all if we remove the punitive consequences of not working. The evidence in support of this notion continues to grow. Increasingly earlier retirement, unemployment insurance time, and, lastly, the staggering increases in income transfer payments in the last ten years are added evidence for this argument. These payments went from $79.9 billion in 1970 to $196.2 billion in 1976. That is a lot of people on a free lunch. It is projected that this figure will rise by 340 percent in one decade. How much of this can the economy tolerate?

In a city like New York, social and economic problems are so enormous that they can only be dealt with by quantifying them. When this quantification is applied to service jobs, it has little or no meaning. How many people are occupying beds and how many nurses or aides are employed in a hospital may say little or nothing about the quality of the care. The lack of quality-control measure in the service sector makes it difficult to hold people accountable for their productivity. As commissioner, what could I do about quality or productivity in a program that had hundreds of civil servants who looked upon me as a transitory phenomenon? There was a small group of us who worked in the "central downtown" office who would spend many hours thinking, planning, scheming, trying to get some meaning into this sprawling mass of programs involving thousands of people. We thought, for instance, that if we created an open administrative atmosphere, it would be conducive to learning and creativity. We felt that on the city office level we had a pretty good participative model of operations. There was a formal participative coordinating organization; but aside from that, we went out of our way in our everyday, casual, informal contacts with the operating agencies to make them part of the decision-making process. It worked as well as one could expect on the top, yet it just did not seem to penetrate to those we thought might benefit the most—the black and Puerto Rican program participants.

There were seminars, meetings, and training sessions for staff in the various participating agencies, yet for the most part they had little or no impact on the lower operating levels, which in many cases had very different agenda. This was best expressed by Henry Timmy, a black instructor in one of the skill-training centers. Henry was over six feet, an ex-professional basketball player who grew up on the streets of Brooklyn and had what he liked to call a Ph.D. in streetology. We were having a drink one day at Suerkin's. "Schrank," he said, "it's easy for white people like you who sit on your ass in your comfortable downtown office to tell us who are out here on the ghetto streets that we ought to be democratic and participatory, but you know you don't know shit about this street world. If you're not tough out here, you know what? The people you is trying to help are gonna eat you up alive. Yeah, they'll strip your ass and eat you alive. So you just keep your nice ideas down there, and when I get a job down there in your nifty office, I'll try democracy out here. You know what? It ain't gonna work cause we ain't got nothing to be democratic with or about. We got nothing but poors to share. You want some, come join us. We got to keep discipline. That's the most important thing." I tried to answer because I did not want to accept Henry's cynicism, yet there was a part of me that was now beginning to say that he was right. Life in the ghetto becomes so infected with daily violence that it may be terribly naive to think that an open, participatory organizational model could survive there.

Because we worked hard, most of the regular civil servants thought people like me were nuts. I remember a city finance department employee whom I berated for not pitching in to help us meet a payroll. He pointed to a series of pictures of former commissioners that hung in the corridors. "Don't get so excited, Schrank. See all those fellows in the pictures. I was here before any of them came. They are all gone now, and I'm still here." It was a cold New York winter night; I put on my hat and coat and left wondering what all the sleepless nights worrying about program content were for, when all anyone seemed to care about was the container.

The commissioner's job helped further my understanding of the differences between a job and the work performed. Jobs are concerned with how society orders status. A professional, a white-collar worker is perceived as superior to a manual worker. This is unrelated to any actual significance of the nonmanual work itself; rather, it is the freedom to work one's own will and never face a quota that makes white-collar jobs so much more attractive. This may be the reason that productivity-type jobs are declining in many new areas of the labor force. The greatest inequality is found between the new helping professions and the old in the distribution of labor and its benefits. Nineteenth-century factory work with its prisonlike rules permitted little or no freedom. Unrest will probably continue in the factory until workers find ways to gain for themselves some of the amenities found in the professions.

# Sociologist

I have now finished my graduate education, have earned a Ph.D., and sometimes I consider myself a sociologist. Though there are times I prefer to be thought of as a machinist or plumber, I now have a job at the Ford Foundation, where my responsibilities include monitoring and evaluation of ongoing programs as well as making recommendations for new funding. I work with a community development organization, and I am concerned with the problems of employment and training of blue-collar workers, and problems of the workplace, in a program now called the "Quality of Worklife." Sometimes my opinions are sought by other foundations or government agencies, requiring me to participate in meetings or conferences that may lead to recommendations for policy actions.

As an employee of the Ford Foundation, I work in a most beautiful building with a huge interior garden, two dining areas, a library, and every conceivable resource I might need for my work. There is no noise or dust and no harmful substances. I have a great amount of freedom to do my work, which is reading, writing, conferring, attending conferences and meetings, meetings, meetings. If there is a workplace heaven, I am now in it. And what do you know! I have heard a few people here, just a few, complain for one reason or another about how "lousy this place is." When pressed why— "Oh, it's very dull" or "Nobody tells you what to do" or "There is no accountability."

"Have you ever worked anywhere else?" I ask.

"Oh yes."

"Is it better or worse?"

"Oh, I don't know."

"In other words, it's just a feeling that you have. You're not comparing it to some other job?"

"No, not really, it's just this place." Here is a workplace where autonomy, creativity, even a certain independence is possible, yet there are a few people I know who simply cannot, or are not interested enough to, respond to that.

"Compared to what?" began to ring in my head like some dumb tune you hear and go around humming until it feels as though you will go berserk. "Compared to what other workplace, compared to what?" That was a key element in understanding how people perceive a workplace.

This place seems wonderful compared to my memory of the furniture factory, the plumbing shop, the machine shop, or of giving out leaflets at a plant gate at 6 A.M. on a bitter cold morning—all this relevant information is stored in my head. In a subconscious way, I compare experiences. It is as though I have a miniature slide projector in my head that flashes comparative pictures. If Henry Abelman tells me this place is boring, that triggers a mental switch that pulls out the slide tray indexed "Boredom." I see the dowel machine in the furniture factory, repetitive lathe operations, assembly lines, punch presses, picking beans, and I wonder, what does Henry's "boredom index" look like? We talk about his life, what he would really like to do, and what emerges is that he is in a general state of boredom; the job, like most everything else, is boring. "Compared to what" might be called each person's experiencing bank. The experience or being of the beholder is the filter through which all perceptions pass. The recognition of this has been most helpful to me in trying to understand how people react to their own workplaces, as well as how observers perceive other people's workplaces.

In many ways, my job at The Ford Foundation permits me to continue observing, writing, and thinking about the workplace issues that I have been involved with for so much of my life. My interest is now expressed in my concerns with the work environment, work motivation, productivity, collective bargaining, and occupational health and safety. There is also a more general question of the quality of work life, a merger of the concerns of physical environmentalists, behavioral scientists, and humanists, or, in the broadest sense, how society organizes itself to get its work done. I spend a considerable amount of time traveling and looking at experiments concerned with autonomy, participation in decision making, and the general improvement of life at the workplace. Here I am being well paid to do intellectual work in an area in which I have had a lifetime of interest. Can I be tired or indifferent? Bored? Of course not, because I now have a real opportunity to explore possible alternative ways of organizing work.

I made a memorable trip to Europe some years ago with a group of people to look at experiments in alternative work organizations. We traveled to Sweden, Holland, France, Italy, and Israel. The purpose of the trip was to get an overview of what was happening in workplace experiments and worker participation in Europe and Israel and to see what, if any, implications there were for the United States. Upon arrival at a company that was designated in our itinerary as an experimental site, we would inevitably be taken to a conference room for a briefing by our hosts. The briefing generally consisted of a detailed explanation of the experiment and its context.

One of the people on this trip was Professor Eli Ginzberg, of Columbia University. At each one of the briefings at the plants we visited, he would ask the same question. "What made you undertake this work experiment?" Because the answers were universally similar, I will try to paraphrase them.

At the time of our European trip, unemployment was running at about one-half of 1 percent to 1 percent. The answer went about like this. "In a tight labor market with little or no unemployment, we are having trouble recruiting local people to do repetitive factory type work. Our people [meaning native Swedes, Germans, Frenchmen, or Israelis], given an option, choose not to do factory work. Our people seem to have a clear preference for white-collar jobs. Second, and probably because of the tight labor market, we have increasing problems of absenteeism, particularly on Fridays and Mondays. People decide they don't feel like working, they just do not show up. Now, how can you run a factory under those conditions?"

The point of Ginsberg's question was to help us focus on why in the first place these companies had decided to do work experiments. What problems were they addressing? Was it a concern for how work is organized, or an interest in industrial democracy or in developing an autonomous and creative work force? Or was it to increase productivity through increased worker motivation or by finding better ways of doing the job, or to get better quality control? Perhaps a little of each? It was never quite clear what the companies doing the experiments were trying to get at. I am not even sure they knew themselves. It was as if there were some general problems of a growing resistance to repetitive work, of increasing absenteeism, of some decline in quality control and productivity, which were stimulating a look at some other way to organize how the job gets done. Why not try other work arrangements that might solve some of these problems? It is the application of the Thomas Edison research technique to a social problem. Keep trying different things until you stumble on something that works. Edison kept a notebook of all the things that did not work so he would not repeat unsuccessful experiments. That can be an effective way of solving technical problems, but I have strong doubts about its effectiveness in dealing with social issues because they lack the stability and specificity of technical problems. The Swedes were discovering that their vast generous welfare system had become an alternative to work, that people could do as well economically if they were sick and stayed home as if they had gone to work. For people who do dumb jobs, the option of welfare and not working becomes quite attractive.

Our visit to the Swedish Saab auto plant had special significance. Some years later we would fund a program that sent six auto workers from Detroit to work at Saab to experience a new way of organizing engine assembly. When we arrived at the Saab plant at Södertälje, we were taken to the conference room for a thorough briefing on the autonomous engine assembly group. We asked our usual questions, "Why did you do it? What are the results? Is there any difference in costs or other comparisons between the traditional and autonomous engine assembly? How do the workers feel about the experiment? How much participation of workers was there in setting up the experiment?''

The answers were again somewhat vague. "Swedes don't want to work on assembly lines. Finns, Yugoslavs, and Portuguese are doing this kind of work in our plants. There is little or no difference in costs between autonomous and traditional engine assembly. There is some improvement in quality control. There was consultation with the leaders of the Metal Workers Union and the works council, but not with the workers directly involved.''

"Would you call it a success?''

"No, not yet, it is too early.''

Following the briefing, we were taken on a tour of the plant. The truck assembly floor at Saab struck me as a most cheerful place, a riot of bright red, green, yellow, orange, and white. It was exceptionally clean for an assembly plant, but most of all I was struck by its spaciousness. There was plenty of room for the people to move around the truck chassis as they came down the line, making them easily accessible.

One of the people on our visiting team leaned over to me and said, "Gee whiz, this noise is terrible. I don't know how these people can stand this all day. I have a headache already.''

I did not think the noise level was bad at all. "Hey, have you ever been in a metal-stamping plant?''

"No, what's that?''

I explained, "It's where punch presses, machines that bang out metal being formed over dies, make an incessant pounding, triphammer noise like dozens of hammers beating steel drums.'' No, he had never heard that. Here comes the old jingle, "This is lousy compared to what?'' Compared to a university office or a library, it was terrible.

Traditional assembly is a linear operation in which the product usually moves down a conveyer that intermittently stops while people add parts or components along the conveyer. The length of the stop is called the cycle. The autonomous engine assembly at Saab was done in semicircular bays that came off the regular assembly line. Two women assigned to each bay did the final assembly of a small Saab engine and then sent it on to the test room. The crankshaft, pistons, and connecting rods—the heavy work—had been installed in the engine blocks before they came off the line to go into the bays for completion of the finished engine.

A couple of us from the visiting group went over to one of the engine assembly bays. There were two women, both Finns, putting parts on the engine block, which was up about three feet from the floor, riding on a well-balanced carriage that permitted them to flip the engine around 180 degrees with very little effort. What Saab had called the "autonomous work group" turned out to be two women.

One of the women, a classic Finnish blonde and most beautiful, was receiving an inordinate amount of attention, though she spoke little or no English. Luckily some of the other women did.

"How long do you have to assemble one of these engines?"

"Forty-five minutes."

"What happens if you fall behind?"

"Well, you try to make it up."

"What is your biggest problem?"

"Bad parts, parts that don't fit properly, or are defective."

"How do you feel about testing your own engines? How do you like assembling a whole engine?"

"It's OK, I guess."

"Did you ever work on the regular line?"

"Yes, that was OK too." The women were not very interested in this conversation. They were, if anything, indifferent, and did not seem to do their work with much enthusiasm. We were told that on weekends they rushed back to Finland, to return only on Sunday night. With unemployment high in Finland, they were unable to find work there. As we observed the women, they worked along at a pretty good pace. The "autonomous assemblers" had the option of putting the engine together in a variety of different sequences. This meant they could vary the order in which they assembled at least some parts of the engine, others having to go in a fixed sequence. The forty-five minutes allowed to assemble an engine turned out to be a pretty tight schedule that required considerable attention or concentration and did not permit the schmoozing or fooling around that seemed to me more common in American assembly plants. The level of "fooling around" in European plants compared to the United States has always struck me as being considerably lower.

Because the Finns spoke such poor English, at times we needed a translator, which just added to what was an already awkward situation. "How do you like this group assembly compared to the regular line?"

"I don't know, I never worked on the regular line."

"Do you like this work?"

"Yes, it's OK. It's a job and that's what I need." Not very enthusiastic. Some of this may have simply been Scandinavian coolness and distance, and yet I felt that the women assemblers were saying that this was just another kind of assembly line with a forty-five-minute cycle. This was not an autonomous work group in which there might have been a kind of interaction that could create a work community. If it were a truly autonomous group, they could create many varieties of interaction while they worked. That interaction could prove to be far more interesting than the work itself.

My impression of the two-person assembly team was that it required considerably more attention for quality control than the traditional line. The company said this was a real challenge to the employees. I was wondering, if I assembled 100 or 200, maybe 400 engines, what would the challenge be? A challenge is the ability to overcome a novel problem. After that the process becomes routine, the challenge or novelty has disappeared. Now the need for attention is no longer interesting. It is an attention that is just as fatiguing because it is thoroughly repetitive.

Much of what Herzberg calls "work enrichment" is simply the addition of tasks that require an increased amount of attention. This kind of increased attention may not be at all enriching; on the contrary, it may add to fatigue and boredom—as when the cycle on an assembly line is stretched out. It is still endlessly repetitious. The requirement of more attention does not in and of itself lead to a more meaningful experience.

How workers respond to increased attention requirements is a very individual reaction. Some people say they like to concentrate on what they are doing because it makes the time go faster. Others say they do not care to concentrate at all but prefer to think about other things while they are working. The two-person, forty-five-minute-cycle team assembly at Saab was some kind of an attempt to alter the traditional assembly line, yet I am not sure what the new system actually was. It was not one consisting of autonomous groups. Since the operating workers had little or no input in setting it up, it was not one involving worker participation in decision making.

When our group left Saab, we had a long discussion about what was going on there. From the varying opinions of our group, it occurred to me that a better way to try to learn what was going on in these work experiments was to have workers from a traditionally organized plant come to work in the experimental workplace. In my travels to various workplaces, I had been struck with the universal language of work, particularly manual work. Given only the additional knowledge of the metric system, I could have easily run machine tools in foreign countries. This kind of work has much of the universal language of music. It is with that universality in mind that the idea of having workers from one country visit another to experience new work arrangements was born. As part of the visiting group, they would have a participant-observer along to record their reactions to the new way of working. The idea of a workers' exchange program eventually led to four different groups of people from the United States going to work in Europe.

One of these groups consisted of six auto workers from Detroit, two men and four women, who went to Södertälje in Sweden to spend a month working in the Saab plant. Unfortunately, because of an excessive amount of public relations activity, the experience tended to be very cloudy. The press reports of the experience of the Americans at Saab tended to distort their view of workplace experiments in general instead of sticking to what actually happened at Saab. In retrospect, the Saab experiment was a poor choice for the American workers to participate in. As I indicated, the team engine assembly was not an autonomous work group, and it was a mistake to treat it as such. As it turned out, the auto workers who went to Saab gave a good description of the two-person assembly team and found it not much better, and in some ways worse, than the traditional line. The mistake of the planners, including myself, was in not realizing that what was going on at Saab was not an autonomous work group but rather a final, long-cycle, team engine assembly. The six American workers who went to Saab were probably more insightful in their analysis than we were in the planning effort.

When our group visited the Philips Electric Company plant in Eindhoven, Holland, we got a chance to see a real autonomous work group in action. This plant manufactures light bulbs and television sets. We traveled from Amsterdam to Eindhoven by train, and we had a rare opportunity to see the Dutch countryside ablaze with tulips. At the plant we were given the usual conference room briefing by the plant manager, personnel director, and the chief of the television production division. Ginzberg asked his questions and the answer was somewhat evasive—"We want to try some other way to assemble television sets."

This plant was much older than the Saab plant, more like some of our old New England textile mills. We were first taken to a traditional television assembly, with its conveyer moving the sets along in about a seven-minute cycle. Women workers along this line seemed relaxed, carrying on various conversations while they did their work. In contrast to Saab, the assembly floor here was crowded, with little or no extra room to move around. This kind of crowding can be oppressive for the people working there, since it is difficult to get away from the work area.

We were then escorted to the experimental workplace. Here, in the middle of a crowded room with cartons of parts, testing tables, and television chassis was a large round table. About seven or eight people sat around it assembling television sets. The whole table top turned, permitting each unit to be moved on to the next person. One of the workers explained how they would meet at the start of the shift to decide how they would work that day. "We can decide to have each person assemble a whole television set or work on whatever cycle we agree to—five minutes or thirty minutes. As long as we make our daily quota of sets we are OK." The manager added, "We expect them to do a specific number of sets a day and they usually do a little better than expected. Each one of the group-assembly employees has been so well trained he can assemble and test an entire television set. This training is expensive for the company, and many of the employees have learned enough about television to be able to open their own repair businesses on the side." As I talked with people, I was impressed with their feeling of pride in being part of an experimental group, as well as with their knowledge of the work.

The Eindhoven experiment was far closer to what I would conceive of as an autonomous work group than the two-person team assembly at the Saab plant. Not only did they decide how they would assemble television sets each day, but if group members were absent, those present assumed responsibility for achieving the production quotas, and deciding how to proceed with the smaller group. They were "autonomous" within the limits of their responsibility to assemble a certain number of sets per shift. Unlike Saab, where new employees were recruited for the team engine assembly, at Philips employees from the traditional assembly line volunteered for group assembly. Obviously there was a self-selection of people who had some interest in working as an autonomous group.

I was quite enthusiastic about it and that night back in the hotel in Amsterdam, I read the material that Philips had given us about the work experiment. I was surprised to learn that this workplace experiment had been going on for years. I was curious to learn why the experiment had not been expanded to include larger segments of the Eindhoven plant or the other Philips plants around the world. Some time later I had occasion to talk with one of the Eindhoven managers, and I asked him, "Are the production costs for the autonomous work group greater than the traditional assembly line?" No, in fact it was about the same, a little slower, but yielded much better quality control and almost zero rejects. Why hadn't it been expanded at Eindhoven or in other Philips plants? He seemed reluctant to answer, but I continued to press him. After some schmoozing and drinking, he finally said, "Well, the fact is we would have a foremen's strike on our hands if we tried to expand the autonomous work group. You know, unlike plants in the United States, our foremen are well organized. Lower management levels are extremely threatened by this sort of thing. After all, it makes them superfluous."

Whether that is the explanation for why Philips has done so little to expand or diffuse the autonomous work group concept, I do not know, but it remains a tiny fragment of a very large company. This seems to be the case with experimental workplaces in a number of major corporations. Some time later I would learn of some work experiments at General Electric that also eliminated first-line supervisors. The experiments were considered by both the company and union observers as quite successful in giving workers greater autonomy and saving costs through improved quality control, much like the Eindhoven experiments. Yet G.E. discontinued the experiments without much explanation to anyone. One union official, who was closely involved through his members, said that in his opinion the work experiments at G.E. were discontinued because of an underlying fear, mostly from middle management, that the company would lose control of the workplace.

As I look around at the experiments in work reorganization, even in cases where they are considered quite successful they have not been replicated within the company or by other companies. Within major corporations, with the exception of Volvo, experiments in workplace redesign have not been expanded. I believe there is a strong resistance to changing the structure of the work organization if the change implies any shift in the nature of control. In our enthusiasm for a more humanistic way to run a plant or an office, we tend to forget that in the first instance the purpose of hierarchy is control. Any shift in the nature of control, whether real or imaginary, is conceived of as a threat by those who might lose some authority.

I spent a few days at the Volvo Göteborg auto and truck plant in Sweden, observing "autonomous work teams" assembling trucks. This assembly plant, unlike Volvo's new Kalmar plant, has a traditional linear assembly line, but they do use a team assembly approach. Because these trucks have so many custom features ordered by the customer, their manufacture readily lends itself to a team assembly concept.

I arrived at the truck assembly plant early enough for the manager to introduce me to a fifteen-man assembly-team meeting. As agreed, he then left me in the plant on my own devices for a few days to observe or talk with whomever I wished. Volvo is one of the few large work-experimenting institutions that is quite open about their experience. For that they need to be complimented. In this meeting the men were deciding how they would work that day. There were about fifteen minutes of discussion and no formal vote. A consensus emerged on how they would assemble trucks that day, and off they went to the assembly area. They had agreed on who would work the rear section, midsection, cab, and front end. As I observed the group, they seemed to work extremely well together. They knew the work; more important, they knew and liked each other, creating a warm feeling of camaraderie and support among themselves. I would describe this group as a well-integrated cooperative effort that created a community of workers concerned about each other's welfare. I learned that they were also strong union supporters. At 3:30 the team I was observing began to wash up, although quitting time wasn't until 4:30. There did not seem to be a foreman within the team, so I asked one of the men, Hans Bargman, a lead man or parts expediter, what was happening. "Oh, we have finished our division quota of thirty-one trucks for today, so that's it. The men won't do even a half more." (I remembered Max's "We give so much and no more.") I asked him if I could talk with the union representative about the team assembly. "Of course," he said, and scuttled around the plant looking for the representative as the men sat around on a bare truck chassis, wiping their hands, cleaning up, drinking coffee, talking, killing time.

The union representative, a short, jolly fellow still in his work clothes, gave me a hearty handshake, saying, "I hear you vas a union man so dat's good. Yah, vot vould you like to know?"

"Well, why did the men stop working? You still have an hour to go and it's only 3:30."

"Ve made da quota, und dat's it. Ve don't make more just because it's team assembly. You see, ve agree to team assembly if dey don't try to use it as a vay to shpeed up da line. So, ve say, OK, you vant team assembly, it's OK. But ve produce same number of trucks. The union vatches all the time vot the company is doing. Ve vant to cooperate, but no shpeedup." He kept rubbing his hands on a wiping cloth. He had a lot of dignity, which reminded me how a union affiliation can give workers a sense of pride and power.

"How do you like the team assembly?" I asked.

"Vell, it's OK if you got a group of men who vork together vell. You know vot? Dat's da vay you gotta vork on da regular assembly line or it's no good for nobody. If da mens don't vork together, tings is bad no matter how you do da job."

"Did the company consult with the union about the team assembly?"

"Oh yes, dey ask us. Ve say OK, but no more production. You gotta vatch all the time. The company try to shpeed up line, and dat's bad for da men, for den dey go home tired and have trouble mit da families."

Later on I spoke with the plant manager, who affirmed the quota and felt hopeless about ever doing anything about it. He was clearly the person in the middle, squeezed by management for more production and resisted by the union. "It is clear that they could assemble at least two more trucks a shift, but they won't do it. As the workers see it, the team assembly is just a way to get out more work." How much discussion or training was there for the assembly team work groups? He confirmed what the union representative had said, that there was little or no discussion with the workers on the plant floor about team assembly concept. Unions in Sweden tend to be run much more on the national level than unions like the United Auto Workers in the United States. While the UAW signs a basic national agreement, local issues such as a work experiment in a particular plant would need agreement of the workers in that plant. At

Volvo-Göteborg there was an agreement with the national union and then implementation at the plant.

This was also the case at Saab. The union had agreed to the engine team assembly, but there was little or no participation of the workers on the shop floor in its design or implementation. A real paradox is created when management decides to increase worker participation or increase their autonomy or enrich the job. In most workplace experiments I have studied, I observed little or no input from the people affected by the changes. Though the workers at the Volvo truck plant thought team assembly was OK, they did not feel it was theirs, they did not own it. The Saab team engine assemblers said this is OK, it's a job, the company set it up this way, so we will do it. What would happen if workers were actually involved in the planning process?

The potential role the union can play in rearranging work, as well as the difficulties involved, was dramatically illustrated to me during a visit to the UAW education center at Black Lake, Michigan. The Black Lake center is deep in the woods of northern Michigan. It could easily be confused with a handsome modern resort hotel. It is of Scandinavian design, almost all wood, much of it huge, laminated beams that fly across the high ceilings of the meeting halls. The place can accommodate hundreds of people. The buildings, scattered about in the deep woods, are all connected with a series of weblike, glassed-in, wooden passageways that make it unnecessary to go outside in the winter cold.

Walter Reuther was the architect, planner, the dreamer and builder of this center. I sense that he probably did it to demonstrate that the American labor movement could build workers' country clubs similar to the workers' rest or vacation homes in the Eastern European countries and in the Soviet Union.

Local union officials, committeemen, and stewards of the UAW come from all over the United States to Black Lake for a month or six weeks of vacationing and learning with their families. While there, they set up a functioning union, beginning with the plant committees, then through the local and the regional offices, right up to the national office and into the convention. It is a simulation of union life packed into a few intensive weeks of learning.

The UAW invites some outsiders, resource people who can be consulted on issues as they arise. I was invited to come as a consultant on the European work experiments. I made a few formal presentations about what I had observed in Europe. Then one evening in a very informal seminar, I asked some stewards and committeemen from a large General Motors plant the following question: "If you had the option of running your plant in some way other than what is now being done, or any way you thought would be better for the people working there, how would you do it? Here's a blackboard, a flip chart, magic markers, if you want to draw pictures you can. Do it the way you want." There were about fifteen or eighteen people, mostly men, at the seminar, who had all been in the auto industry for quite a few years. Some were experienced, skilled workers, others had been on a line for some time. I would characterize them as a group of seasoned automobile workers. The suggestions they had for alternative ways of running an auto plant ran something like the following:

Establish a four-day work week.

Clean the place up. Get the oil off the floor.

Reduce the noise level.

Improve the ventilation over the automatic welders and the paint department.

Have a better and more constant supply of parts so you don't have to run around looking for them.

Get rid of all the foremen, or at least some of them.

Raise and lower the height of the line so that you can work at hand level instead of up over your head or low down on the floor.

Provide lighter hard hats, improved safety goggles, more work clothes changes.

Provide better lunchroom areas.

That was about it. I found myself upset by the limited nature of the discussion. Here was an experienced group of union workers speculating on what could be done to improve the workplace, and they could only come up with more collective-bargaining demands. Of course, I thought, this is their frame of reference, the way they perceive, how they are expected to think, their experience bank, what they know.

I went to the blackboard and I began to sketch an assembly line with semicircular bays. Then I sketched the new star-shaped Volvo-Kalmar plant. I made diagrams of an autonomous work group, eliminated foremen and supervisors, had people doing their own quality control, a variety of things suggestive of new options. I said, "Now, what about doing some things like this?" There was a long silence. Then the discussion started. "That's ridiculous. I mean the company knows more about this stuff than we do, and if this was a good way of doing things, wouldn't they do it that way? Shit man, we could dump all the parts for an Oldsmobile in the middle of the floor and given enough time, we'd assemble it. But Christ, that would cost a fortune. This company is in business to make money, not to run Mickey Mouse programs."

There was general support of the notion: "If there is a better way of running a plant, the companies know how to do it." Then one fellow said, "Wait a minute, fellas. What about Lordstown—that place stinks. We could run a place better than that, like two smaller lines instead of one big one."

"How do we know it would really work, and I'm not sure the guys would like it."

"Damn it, we just haven't thought about it. If we had time to think about stuff like that, we could come up with plenty of ideas, but who would listen to us?"

The point I'm trying to make here is that the frame of reference of these workers was the linear assembly line as they experienced it. Even to think beyond that seemed difficult at first. After some beer was drunk, and we got to know each other better, we began to do some planning-group exercises. We broke up into groups of three and four people. Each group was to come in with an original way to assemble automobiles. The groups began to cook up ideas ranging from dumping the 3,000 automobile parts in the middle of the room with fifteen guys in a competition with fifteen others to see who could assemble a car fastest, to a group assembly with a series of bays all along the assembly line to eliminate the sequential nature of linear work. There were suggested variations of the Kalmar electronic cart, which moves the car around as it is being assembled. Then came a series of interesting discussions about the nature of responsibility and how we would work without foremen. There was a mixed feeling as to whether workers would work if you took the foremen away. Toward the end of the discussion, it was generally agreed that there were alternative ways to run a plant but that there would have to be a major learning of new, more cooperative attitudes in order really to achieve a more human workplace.

That night as I sat in my cabin on the shores of Black Lake, I thought, How can we create new kinds of workplaces with what we know? The workers were saying, "Look, we need to learn to think in an entirely different way. We need a new kind of person. We are all trained to live in a hierarchy, we are trained to take orders." The average worker might say, "Just-tell me what you want me to do, and I'll do it. I don't know what participation is. I don't even know if I want much more responsibility. Just tell me what I should do." It is not because he or she does not want to participate or does not want additional responsibility. The resistance to change grows out of the nature of "participation." Broad-based participation is a literal unknown in our society, and perhaps in most other modern industrial societies as well. I have a hunch that the majority of work reorganization experiments are failing because they are not truly participatory; they do not develop a grassroots constituency that will advocate the new approach. At Black Lake, I realized that the problem is even more profound—managers, behavioral scientists, owners, and workers all know very little about *how* to organize institutions in a way that makes them truly participative. We suffer from collective ignorance when it comes to this form of social action.

Based on our individual experience, we have little or no way of learning what the notion of a participative organization is about. All of our learning about institutions, from the family in childhood through adolescence and young adulthood, is based on the acceptance of hierarchy. Schools, children's camps, scouting organizations, fraternities, the military, the police—in a word, all institutional life—assumes a hierarchical order of things. After this lifetime of preparation, the auto workers I met at Black Lake, like the rest of us, arrive at the workplaces prepared for a hierarchy and nothing else. So we settle into our positions on the pyramid and let the person above do the worrying. Then some behavioral scientists and humanists suggest that it might be more fulfilling, satisfying, more human, a better place to work if the employees could somehow have some autonomy, creativity, participate in the decision making, and in general help run the place as part of a team or group. An experiment in autonomy is launched, sometimes with a lot of P.R. flimflam. It runs into problems, the launchers leave, and things settle back into the old pyramid. From this experience, I now believe if we are to take part in the process of thinking creatively—about what we might want from our working life—we will need to learn the alternatives to the traditional hierarchical organization.

The six UAW members who went to work at Saab and expressed so little enthusiasm for the team assembly were also saying that they missed some of the things that go on in the UAW plants in the United States. The union has not only improved working conditions through its contract negotiation, but it has established tough, hard grievance procedures that are continually in action on the plant floor. This adversary relationship is functional. It is, after all, a form of participation; it also reduces boredom by creating interesting kinds of conflicts. These activities occurring in the plant may prove to be far more compelling than the work itself. This is the fabric of community, the social life of the plant, in contrast to the repetitive mechanical tasks. The conflict, whether between individuals or between groups of workers and the company, turns out to be the most human activity in the place.

I have witnessed workers fighting on the plant floor in the middle of the day over some miniscule problem. One guy opens a window, another slams it shut; or someone turns on a ventilating fan, someone else snaps it off. They argue, yell, come to blows, and everybody gets excited. "Man, this is neat! The best thing that happened all day. Wow, what a fight!" A little excitement to break up the boring repetition of doing the same thing over and over again. In a desperate need for variety, conflict can break up routines.

At least some of the aggressive, conflict-generating collective bargaining that is most characteristic of American unions may be a way of dealing with the frustration of not being heard. Scandinavians are less prone to our kind of cowboy-and-Indian behavior. On the other hand, in France and Italy, particularly in certain plants, there is a growing level of conflict that is probably being generated by the younger, better-educated workers who are bored with uninteresting, unchallenging work. European workers, who are traditionally more class-conscious, see the *system* as evil. American workers see it as "them against us" with the workers as the good guys, and the foremen, managers, or supervisors representing the bad guys. Authority in American plants does not necessarily represent an evil system, just an evil foreman. The distinction is significant in that it may be the reason that the American labor movement tends not to get far beyond demands for greater economic concessions and increased benefits. American labor is most consistent in its tradition of not wanting to get involved in the responsibilities of managing the plant. It is in this sense that the adversary relationship of workers and management, so common in many plants, needs to be transcended and integrated into some new work arrangement. To ignore it, as happened in the Rushton Coal Mine experiments in Pennsylvania, only exacerbates the conflict.

These same issues are somewhat similarly illustrated in a well-known American experiment at the new Gaines pet food plant in Topeka, Kansas. Some time ago I had occasion to spend a week there. It is located on the outskirts of Topeka off a main highway, in what not long ago must have been a wheat field. The plant looks like a windowless fifteen- or twenty-story office tower. It is painted white and is lit up at night.

The Topeka dry dog food plant is run around the clock by 120 employees. It offers an interesting contrast between a continuous process operation and a more traditional manufacturing-type operation in packaging and warehousing. The first employees were recruited specifically for this new experimental plant more than five years ago. About 1,200 people applied for jobs. Sixty-three were hired. In hiring, the emphasis was on a high level of initiative, decision-making ability, and most important, the ability to work as part of a team.

Topeka has a forty-hour, five-day work week and no time clocks. Benefits include nine holidays, two weeks' vacation a year, five days' sick leave (approved by the group team leader), and hospitalization through a major insurance concern.

The management people, who are identifiable from the rest of the work force, emphasized to me repeatedly that it is easier to start up a new plant based on autonomous work teams than it is to introduce these concepts into an existing plant, and that things are made more difficult if there is a union contract. One manager said, "When you have a union situation, you have very different problems. You are limited by the collective-bargaining process."

The number of people in the Topeka plant is small, and employees do express the feeling that they have freedom to communicate with anyone they want, but the size of the plant was not considered a critical factor in developing the autonomous work teams. The Topeka managers felt a critical variable was the size of the work group, not the plant. The number seventeen seemed to be maximum workable group size, affording optimum communication within the team. They then cited a second critical element for a successful work group: The need for a basic trust relationship between the employees and management. One manager said, "If you can win trust, then employees will accept what you are doing; and in order to win trust there must be full participation, good communication, and an open atmosphere in the plant."

There is some evidence, however, to suggest that the question of participation and openness is very much related to plant magnitudes. It is one thing to have an open administrative management style in a plant of thirty or forty people per shift. It is yet another thing in a plant of two thousand or ten thousand. It is like comparing a mom-and-pop grocery with A & P. The number of people working in a plant is a critical variable determining the level of openness, for in a large organization there is an inevitable control factor. I believe that to achieve a participative atmosphere, small operating units are required.

Gaines dog food consists of corn, soya, premixed vitamins, and meat meal. The processing section is automated and percentages of the mix are predetermined. The processing group, or team, consists of eight people per shift. They run the entire processing operation, beginning with the receipt of raw materials by freight cars that dump them into floor bins, where they are weighed and then conveyed to storage. The raw materials are then mixed, coated with tallow to make the dogs eat it, and colored red so the dog owners think it is meat. This whole operation is monitored by a computer on the fifth floor with an eight-by-thirty-foot control panel divided into five or six different sections full of red pilot lights. Two or three people might be in the control room at any one time, monitoring the process computer. The objective of the processing group is to produce a minimum of 100 tons of dog food per shift, as well as to assure the packaging room that they never run out of material for packaging.

The processing team has few routine functions. They do a small amount of maintenance, such as periodic lubrication, and monitor the equipment to try and avoid breakdowns. They may attempt to speed up the equipment and try to surpass the 100-ton-a-shift objective. A red light may go on, signaling a malfunction; the men in the control room will decide what to do. They say that sometimes dog food clogs a chute, or is hung up in one of the feeder bins, and it has to be cleared. The processing team is a somewhat typical maintenance crew, where initiative, decision making, and teamwork are essential to the smooth functioning of the process—not that unusual for this type of operation. But there is something else here; this group of workers, like other maintenance people, have a lot of freedom at their workplace, which may contribute to a high level of satisfaction. This is a correlation that may be more universal than is now acknowledged. One of the processors, who had been a machinist on the Santa Fe railroad, said, "I like the Gaines plant 300 percent better because I am not stuck in one place turning railroad wheels on a lathe. Now, as a troubleshooter, I am free to roam around the plant anyplace, anytime. I can stop and talk to people. The day goes like that."

While they kept an eye on that big board, we schmoozed about whether it is better to live in the city or the country, whether girls in Topeka had given up wearing brassieres, and what unions can do for you anyhow. Somebody suggested, "Why don't we speed the mill grinder or the conveyer a bit?" That precipitated the pushing of a button. Then we went back to schmoozing. Schmoozing is common in offices, universities, processing plants, and many service industries. It occurs less in manufacturing plants, and ofttimes workers have figured out the most ingenious ways to do it surreptitiously.

The degree to which employees are permitted to visit, have access to a variety of areas, use the telephone may be a critical element in humanizing a workplace. The scope of schmoozing does not have to do with the work itself, as suggested by Herzberg and others, but is influenced by the nature of the work and how it is organized. Most manufacturing plants, unfortunately, are designed with a maximum amount of employee time at a given place. I consider this an important dissatisfier because it deprives factory workers of freedoms enjoyed by many white-collar and service workers.

One of the first things I would do for blue-collar workers to increase their work satisfaction is to grant them one equal right that the rest of us take for granted, the free use of a telephone at work. Those of us who can reach for a phone any time we wish underestimate its role as a socializer and reliever of daily monotony and boredom. How many times during a working day might a white-collar worker or a professional pick up the phone and dial a friend? The phone conversation may be inconsequential or silly, but it helps relieve tedium and routine and so makes the workday seem easier.

The telephone creates a vast network of intimate human contact in an otherwise impersonal world. Some people have thought this notion is quite impractical, yet I know at least two large manufacturing plants that have tried it and found no serious difficulties or abuses. Needless to say, the employees love it.

Like most people in other kinds of workplaces, workers understand the limitations on satisfying their needs and desires in the factory. They are very much aware of both the magic and the curse of mass production technology. It is magical to see raw material start in at one end of a plant and come out as a working thingamajig on the other. It may also be a curse to keep doing the same little task over and over again, but workers know that this is the secret of the magic. They understand this as a group; it is "our secret." They make the best of the life in the plant with humor and camaraderie. When they do participate in decision making, it is mostly through collective bargaining for controls over safety, agreements on productivity levels, and so forth.

While the processing part of the Topeka plant is a modern, automated operation, the warehousing and packaging is in many ways quite traditional. Workers stand all day long at filling stations, holding or feeding boxes or bags under a chute that fills them with a preweighed amount. The containers then go onto a conveyer to a sewing machine that closes the bags, and then to a pallet for warehousing. I would characterize this work as highly repetitive, with little room for autonomy or growth, and no position to rise to but processing. Here there is also a lack of that critical job satisfier, the freedom to walk around and schmooze. (Yet, because workers, like the rest of us, are not of one mold, one worker said, "I like packaging because I do not want to think about the work anyway.") There may be a lesson in this example of two very different types of jobs in the same plant. Given the premise that some jobs like packaging and warehousing are lousy, and some lousy jobs are with us to stay, then maybe we need to rotate the "lousy work."

Much of the literature dealing with workplace problems uses Maslow's concept of a needs hierarchy as the theoretical base. I would argue that a more basic issue at stake is the relationship of the individual to the institution. Can an individual worker achieve autonomy, creativity, or self-actualization in an institution which has as its primary, and in many cases sole, objective increased profit? Some of us have argued that it is in the company's best interest to assure workers their higher order of needs. The trouble with this argument is that we have little evidence to support it. I am fearful that at least some of the definitions of workplace problems have grown out of the behavioral science gardens of people's needs, satisfactions, wishes, and wants. Some of the difficulty may be semantic; concepts such as needs, autonomy, and control are highly relative. I have been amused by how some intellectuals tend to view manual work as a kind of horror. They would be surprised that many manual workers are horrified at the prospect of having to sit at a desk and write all day. Our frame of reference may have more to do with how work is perceived than the claimed objectivity of a test or questionnaire. This raises our old question, "Compared to what?" Terms like needs, satisfaction, autonomy, growth, and, most important, alienation, have become so all-encompassing that I am not sure they have any distinct meaning any longer.

A basic difference between Marx and Maslow is that Marx's assumptions about alienation are based on the conflict between the private ownership of the means and products of production, and the social nature of the factory. Marx uses the term alienation to describe the factory worker's lack of control in his relationship to the raw material, the process or means, and the finished product. This concept is based on an economic and social relationship. Maslow's concept of alienation, on the other hand, is based primarily on the psychological needs of individuals.

It seems odd that many writers dealing with workers and workplace problems seized on the Maslow schema as an explanation of worker dissatisfaction without at least questioning the basis of such concepts as autonomy, participation, creativity, or self-actualization as they apply to mass production workplaces. I have a feeling that behavioral scientists who believe that these concepts can be easily applied to mass production technology are either ignorant of what goes on in manufacturing plants, or vulgarize the meaning of the concepts—which could be interpreted as creating straw men to avoid dealing with real ones, that is, excusing inadequate pay and poor working conditions by concentrating on individual psyches.

Any discussion of workplace problems requires some agreement on the definition of mass production technology. Mass production technology requires an operation that is predesigned, preengineered, and preplanned to the smallest detail in order to guarantee interchangeability of parts. In order to assure cost replication, every step of the production process is costed out and engineered to time. Schedules must be strictly adhered to. No deviation from a specification can be permitted or interchangeability would be threatened. Even the experimental Topeka plant embodied a natural hierarchy of jobs in the difference between packaging and processing. The successful completion of the final product, including costs, depends upon everyone adhering to a master plan. Given this as the basic nature of mass production, where can there be opportunities for autonomy, creativity, and self-actualization? Only by participating in an overall planning process where their inputs can be incorporated can workers really achieve those goals, yet that is the very aspect of work from which they have been excluded. I do not consider worker representation on corporate boards as addressing this problem. It is not an issue of formal representation but of a participatory process. If workers are barred from the planning, they are not represented.

Contemporary difficulty with Marx's concept of alienation grows out of our doubts about whether what is called socialist, or worker, ownership and control over the means of production has given the workers on the plant floor any greater autonomy or participation than workers in capitalist countries. In so-called socialist countries, factory workers find themselves in a relationship with the means of production that seems to be endemic to factories: highly repetitive work, preplanned and preengineered with little or no participation in decision making. In Yugoslavia things seem to be different to the extent that workers have some say in how plants are run and who manages. The organization of the work and task performance remain similar to all factory production techniques.

Marx's concept of alienation failed to note that alienation may be inherent in the nature of mass production technology *regardless of who owns it*. The socialist countries, far from finding a new way to produce things or a new model of work organization have, if anything, emulated the worst features of the capitalist efficiency system to its smallest detail.

The American labor movement has traditionally dealt with "alienation" by seeking more for its members in pay and benefits, while reducing the amount of time they have to spend at the job. Until we have found an alternative to our traditional way of organizing work, history may reveal that this has been the best response to a negative situation.

I believe that at least some of the suggestions for improving the quality of work life reflect a certain nostalgia for the return to craftsmanship. In his 1844 manuscripts, Marx expresses a sadness over the decline of the renaissance craftsman. Such concepts as autonomy, creativity, decision making, and control of one's tools are qualities that are associated with craftsmanship, and, to some extent, hand tools. While being extremely empathetic with that nostalgia, I am also convinced that notions of bringing back craftsmanship are based on either fantasy or ignorance about mass production. So little of the traditional craftsman survives that I hardly think we know anymore what the term means.

As a skilled machinist or toolmaker in the traditional sense, I was not a craftsman. I made no decisions about the raw material, the process, or the product. As distinguished from craftsmanship, my skill was the ability to follow extremely detailed instruction to very fine tolerances. That requires a certain kind of skill, not craftsmanship, and above all, not creativity. I remember an old boss repeating over and over, "Follow the instructions. Follow the prints. Do not deviate from the specifications."

What happened to craftsmanship? How did we evolve from craft to skill, from creativity and inventiveness to a life of following the instructions without deviation? In *Art and Industrial Revolution*, Klingender talks about the end of craftsmanship. The beginning of the end was signaled in 1830 when owners of the Wedgwood Pottery in England hired its first salesman to go out and find out what kind of pottery people were interested in buying. He came back with his report, "Make as many queen-on-a-horse motifs as you can. They'll buy them like hot cakes." Instead of leaving the design to the individual potters, as had traditionally been done, Wedgwood decided to hire a designer to create a series of ceramics with a queen-on-a-horse motif that could then be copied by the potters. That act of engaging a salesman and a designer, both of whom were responding to a market, was the beginning of the end of craftsmanship. Klingender says that because of the designer, the Wedgwood potter became, at best, an "inventor" who could now decide how to do it, but no longer what to do.

As engineers moved into factory production, the "how to do it" became the next victim. Now *companies* decided what was the best way to do it. The best known of these work engineers was Frederick Taylor. He was obsessed with the idea that a man should be a part of the machine. Thus, even the "inventor" trying to decide "how to do it" soon disappeared when equipment and machinery were designed for specific functions, and workers lost control over the method as well as the product.

The final blow came with the notion of interchangeability of parts. The result was Taylor's phenomenally successful effort to fragment all tasks to their smallest element so as to eliminate any possible judgment on the part of the worker—thus assuring no variation in the final product. And it worked. The factory proved to be productive beyond the engineers' wildest dreams. This success is called the industrial revolution; and that it was.

Many behavioral scientists who write on this subject fail to mention the role of the union at the workplace. Union people argue that factors which behavioral scientists refer to as autonomy, participation in decision making, self-esteem, openness, can be achieved only if employees feel they are not subject to the whims and fancies of management, particularly first-line supervisors. This was well illustrated in the Volvo plant. Trade unionists point out that people at the production level are often the victims of new production schemes that ignore their interests. The General Foods planners consulted with the first-level supervisors in the planning for Topeka, but participation of the workers in the planning process was nonexistent. Could the union have been involved in the planning for Topeka? This is a difficult question to answer since the union was not asked, and even if it were, I am not at all certain that it would have been able or willing to do so. Yet it seems clear that it needs to be part of the total planning effort.

On the plant level, a well-functioning union may be an expression of the best humanitarian qualities of the work force. People concerned with quality of work life need to understand more about the role of unions beyond strict contract bargaining. Unfortunately, many consultants on work reorganization are employed by management, and so they tend to be less than fearless on this issue. However, if the unions insist on limiting their role to traditional collective bargaining issues, the question of workplace reorganization may just pass them by. The UAW has begun to recognize this in bargaining with the auto industry. Joint committees have been established to examine issues of workplace organization and operation. This is a step forward for a major union. People concerned with workplace changes need to understand that unions have been dealing with these problems for a long time and therefore are an important arena for participation. Without their involvement, the suspicion that workplace changes are designed to counter union organization will continue to grow.

Even the most recent American experiments that do include union involvement, the autonomous work group at the Rushton Coal Mine in Pennsylvania and the Harmon Industries plant in Bolivar, Tennessee, are experiencing serious difficulties with their work reorganization experiments. The troubles they are encountering lend at least some credence to my fears.

The Rushton experiment took place in a mine of 120 workers. As a result of extensive negotiations between the company, the United Mine Workers, and a group of behavioral scientists at the University of Pennsylvania, an agreement was reached to develop an autonomous work section in the mine. An autonomous work group was formed by seventeen volunteers working on two shifts.

Rushton's troubles have grown out of conflicting motives of the principal groups involved in the experiment. Miners who volunteered to participate in the experiment were hopeful of better salaries and a more satisfying way of going about their daily work. The company's primary interest was the possibility of increased production. The United Mine Workers wanted to find ways to improve the safety conditions in mining work. The behavioral scientists wanted to develop an experimental setting in which they could test some of their ideas regarding autonomous work groups. It is to be expected that each of these participating groups would have their own goals. What they needed was an understanding of their respective motives, and this is a process of negotiation and compromise. What could have emerged from such a procedure were common goals that all groups felt they could work toward. It was when the goals of the "others" were undermined or ignored that trust began to fade and the alliance was in trouble.

At Rushton, an agreement had been made by the company to share the benefits from increased productivity with the workers. When it was time to come through, the company hesitated, insisting that it was unable to detect measurable increases in production. This argument continued for the duration of the experiment, seriously eroding the trust of workers in the entire process. Similarly, the union felt its power eroding when the company decided, without consultation, to expand the experiment to the whole mine. As grievances were increasingly handled through the autonomous group structure rather than through the traditional union procedure, it was perceived as an additional threat to the union's authority to represent the workers.

The insensitivity of the behavioral scientists to the union's position, and to the traditional adversary relationship between company and workers, seemed to weaken their ability to confront the power issues squarely and try to help the concerned parties to achieve a solution. The confrontation might not have worked, but then in the last analysis neither has the experiment.

From the behavioral scientists' point of view, there were further difficulties with the Rushton experiment. How could a small autonomous section of a mine exist within an operation that was thoroughly hierarchical? Similarly, this problem of experiment in isolation was experienced in the Topeka plant, a fragile oasis in the General Foods conglomerate. Perhaps one answer to this problem is that the rest of a work community where an experiment is taking place needs to be informed, and, if possible, included in the process. They cannot be treated as outsiders, for eventually their lack of information will lead to resistance and even sabotage, as seems to have occurred at General Foods. Another possible way to address the problem of isolation is to prepare the participants in the experiment for the experience. A question that needs to be asked is, how do we train or help people learn how to be autonomous or how to accept authority for themselves? One of the weaknesses of the Rushton experience was that the experimental group-training sessions of workers and supervisors centered almost exclusively on safety issues. They might have done better had they focused on how to prepare people for autonomy, since this is such an uncommon feature of our social life. How could we expect coal miners or any of us to begin magically to function autonomously? The work experiment had been sold to the union leadership as a way to improve safety practices in the mine. This became the union's public position. Had the union been able to embrace the issue of autonomy, it could have probably been taken more seriously as a training focus. This means that the union itself should be willing to examine its own attachment to authority and hierarchy if it is to contribute to the problem of reorganizing work—not easily achieved in an organization with the tradition of John L. Lewis and Tony Boyle, who are not exactly your participative types.

The Harmon Industries International, Inc., Automotive Division's mirror manufacturing plant in Bolivar, Tennessee, has been the site of another experiment in participation. The leadership of this innovation included the president of Harmon International, a vice president of the United Auto Workers, and a behavioral science consultant. Like all of the experiments I have looked at, this effort did not grow out of any grassroots efforts of the workers themselves. I am doubtful that even after three years of efforts at

Bolivar the workers have embraced the experiment as theirs. In the long run, this will be a most serious shortcoming; without broad-based support, there will be little to maintain the experiment's integrity when there is a change of ownership or when the consultant's relationship comes to an end.

The way the program was developed at Bolivar tended to negate grassroots support. The start-up activities included elaborate and intimate question aires and tests that in effect said to workers, "Look we think you have problems; maybe we can even give them a psychological label. We want to help you." This sort of initial approach from consultants can only confuse any further efforts toward mutual control. No wonder then that an evaluation report from the Institute of Social Research shows that only 30 percent of the workers interviewed at Bolivar felt that the program was at all participatory.

This situation is further evidenced in one of the more publicized achievements of the Bolivar project, Earned Idle Time (EIT). Workers here demonstrated their enthusiasm for the opportunity to knock off early when they had filled their daily quotas. The support for EIT lends accuracy to the trade unionist's argument that shorter working hours and increased benefits are the real contributions to the improvement of the quality of working life. On the other hand, earned idle time may be the most attractive alternative to workers who do not feel real inclusion in the change effort. This was the view expressed by the auto workers at Volvo who stopped working when they had assembled their thirty-one trucks.

The Bolivar plant has now been sold to the Beatrice Foods conglomerate. I predict that, like Topeka, the innovations at Bolivar will slowly disintegrate and the plant will go back to its traditional model. This seems to me the inevitable result of the absence of grassroots support. It means that workers involved in such projects need some real commitment to an autonomous workplace if they are to be the ultimate source of ongoing support for such projects. This can be encouraged by the show of genuine good faith and partnership on the part of the company.

The issues of humanizing work and creating participatory structures have not caught on in the United States, though they frequently find support and interest in Europe. In criticizing the Rushton, Bolivar, and Topeka projects, I have tried to treat them as learning opportunities, for that, after all, is what an experiment is about. I do not believe that we should cease experimentation because we have not yet been able to get any broad support for workplace change. On the contrary, experimentation helps us become more aware of the issues, and the pitfalls that should be avoided.

A dialectic of workplace change emerges from this discussion. The polarities that I have discussed are those of power and creativity. Workers who want to move in the direction of participative structures will need to confront the issues of power and control. The process of change needs to be mutually shared by all involved, or the outcome will not be a really participative model. The demand for a structural redistribution of power is not sufficient to address the problem of change toward a humanistic, as against a technological, workplace. If we are to change our institutional arrangements from hierarchy to participation, particularly in our workplaces, we will need to look to transformations in ourselves as well. As long as we are imbued with the legitimacy of hierarchical authority, with the sovereignty of the status quo, we will never be able to generate the new and original participative forms that we seek. This means if we are to be equal to the task of reorganizing our workplaces, we need to think about how we can reeducate ourselves and become aware of our own assumptions about the nature of our social life together. Unless the issue is approached in terms of these complexities, I fear that all the worker participation and quality-of-work-life efforts will fail.

I believe that the journey of my own growth has helped me to perceive at least some of the complexity of these issues. As a labor union organizer, I used to believe that by securing more benefits workers were increasing their power and thus paving the way for a more egalitarian system. I now believe that merely achieving economic security or creating structures that assure a limited amount of worker participation through union representation will not achieve these changes. An egalitarian world through participation means that people must behave together in a new way. Many of the things I fought for as a labor leader have now come to pass, yet we are no closer to nonauthoritarian social life than we were in 1930. Perhaps because of the hierarchical mushrooming of our system, I think at times that we are even further away.

My observations of workplace experiments have convinced me that autonomous and participatory behavior will not result from mere structural manipulation. Yes, we may organize work so as to minimize hierarchy or redistribute decision-making prerogatives, but nothing firm will be achieved unless we somehow help people, and help ourselves, to become aware of our own behavior and how we must change. I have spent the last twenty years of my life searching for workable alternatives to authoritarianism, only to find that ultimately I must fight the authoritarian within myself. Only when in my routine behavior I can embody the ideals I have been fighting for—only then can I understand what is truly involved in reorganizing work on a participative basis.

One last sociological word about the decline of the Protestant work ethic and the rise of schmoozing: Manufacturing and farming jobs are decreasing in the labor market. Service jobs in the private and public sectors are on the increase. Income transfers, such as social security, unemployment insurance, welfare, and food stamps, money people receive for which they do no work, have increased almost geometrically to the point of 200 billion dollars a year and steadily rising. All of this is to say that there are increasingly attractive alternatives to hard work and people are learning how to use them. Why work hard if we have a choice? The answer is, we may not, unless somehow work can be made more rewarding.

# References

Bennis, Warren. "Review of Current Trends in Business and Finance," *Wall Street Journal*, March 1977.

Cloward, Richard, and Lloyd Ohlin. *Delinquency and Opportunity: A Theory of Delinquent Groups.* New York: The Free Press, 1960.

Galbraith, John Kenneth. *New Industrial State.* Boston: Houghton Mifflin Co., 1967.

Herzberg, Frederick. *Work and the Nature of Man.* New York: New American Library, 1966.

Khaldun, Ibn. *The Mugaddimah: An Introduction to History*, Vol. II. Princeton, NJ: Princeton University Press, 1958.

Klingender, F. D. *Art and the Industrial Revolution.* New York: Schocken Books, 1970.

Maslow, Abraham. *Motivation and Personality.* New York: Harper and Row, 1970 edition.

Miller, S. M. "On Socialism Now," *Social Policy*, January/February, 1974.

Mumford, Lewis. *The Pentagon of Power.* New York: Harcourt Brace Jovanovich, 1964.

Pinkerton, Allan. *Strikers, Communists, Tramps, and Detectives.* G. W. Dillingham Co., 1878.

Vickers, Sir Geoffrey. *Value Systems and Social Process.* New York: Basic Books, 1968.

Weir, Stan. "The Informal Group," *Rank and File: Personal Histories by Working Class Organizers*, edited by Staughton Lynd. Boston: Beacon Press, 1973.